THE END OF PROSPERITY

How Higher Taxes Will Doom
the Economy—If We Let It Happen

Arthur B. Laffer, Ph.D.

Stephen Moore

Peter J. Tanous

THRESHOLD
EDITIONS

New York London Toronto Sydney

Threshold Editions
A Division of Simon & Schuster, Inc.
1230 Avenue of the Americas
New York, NY 10020

First Threshold Editions hardcover edition October 2008

THRESHOLD EDITIONS and colophon are trademarks
of Simon & Schuster, Inc.

For information about special discounts for bulk purchases,
please contact Simon & Schuster Special Sales at
1-800-456-6798 or business@simonandschuster.com.

Designed by Carla Little

Manufactured in the United States of America

10   9   8   7   6   5   4   3   2

Library of Congress Cataloging-in-Publication Data

Laffer, Arthur B.
   The end of prosperity : how higher taxes will doom the economy—
if we let it happen / by Arthur B. Laffer, Stephen Moore, Peter J. Tanous.
      p.   cm.
1. Fiscal policy—United States.   2. United States—Economic policy—2001–
3. United States—Economic conditions—2001–   I. Moore, Stephen, 1960–
II. Tanous, Peter J.   III. Title.
   HJ257.3.L34   2008
   339.5'20973—dc22   2008017196
   ISBN-13: 978-1-4165-9238-9
   ISBN-10:   1-4165-9238-5

TABLE OF CONTENTS

CONTENTS

The Second Coming

Turning and turning in the widening gyre
The falcon cannot hear the falconer;
Things fall apart; the centre cannot hold;
Mere anarchy is loosed upon the world,
The blood-dimmed tide is loosed, and everywhere
The ceremony of innocence is drowned;
The best lack all conviction, while the worst
Are full of passionate intensity.
Surely some revelation is at hand;
Surely the Second Coming is at hand.
The Second Coming! Hardly are those words out
When a vast image out of *Spiritus Mundi*
Troubles my sight: somewhere in the sands of the desert
A shape with lion body and the head of a man,
A gaze blank and pitiless as the sun,
Is moving its slow thighs, while all about it
Reel shadows of the indignant desert birds.
The darkness drops again; but now I know
That twenty centuries of stony sleep
were vexed to nightmare by a rocking cradle,
And what rough beast, its hour come round at last,
Slouches towards Bethlehem to be born?

—W. B. Yeats, 1920

FOREWORD

PROSPERITY IN THE BALANCE

By Larry Kudlow

When I came to Washington as a young man in late 1980 to work as an economist for Ronald Reagan, the new administration was set to launch a bold and controversial domestic program based on something called supply-side economics. My dear friend Arthur Laffer was one of the principal designers of this program, which threw out the failed Keynesian tenets of government planning and demand-side management.

From the late 1960s up until Reagan's election, all manner of government tinkering and targeting completely ignored the crucial role of producers, investors, and entrepreneurs in the economy, as well as the need for stable money and low inflation. These interventionist programs produced the twin evils of high inflation and equally high unemployment. But Laffer's handiwork helped resurrect the long-forgotten classical model of economic growth that emphasized free-market capitalism as the engine of prosperity.

Fighting off attacks from establishment economists who were baffled by what came to be known as stagflation, Laffer and others argued that monetary control by the Federal Reserve was necessary to curb inflation, and that significantly lower tax rates were essential to reignite economic growth. It must pay sufficiently, after tax, for investors to supply capital, for workers to supply their labor, and for entrepreneurs to risk life and limb to re-electrify the market's animal spirits and generate Schumpeterian gales of creative destruction.

Along with industrial and financial deregulation, and an aggressive lowering of barriers to free trade, these principles launched a twenty-five-year-long prosperity boom, the likes of which has seldom been seen in American or world economic history. Defying the critics, Reagan's supply-side policies took effect quickly and lasted a long time. The U.S. reclaimed the status of economic superpower. Reagan's economic miracle dealt a crushing blow to the liberal academics, and their fellow travelers among the chattering classes, who had touted the state-planning socialism of the Soviets, or the rampant welfarism of Western Europe, or the industrial planning of Japan. Even worse for the critics on the left, as America moved back to the epicenter of the world economy, the Reagan model was adopted in nearly all corners of the planet.

Imitation is the sincerest form of flattery. Indeed, not only did the entire Soviet system collapse, but market economics and flat tax rates have appeared everywhere—from the old Soviet-bloc Eastern European nations, to the former collectivist bureaucratic Keynesian nation of India, and most remarkably, to that last bastion of red communism called China. Capitalism has also made its mark throughout Latin America. It has even infiltrated some of the most difficult areas of the Middle East, with radical Islam losing badly to new economic freedoms in Bahrain, Abu Dhabi, Jordan, Egypt, and even Saudi Arabia.

Literally hundreds of millions of formerly impoverished people are moving into the middle class around the globe, proving that market capitalism is the greatest anti-poverty program ever devised by man.

Turning back home, the twenty-five-year supply-side boom launched by Reagan has been in prosperity 95 percent of the time with only two brief and shallow recessions occupying the other 5 percent. Stock markets during this period have increased twelve-fold. The economy has expanded from $5 trillion to roughly $12 trillion in gross domestic product. More than 40 million new jobs have been created. Household wealth has exploded from roughly $15 trillion to nearly $60 trillion. More than 100 million Americans now own equity shares, either directly through their brokerage accounts or indirectly through proliferating 401(k) and other pension plans. Literally, in America, the workers now own the means of production. Karl Marx is now both dead and wrong.

Partnering with all this, we also have witnessed the most breathtaking technological transformation ever recorded in history, with the information revolution having modernized and changed every nook and cranny of the new American economy.

And yet, the current economic slowdown has spurred voices of the Left to once again plot to overturn the low-tax, free-market, free-trade principles that transformed us from impoverishment to prosperity nearly three decades ago.

Tax hikes are in the air, especially tax hikes on the so-called rich. Businesses and corporations are being lambasted as villains. Financiers and traders are being blamed for all that seems to ail us. The global free-trading system and the free movement of labor and capital worldwide are being attacked as part of the problem, instead of hailed as the source of solution. So-called global warming and climate change—still matters of much debate in the scientific community—are being used as an excuse to replace free markets with a Gosplan approach to central planning and regulating that would be the biggest expansion of the state's role in the economy in our history.

These developments have been a call to action for economist Arthur Laffer, Steve Moore of the *Wall Street Journal* editorial page, and investment adviser Peter Tanous. Together my friends have produced a book that is nothing short of a loud-sounding siren—a critical warning about the threats to prosperity that are now gathering force in Washington and out on the campaign trail. To that end, this excellent book details the economic successes of the past three decades, and chronicles the new economic-policy threats that face us today.

Regarding the almost manic liberal effort to repeal supply-side tax cuts, I am amused at the idea that raising the top tax rate on the so-called rich is some sort of economic panacea. With the exception of President John F. Kennedy, Democrats have been saying this for seventy-five years. That they keep losing presidential elections with this platform seems not to deter them. Neither does the fact that the top 1 percent of income-tax payers now shoulder 40 percent of all income-tax collections, while the top 5 percent of payers today generate 60 percent of tax collections. In fact, we have learned that reducing tax rates on the attendant incentives to economic behavior produces not only economic booms, but booms in tax collections from upper-income earners. But it's almost impossible to dissuade even the most charismatic graduates of Harvard Law School from wanting to tax these earners more.

I am also amused that liberals do not understand that taxing capital at prohibitive rates is akin to attempting to have capitalism without the very capital that makes it run. How does the average worker get a job when businesses cannot create jobs because they are starved for capital? The point of the U.S. experience of the past thirty years, and the reason for its imitation around the world, is that modern economic thinkers understand that capital and labor work together.

Energy is another area where today's liberals are proving to be completely separated from reality. At a time when the world oil price has jumped to $140 a barrel, pulling up gasoline prices at the pump to more than $4 a gallon, the American people know full well that we should be maximizing our natural resources with environmentally sound policies to find more oil, more clean coal, more nuclear power, and more natural gas, while at the same time exploring alternatives such as wind, solar, or cellulosic energy.

The new fashion for cap-and-trade, which would create a remarkable regulatory state, will do nothing less than cap our resources and kill the economy. The economics of cap-and-trade would produce a constant state of less prosperity, not more. Americans know this and are rejecting it.

They also reject the notion that a weak dollar is somehow good for us, even if the idea comes from the sacred temples of the Treasury and Federal Reserve. It was Reagan who promoted the strong dollar—not only as an inflation-slaying tool, but also as a symbol of America's economic strength around the world.

Looking at the current lull in economic growth, I would modestly suggest a three-part supply-side agenda. First, appreciably strengthen the value of the greenback. Second, keep marginal tax rates low and move to reform both the corporate and personal tax codes to keep America competitive in the global race for capital and labor. Third, enact a drill, drill, drill program aimed at offshore and onshore oil and gas, including the extraordinary oil-shale resources that bless our nation. Moratoriums on the outer continental shelf, shale, or Alaska should be quickly eliminated. We should adopt an America-first energy program that completely decontrols and deregulates our natural resources and unleashes the entrepreneurship of our energy sector, which is a world leader if we let it be. Rather than return to the hackneyed past of higher taxes, higher spending, and overregulation, we should stay on a free-market supply-side path that will generate another twenty-five years or more of economic growth and prosperity.

The End of Prosperity is an essential warning that bad policies will produce a bad economy. Not for months or a year, but for a long, long time. That's why this is such an important book.

I'll note that I am more optimistic than my good friends the authors. I believe that in our free democracy, the good common sense of American voters will reject mistaken ideological attempts to move our great nation backward. I believe that American investors, workers, and small-business owners will once again use the ballot box to turn down the sure failure of a planned economy. I believe that the historical and inherent successes of economic freedom will continue to prevail. But I know that Goldilocks, as I often call the U.S. economy, must be nurtured and incentivized for growth.

Every night on CNBC I repeat the creed that free-market capitalism is the best path to prosperity. I know that Messrs. Laffer, Moore, and Tanous agree with me. And I have faith that the American electorate stands with us, too.

Larry Kudlow is the host of CNBC's *Kudlow & Company*.

THE END OF PROSPERITY

1

THE GATHERING
ECONOMIC STORM

On the hope of our free nation rests the hope of all free nations.
— JOHN F. KENNEDY

AMERICA: WHAT WENT RIGHT

It was difficult for the three of us to write a book titled *The End of Prosperity.*

We're not doom and gloom people; we're natural optimists. And we're not part of the trendy set of intellectuals who like to trash our nation, blame America first for all the world's problems, or worst of all, predict with glee America's downfall as some kind of punishment for our alleged past environmental crimes, racism, financial mismanagement, greed, overconsumption, imperialism, or whatever the latest chic attack on the United States is.

By contrast, we *do* believe in the idea of American exceptionalism and that this nation is, in the words of our hero Ronald Reagan, "a shining city on a hill." The Gipper said it eloquently in his 1980 speech at the Republican National Convention in Detroit when he proclaimed that it was "divine providence that placed this land—this island of freedom here as a refuge for all those people in the world who yearn to breathe freely."[1] Yes, we certainly agree.

We're also well aware that American skeptics who have written over the last two or three decades about the end of the United States' economic might have gotten the story 180 degrees wrong. There've been dozens of wrongheaded books, many which became best sellers, from *America: What Went Wrong?* (Bartlett and Steele), to *Bankruptcy 1995: The Coming Collapse of America and How to Stop It* (Figgie and Swanson), to *The Great Depression of 1990* (Ravi Batra), to *The Rise and Fall of the Great Powers* (Paul Kennedy), to *The Day of Reckoning: The Consequences of American Economic Policy Under Reagan* (Benjamin Friedman), all forecasting America's impending economic collapse. So much gloom. These pessimists were about as right as the record producers who turned down a contract with the Beatles in 1962 because in their famous assessment, "guitar groups are on the way out,"[2] or the venture capitalists who rolled with laughter over the idea of a computer in every home, and then told Bill Gates to go take a hike.

Many of today's leading liberals who are advising Barack Obama and the Democrats in Congress are the same people who predicted in the late 1980s that Japan, with its sophisticated government-managed industrial policy economy, would take over the world in the 1990s and the early twenty-first century. Yes, those predictions were made at the early stages of one of the greatest and longest financial collapses in world history. Lester Thurow wrote after the Berlin Wall came down: "The Cold War is over. Japan won."[3] The Nikkei Index stood at 38,000 in 1989 and fell to below 8,000 in 2003, an 80 percent decline.[4] So in the 1990s while the U.S. stock market more than doubled, the Japanese stocks fell by about half.

Where the declinists on the left foresaw America's demise in the eighties and nineties and predicted a future that looked like the grim portrait of cities in movies like *Blade Runner* and *Batman*, we forecast growth and a cornucopia of financial opportunity and

2

a coming burst of prosperity. We believed that Ronald Reagan had the right prescription for the malaise of the 1970s. Reagan focused like a guided missile on the big problems that had come to cripple the U.S. economy: rampant inflation, high tax rates, a crushing regulatory burden, and runaway government spending. Call the Reagan economic agenda Reaganomics, supply-side economics, or free market economics—critics can even keep on calling it Voodoo or "trickle down" economics—but what is undeniable is that the economy surged in the 1980s and 1990s as if injected with performance-enhancing steroids.

Movin' On Up

Anyone who followed the declinists' advice about selling America short lost a lot of money. After the Reagan tax cuts and the conquering of inflation in the early 1980s America's net worth—or what we call America, Inc.—climbed in real terms from $25 trillion in 1980 to $57 trillion in 2007.[5] More wealth was created in the United States over the past twenty-five years than in the previous two hundred years. The economy in real terms is almost twice as large today as it was in the late 1970s. Or consider these income gains:

- Between 2001 and 2007 alone the number of Americans with a net worth of more than $1 million quadrupled from 2.1 million to 8.9 million, according to TNS Financial Services.
- In 1967 only one in 25 families earned an income of $100,000 or more in real income (in 2004 dollars), whereas now, almost one in four families do. The percentage of families with an income of more than $75,000 a year has more than tripled from 9 percent to almost 33 percent from 1967 to 2005.
- The percentage of families in all of the income groups between $5,000 and $50,000 has dropped by nineteen percentage points since 1967.[6]

These figures confirm what we believe to be the most stunning economic accomplishment in America over the past quarter century: the trend of upward economic mobility in America. A poor family in 1979 was more likely to be rich by the early 1990s than to still be poor.[7] This is the sign, not of a caste economic system, but of a meritocracy where people get ahead through hard work, saving, and smart investing. And moving up the ladder is the rule, not the exception, in America today.

There's a wonderful new video on Reason.tv called "Living Large" that can be viewed on YouTube. In it, comedian Drew Carey goes to a lake in California where people are relaxing on $80,000 twenty-seven-foot boats and goofing around on $25,000 jet skis that they have hitched to their $40,000 SUVs. Mr. Carey asks these boat owners what they do for a living. As it turns out, they aren't hedge fund managers. One is a gardener, another a truck driver, another an auto mechanic, and another a cop.[8]

Today most of the poor own things that once were considered luxuries, such as washing machines, clothes dryers, refrigerators, microwaves, color TV sets, air conditioning, stereos, cell phones, and at least one car. Table 1-1 shows that, amazingly, a larger percentage of poor families own these consumer items today than the middle class did in 1970.

One of the big dividends of this technology age is how rapidly new inventions become affordable to the middle class. It took more than fifty years for electricity and radio to reach the average household, but newer inventions, such as cell phones, laptop computers, and color TVs, became affordable within a matter of a few years (see Figure 1-1). We are democratizing wealth in America, and new things that were once the exclusive purchases of the rich are now regarded by Americans of all income groups as not just necessities, but entitlements. Young people today can't even fathom a society without cell phones, iPods, laptops, DVD players, and the like. They think that to live without these things is to be living in a prehistoric age. But watch a movie from twenty years ago and you will laugh

Table 1-1: The Ownership Society

Percent of Households That Own	All Households 1970	Poor Households 2005
Washing machine	71	72
Clothes dryer	44	57
Dishwasher	19	37
Refrigerator	83	99
Stove	87	99
Microwave	1	73
Color TV	40	97
Videocassette/DVD	1	78
Personal computer	3	25
Telephone	93	96
Cell/mobile phone	1	60
Air conditioner	34	82

Source: Dallas Federal Reserve, based on Census Bureau data.

out loud seeing big clunky black machines that weighed as much as a brick, gave crackly service, and cost $4,200. Now cell phones are about forty-two dollars—even disposable. And the cost of making calls has dropped dramatically, too.

Here's an even more amazing statistic: Americans in 2007 spent more than $1 billion just to change the answer tune on their cell phones.[9] And yet Americans are still far and away the most generous citizens of the planet, giving more than $306 billion in 2007 to charity to help others, while 60 million Americans volunteer time for nonprofits, hospitals, churches, and other causes.[10]

In the late 1990s Barbara Ehrenreich asked in the *New York Times,* "Is the Middle Class Doomed?" She then noted that "some economists have predicted that the middle class will disappear altogether, leaving the country torn, like many third world countries, between an affluent minority and throngs of the desperately

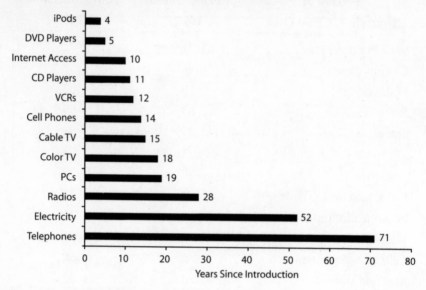

Figure 1-1: **Number of Years for Major Technologies to Reach 50 Percent of American Homes**

Source: Heritage Foundation.

poor."[11] Here's the truth. The purchasing power of the median-income family, that is, families at the midpoint of the income continuum, rose to $54,061 in 2004, an $8,228 real increase since 1980.[12] The middle class is not disappearing, Barbara, it is getting richer, as shown in Figure 1-2.

There's no question that the poor and even the middle class face real financial challenges—paying for health care, college tuition, making mortgage payments in a downward spiral of housing values, and filling up the gas tank at the pump. But we always have to ask the question: compared to what? Today the poor generally have access to more modern goods, services, and technologies than the middle class did in the middle of the last century. As Nobel Prize–winning economic historian Robert Fogel wrote in 2004: "In every measure that we have bearing on the standard of living . . . the gains of the lower classes have been far greater than those experienced by the population as a whole."[13]

Figure 1-2: Middle Class Getting Richer

Upper and Lower Income Limits for Middle Class Families

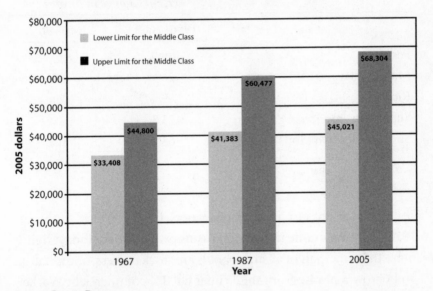

Source: Census Bureau.

A recent study by the Congressional Budget Office came to the eye-popping conclusion that from 1994 to 2004 Americans in the bottom 20 percent of income actually had the highest increase in incomes.[14] Yes, you read correctly: The poor got richer faster than the rich did. A subsequent study by the Treasury Department found the same thing.[15] When you track real families—real people—over time, you find that people who are poor at the start of the period you examine have the biggest subsequent gains in income. Amazingly, the richer a person is at any given point in time, the smaller the subsequent income gains. Those in the top 1 percent actually lose income over time. You won't read that in the *New York Times,* because the media treat facts like this as if they were closely guarded state secrets. And for the media, good news is practically a contradiction in terms when covering the American economy: If it's good, then it's not news. But no matter how you slice or dice the data, this has been a shared prosperity (see Table 1-2).

Table 1-2: **Poor Are Getting Richer**

	Percent Change in Income	
	1996–2005	**1987–96**
Poor	109%	81%
Middle class	26%	9%
Rich	9%	−2%
Super rich (top 1%)	−23%	−24%
Super duper rich (Top 0.01%)	−65%	n.a.

Source: Treasury Department, 2007.

Today we are not just a nation of earners, but of owners. In the late 1970s only about one in five Americans owned stock. Today slightly more than one-half of all households are stock owners, or capitalists. To borrow a phrase from the Prudential TV commercials: Workers and families own a piece of the rock in America. This is one of the most important and uplifting demographic changes of recent times in the United States. We are becoming a nation of worker/owners. Americans now increasingly own the means of production. Marxism is dead. There is no inherent death struggle between workers and capitalists because in America they are one and the same.

We could go on, but the enduring lesson we hope we've documented is how much the standard of living of Americans rose in the short time period since 1980, once we got our economic policies in order and rewarded growth. We only wish that this were the end of the beginning of this golden age of prosperity, not the beginning of the end.

Don't Know Much About History

So what explains our sudden turn toward pessimism? Why do we now forecast the End of Prosperity?

The short answer is that we aren't just optimists, we are first and foremost realists. And we are now witnessing nearly all of the economic policy dials that were once turned toward growth being twisted back toward recession. The problem is not a crisis of the American spirit or work ethic, or value system, or some inevitable decline due to complacency. It is that our politicians in both parties, but especially the liberal Democrats, are getting everything wrong—tax policy, regulatory policy, monetary policy, spending policy, trade policy. We call this the assault on growth. The political class seems to be almost intentionally steering the United States economy into the abyss—and, to borrow a phrase from P. J. O'Rourke, the American electorate, alas, seems ready and willing to hand them the keys and the bottle of whiskey to do it.[16] Almost all of the catastrophic policy mistakes are being coated with good intentions: to help the poor, the middle class, the environment, or the unemployed; to hold down prices, "obscene profits," or irresponsible CEO pay; or to close the gap between rich and poor.

Let us interject an anecdote that goes a long way toward explaining the backwardness of the current political environment. In a Democratic presidential primary debate in Philadelphia, the following interchange occurred between Charlie Gibson of ABC News and Barack Obama on the senator's plan to raise the capital gains tax. The discussion went like this:

> **Gibson:** Senator, you have said you would favor an
> increase in the capital gains tax. You said on CNBC, and
> I quote, "I certainly would not go above what existed
> under Bill Clinton," which was 28 percent. It's now 15
> percent. That's almost a doubling, if you went to 28
> percent. But actually, Bill Clinton, in 1997, signed legisla-
> tion that dropped the capital gains tax to 20 percent.
> **Obama:** Right.
> **Gibson:** And George Bush has taken it down to 15
> percent. And in each instance, when the rate dropped,

revenues from the tax increased; the government took in more money. And in the 1980s, when the tax was increased to 28 percent, the revenues went down. So why raise it at all, especially given the fact that 100 million people in this country own stock and would be affected?

Obama: Well, Charlie, what I've said is that I would look at raising the capital gains tax for purposes of fairness. We saw an article today which showed that the top fifty hedge fund managers made $29 billion last year—$29 billion for fifty individuals. And part of what has happened is that those who are able to work the stock market and amass huge fortunes on capital gains are paying a lower tax rate than their secretaries. That's not fair.

Gibson: But history shows that when you drop the capital gains tax, the revenues go up.

Obama: Well, that might happen, or it might not.[17]

This amazing exchange left us scratching our heads and wondering whether this gifted orator who can fill stadiums with 70,000 or more adoring fans and followers and says that he is promoting "The Audacity of Hope" has even the slightest clue about how economics works in the real world. How jobs are created. How entrepreneurs and risk takers create wealth. Mr. Obama admitted in front of a national television audience that he would raise the capital gains tax even if the revenues would fall—because this is the "fair" thing to do. Fair to whom? Everyone—and we mean everyone—loses when a tax increase lowers revenue. The government, the taxpayer, the economy, American workers.

But this was only the beginning of the onslaught, not the end. We're worried that tax rates are going to go up across the board over the next few years—income tax, capital gains taxes, dividend taxes, Social Security taxes, and estate taxes. Even many of our friends who believe in limited government say that taxes must rise over the next five or ten years to pay for the stampeding cost of

Medicare, Medicaid, and Social Security. We're worried that the dreaded alternative minimum tax, which is now paid by some 5 million upper-income families, will be expanded to 25 million mostly middle class families as early as 2009. We've seen the greatest era of tax rate reduction in decades all over the globe in Iceland, Ireland, Britain, Sweden, even France. By 2010 the United States could be the nation with the highest tax rates on investment, savings, corporate profits, and stock ownership of any nation in the world. How will America compete and win in a global economy with that millstone around the neck of U.S. businesses? That can't be healthy for the U.S. economy.

One thing is certain: If Washington turns all the policy dials in the wrong direction, just as sure as the sun rises in the morning, the U.S. economic growth machine will grind to a halt. It's already happening, as evidenced by the housing crisis, high gas and food prices, and the collapse of the dollar. That is, in fact, the central premise of this book: Economic policy matters. Incentives matter. Prosperity doesn't happen by accident, and growth is not the natural course of events; it has to be nurtured and rewarded.

A corollary to this premise is that when the politicians start to get the wires crossed, as on the engine of a finely tuned race car, bad things can happen in a hurry. When we got our policies terribly misaligned in the 1930s during the Great Depression the economy didn't recover for twelve years, and then only because we entered a world war and the economy became a military emergency mobilization operation. The explanation of the Great Depression and the human misery it wrought is not an unsolved mystery.[18] The twelve-year economic slide was a result of trade protectionism, high tax rates, a contractionary monetary policy, and a New Deal mishmash of government programs that were well intentioned, but made things worse, not better. The result was the worst stock market performance in history, bread lines and one in four Americans out of a job.

Then in the 1970s, during the era of malaise and stagflation, the over-regulated, overtaxed and overinflated U.S. economy sank from the exhaustion of carrying around these economic Quaaludes, and the stock market went Helter Skelter. We should have learned from these eras of despair that policymakers can do a lot of harm to financial conditions, family incomes, and American competitiveness—and they can rain down destruction in a hurry.

If anything, now that we live in a globalized economy without walls and with information traveling at warp speed, the penalty for getting economics wrong is more swiftly imposed and more punitive than in earlier times. Capital markets adapt to policy changes not within months or weeks but within hours, minutes, and even seconds. Tens of billions of dollars of capital investment can move from one nation to another in the time it takes global capitalists to right-click on the computer terminal. That we live in an era of quicksilver capital is a liberating force for good, not evil—it disciplines rogue governments for intervening in markets and for making horrendous policy mistakes. But it doesn't guarantee that politicians won't screw up in the first place.

The Four Killers of Prosperity

The tanking of the U.S. economy in the 1930s and the 1970s demonstrates the dangers of the four great killers of prosperity and bull markets. Those killers are:

- Trade protectionism.
- Tax increases and profligate government spending.
- New regulations and increased government intervention in the economy.
- Monetary policy mistakes.

So what can happen when we get these policies wrong? Again, the 1970s is instructive. Prices started the decade rising at 5 percent, then 6 percent, then 9 percent, then 11 percent, and then, in Jimmy Carter's last months in office, at a 14 percent inflation rate. And when unions scored three-year contracts with 30 percent pay raises in the late 1970s, the hard-hat workers finally discovered they had been hoodwinked: Their fat raises were falling behind stampeding price increases. Families saw their biggest decline in real after-tax incomes since the Great Depression, with the median family *losing* almost $3,000 of income (in today's dollars) thanks to high unemployment and high inflation. The highest tax rates hit 70 percent, and in some states the combined federal and state tax rate exceeded 80 percent. That meant that the government was entitled to four-fifths of the last dollar earned on investment. Regulations and government spending also went berserk. Investing, working, starting a business, taking risks—all of which are economic virtues in our book—were punished rather than rewarded. The result, as we see in Figure 1-3, was the worst stock market performance since the Great Depression. After-inflation, stocks lost 6.1 percent of their value compounded annually for sixteen years.

But now take a close look at the second half of the chart and you will see the astonishing and nearly uninterrupted surge in stock values starting in the early 1980s when taxes and inflation were cut. Our friend Larry Kudlow of CNBC TV's *Kudlow & Company* calls this "the greatest story never told." And we agree. Instead of losing 6 percent per year the S&P 500 rose at an annual real rate of just under 8 percent. The Dow Jones Industrial Average soared from 800 in 1982 to 12,500 at the time of this writing in early 2008. If we have another quarter-century run like that, by 2033 the stock market will be at 120,000.

In the 1980s, we rediscovered prosperity through the new agenda of supply-side economics. Ronald Reagan embraced as a centerpiece of his economic philosophy the idea of the Laffer Curve, which in shorthand tells us that when tax rates get too high, they smother growth and can cost the government more revenue than they raise.

Figure 1-3: From Bust to Boom:
Before and After-Inflation Stock Market Performance*

Stock Market Performance Before and After Inflation

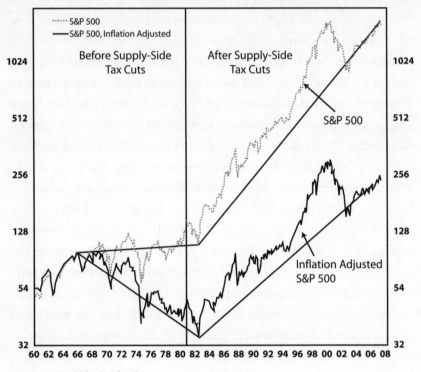

* Does not include dividends.
Source: SAP, W&J, BLS.

In the 1980s and 1990s and early 2000s most of the obstacles to growth were cleared away. Taxes, tariffs, regulations, and inflation weren't eliminated, but they were tamed. Yes, there were policy mistakes along the way, there were periods of irrational exuberance in tech stocks and housing and savings and loans, there were tax increases under Reagan and Clinton that did more harm than good, there were protectionist tariff policies that set back the trade liberalization agenda. But the unmistakable trend over the period was toward stable prices, a dependable and strong currency, lower and flatter tax rates, freer trade, a lighter hand of regulation in key industries ranging from financial services to transportation to tele-communications and energy, somewhat moderated levels of federal spending, welfare reforms that rewarded work over dependency, the elimination of most price controls, and so on.[19]

Without these interferences the economy blossomed and U.S. industries reawakened from the wicked spell of stagflation. The United States was unquestionably the global winner in the race for capital around the world. America soaked up some $5 trillion in net capital investment from around the world.[20] Smart money got parked in America, because this is where the growth and innovation occurred and where the value was added. (Think of the Silicon Valley high-tech revolution.) The after-tax, after-inflation return on a dollar of investment was more than doubled in many cases, so the dollars flowed in. These growth policies also attracted human capital, as smart and ambitious people knocked down the doors to stream in to fill many of the 40 million jobs that appeared practically out of thin air.[21] And the United States became the world's premier economic superpower. By 2005, according to the U.S. Department of Labor, the amount of production per person in America was $42,100, versus $34,000 in Canada, $31,000 in Japan, $30,200 in France, $29,800 in Germany, and $25,500 in Italy.[22]

Much of this growth was also fostered by the dawning of the age of the microchip and all the attendant fabulous technological advances, which have played such a vital role in this wild and wonderful ride. Ingenious and daring entrepreneurs from Bill Gates to Fred Smith to Larry Ellison to Google founders Sergey Brin and Larry Page launched whole new industries and made billions of dollars for themselves and billions more for workers and society. One of the often-repeated lies about the U.S. economy is that "we don't make anything in America anymore." Nonsense. We have created whole new 21st-century knowledge-based industries. Our point is that supply-side economic policies created the fertile environment for the entrepreneurial spirit that has made the information age economy such a brilliant success. The technological explosion and the Silicon Valley revolution might not have happened when it did and where it did had it not been for the pro-investment climate fostered by supply-side policies. It's a lot harder to raise the money to start a new technology firm with 70 percent tax rates and a 40 percent real capital gains tax rate than with tax rates half that high.

Around the world other nations observed how the American economy raced forward and ran laps around their own economies. And these nations in effect shrugged their shoulders and said: If you can't beat 'em join 'em. They moved gradually, but recently with increasing urgency, to adopt the supply-side, or "the American model" of free markets and low taxes, to emulate what they saw had worked so brilliantly in the United States. Tax rates in the developed nations around the world are on average twenty to twenty-five percentage points *lower* today than they were in the early 1980s. China, India, Vietnam, Eastern Europe, and now—we never thought we would see the day—even the nations of old Europe, Germany, Sweden, Italy, and yes, France, are shedding the welfare states' state-owned enterprises, and the confiscatory tax policies and are re-engineering their economies in a more capital-friendly way. Good for them. Why aren't we doing the same?

Which Brings Us to Today

We now live in troubled and turbulent economic times. In mid-2008 Americans are feeling uneasy and even slightly panicked about their financial future. They are worried about jobs, health care, and the high price of energy and food. They are also concerned about the housing crisis and making mortgage payments on homes that are falling in value. Many people have told us: The End of Prosperity is *already here*. Polls reveal a widespread gloom among voters not seen since the early 1980s.

So what course will we take to fix things?

16

We are now told by politicians that government will solve all these problems for us. The *New York Times Magazine* ran a lengthy article about the end of laissez faire economics in America—as if we ever had that. The *Times* advised that once upon a time free market champion Milton Friedman taught us that it was the botched job of government and politicians that created the Great Depression. But now in 2008, "a bipartisan chorus has declared that unfettered markets are in need of fettering. Bailouts, stimulus packages, and regulation dominate the conversation—on Wall Street, main street, and Pennsylvania Avenue."[23] We are now told that America can survive only with more government tentacles and do-gooders and controls and rules and programs to help save people and businesses from their own bad decisions. We're back to cradle-to-grave safety nets and cradle-to-grave dependency.

Consider the financial and political fallout from the subprime mortgage crisis. A subprime mortgage is a mortgage given to a borrower with a less-than-stellar credit rating, hence sub, or below, prime. Over the last two to three years, while real estate prices were setting records around the country, a boom in real estate financing followed closely on the heels of the rush to buy property. To capitalize on the market frenzy, lenders devised novel means of financing to help buyers purchase properties they might not otherwise have been able to afford.

But home prices went down, not up, as the real estate crisis spread, and now millions of Americans have mortgages that are more than what the house is actually worth. No bank is going to refinance a house for an amount higher than what it is worth. To add to the misery, subprime mortgage interest rates ballooned, hiking payments on the original loan, which many borrowers couldn't afford. What happened in thousands upon thousands of cases is that the hapless owner dropped the keys off at the bank ("jingle mail") and moved, likely to a rental unit. Another mortgage gone bad and another house on the block in foreclosure.

What happened to these mortgages? The bank no longer had

them. The bank had sold them to some clever Wall Street firms that packaged them into bonds with fancy names like CDOs, or Collateralized Debt Obligations. What happened next is at the heart of the subprime crisis. The wave of defaults on home mortgages cascaded into major losses for the holders of CDOs. As of early 2008, the reported writedowns of major financial institutions reached the staggering sum of $120 billion—and the number keeps climbing. The legendary investment bank Bear Stearns, which effectively imploded in the crisis, was acquired by J. P. Morgan for ten dollars a share (down from $170 in 2007). The fortunes and retirement nest eggs of thousands of Bear Stearns executives and employees were wiped out in an instant, and Bear Stearns stock investors took a bath.

Now here is what is really scary. The federal government now wants a massive $300 billion bailout of the very banks and the borrowers who often got greedy and tried to "play the market." Congress wants the Federal Housing Administration to provide 100 percent taxpayer insurance for these failing subprime loans. Why? Doesn't this just reward the bad behavior and the greed? There are somewhere near 55 million mortgages in America, and some 52 million of those mortgages are being paid on time by conscientious and financially responsible people. Sometimes it's a hardship to make those mortgage payments. But most of us do it. So here's a question about fairness: How is it fair to make 52 million who acted responsibly and are paying their mortgages on time pay more in taxes to bail out those who acted irresponsibly? In the marketplace, if you take a risk and you win, you keep your winnings. But now government is saying if you lose, the government bails you out! This sounds like heads I win, tails the taxpayers lose.

Plummeting home prices are not the only economic adversity we face today. Oil has soared above $140 a barrel, and gasoline prices are up to $4 a gallon. Hard-pressed consumers face higher prices on such necessities as transportation and heating, increased costs they simply cannot absorb without cutting somewhere else.

Stock market volatility has soared. Daily triple-digit movement of the Dow Jones Industrial Averages, once a rare phenomenon, is now common. Indeed, declines of two hundred and even three hundred points occur with alarming regularity, offset by occasional large increases. In just the first half of 2008, Americans lost $2 trillion in wealth.

So, whither prosperity?

The Imminent Economic Danger

Today there is a widespread consensus of opinion that tougher times lie ahead. Employment is down, incomes are down, housing values are down, family incomes are down, and consumer confidence is in the tank. The only thing that seems to be up these days is the price of everything we buy, from groceries to gas.

If in this precarious financial environment a new Congress decides to impose tax increases, the effect on our economy could be devastating. Indeed, a series of tax increases, presumably on "the wealthy," could decapitate the prosperity we have enjoyed for over two decades. These tax increases will also sink the nervous stock market, and accelerate the sell-off of the shrinking dollar.

The danger is imminent and very real. One of the most serious aspects of the problem today is that major tax increases will occur if Congress does *absolutely nothing*, something it has become very adept at. The Bush tax cuts that reduced the tax on capital gains and dividends to 15 percent will simply expire after 2010 if nothing is done to extend them. That would mean that the capital gains tax rate will go from 15 percent to 20 percent, and the dividend tax rate will go from 15 percent back to 39.6 percent or higher for top earners. Barack Obama has suggested raising the capital gains tax rate to as high as 28 percent—higher than the rate when Bill Clinton left office.

Arguably the cruelest tax increase of all will be the death tax increase. The death tax has been declining each year under the Bush tax cuts. In 2010, that tax reaches 0 percent. But, if nothing is done to extend the tax cut, the death tax jumps from 0 percent to 55 percent in 2011. It takes little imagination to understand that in these automatic tax increases, which require no action or initiative, we have the makings of an economic calamity.

Is There a 50 Percent Tax "Baracket" in Your Future?

Under the Obama tax plan that is spelled out in detail on his website, tax rates on income will go back to as high as 50 to 60 percent. Senator Obama believes that "there's no doubt that the tax system has been skewed. And the Bush tax cuts—people didn't need them, and they weren't even asking for them, and that's why they need to be less, so that we can pay for universal health care and other initiatives." [24]

But it could be worse than that. Note these frightening comments by a Democratic "thought leader" and former secretary of labor, economist Robert Reich (Steve Moore's "dynamic duo" debate partner each week on CNBC TV). Reich wrote in December 2006 about the need for "An Economic Populism" (ughh!) to "level the playing field" in education, health care, and the workplace:

> And to pay for all of this, and guarantee upward mobility, the tax system would have to be made far more progressive than it is today—starting with excusing the first $20,000 of income from payroll taxes and removing the $100,000 cap on those taxes, and getting back toward the 70 to 90 percent marginal tax on the highest incomes we had under Eisenhower and JFK. [25]

We think the solution to our economic problems lies 180 degrees in the opposite direction. We favor a low flat tax with everyone paying the same low tax rate. If you make more money, you pay higher taxes, but at the same rate. No more tax shelters. We will show how America could impose a flat tax of just 12 percent on business activity and household income and still generate enough money to run the government. Imagine America with a 12 percent tax rate. Our economy would fly as if powered by rocket fuel.

But the Left says it wants progressive taxes that get higher and higher as incomes rise. In the Eisenhower administration, that rate was as high as 91 percent, and Reich suggests that we go back there! So how hard would you want to work for that last dollar of income if the government would take away ninety-one cents of every last dollar you earned? It is frightening to think that some Democratic leaders are seriously suggesting a return to that type of confiscatory taxation.

Doesn't the flat tax make much more sense?

Fair Trade Means No Trade

In August 2007 Senator Barack Obama launched this rant against free trade:

> Look, people don't want a cheaper T-shirt if they're losing a job in the process. They would rather have the job and pay a little bit more for a T-shirt. And I think that's something that all Americans could agree to.[26]

Really? Well, let's push this example a little farther. Would Americans mind paying "a little bit more" for their cars to keep Americans employed? And what about plasma TVs, home appliances, clothing, and food? Where would this lead? You know the answer. We would become an economy that produces products that are uncompetitive and with zero export value. What would happen to jobs then?

Trade protectionism crosses party lines. Republican presidential candidate Mike Huckabee won the Iowa caucuses running on a message of trade protectionism.

The people who are victimized the most by trade barriers and tariffs are the poor. They are the ones who benefit the most from the lowering of prices that free trade brings. From 2001 to 2006 the prices of food, clothing, and basic modern conveniences like appliances fell, and that is in large part due to the forces of global competition that hold down prices. It is ordinary people who shop at Wal-Mart and harness the greatest economic gain from the low prices of imports from China. In many ways international trade and discount stores like Wal-Mart that sell imported goods have done more to alleviate poverty in America than all the Great Society programs wrapped together. Why don't Barack Obama or Nancy Pelosi or Mike Huckabee or the union chiefs understand this?

We hope the reader can see already that our book is not meant to make a partisan case for one political party over the other. Yes, Barack Obama and Hillary Clinton and Nancy Pelosi scare us. But there are a lot of Democrats *and* Republicans we also think don't have their tray tables in the upright and locked position when it comes to understanding sound economics. The warning we also give here is offered to both parties. It is a call to arms, an appeal to reason to all Americans, and especially to those who seek public office.

If we allow higher taxes, we will face higher unemployment, plus lower or even negative growth, and a declining stock market that will affect Americans at all economic levels, from stock and mutual fund investors to those Americans who depend on their pensions, IRAs, and 401(k)s to ensure their comfortable retirement. Remember, over half of Americans today are investors in the stock market. The best prescription for their investments and for continuing a strong economy is lower taxes and free trade.

Read on.

Heed this message.

Please!

2

HOW A COCKTAIL NAPKIN CHANGED THE WORLD:
THE LAFFER CURVE

Taxes operate upon energy and industry, and skill and thrift, like a fine upon those qualities. If I have worked harder and built myself a good house while you have been contented to live in a hovel, the tax gatherer now comes annually to make me pay a penalty for my energy and industry, by taxing me more than you. If I have saved while you wasted, I am taxed, while you are exempt. If a man builds a ship, we make him pay for his industry as though he has done injury to the state.

—HENRY GEORGE, nineteenth-century American economist[1]

In December 1974, a group of men dined at the Two Continents restaurant at the Hotel Washington in Washington, D.C. The stately old hotel sat right across the street from the Treasury Department, and one building away from the White House, on Pennsylvania Avenue. One of the men dining that night was Jude Wanniski, then associate editor at the *Wall Street Journal* editorial page. The three other men at dinner were Dr. Arthur Laffer, associate professor at the University of Chicago, Don Rumsfeld, chief of staff to then president Gerald Ford, and Dick Cheney, Rumsfeld's deputy and Laffer's former classmate at Yale.

Had it not been for Jude Wanniski's writing a famous article in *The Public Interest* magazine a few years later, this dinner would have been forgotten long ago and would have had no more historical significance than any other of the hundreds of gabfests of Inside the Beltway types that happen every evening in Washington. But it was on this occasion, during a heated discussion of President Ford's Whip Inflation Now (WIN) proposal for fighting inflation and getting the economy out of its rut, that thirty-four-year-old Dr. Laffer grabbed a pen from his pocket and his cloth napkin and quickly sketched some lines and a curve that showed the tradeoff between tax rates and tax revenues. In his article, Wanniski memorialized the tradeoff as the "Laffer Curve."[2]

Each of the participants had different recollections of that evening, and Laffer's only objection to Wanniski's version is that his mother had taught him better manners than to desecrate an elegant cloth napkin, and he had drawn the curve on a paper cocktail napkin.

Whichever version is true, no one could have possibly imagined that this simple economic insight—that when tax rates get too high they injure the economy and produce less money for the government—on that evening thirty-four years ago would launch a new chapter of economic theory and history for the United States and the rest of the world. Some thirty years later the dinner had a big impact on Bush administration tax-cutting policy. Vice President Dick Cheney recently recalled the meeting and the significance of the Laffer Curve revelation. "The point Laffer was trying to make was basic supply-side theory, that by cutting people's taxes you could change their behavior and they would work harder and produce more. I didn't run out and say 'Mr. President, Mr. President [President Ford], you have to cut taxes.' During the Reagan years a lot of us became supply-side advocates. I reached that point where I believe that it is extraordinarily important to keep taxes as low as possible. . . . I also believe it does produce more revenue for the federal government."[3] This was one of the reasons George Bush enacted his investment tax cut in 2003.

Love or hate supply-side economics, there is no doubt that the ideas behind the Laffer Curve transformed national economic policies for nearly two generations, and that during the period of triumph of supply-side economics the world has experienced the largest expansion in living standards in world history. The Laffer Curve has created a growth revolution across the globe from America, to Ireland, to Iceland, to Russia, to China and Hong Kong, to India, and to Ukraine. Ronald Reagan and Margaret Thatcher were the first world leaders to adopt Laffer Curve logic in their economic programs in the early 1980s, but the curve is now well understood—though still controversial—almost everywhere.[4]

For that reason Arthur Laffer's drawing belongs in the Smithsonian Institution, or at least the economics hall of fame—if there ever is one.

What the Cocktail Napkin Taught Us

The idea behind supply-side economics, that tax cuts can spur economic growth, is not new and not so radical. Art Laffer is the first to point out that he did not invent this theory. As with so much of our knowledge in economics, one of the scholars who first explained that taxes affect behavior was Adam Smith, who wrote in *The Wealth of Nations*:

> *High taxes, sometimes by diminishing the consumption of the taxed commodities, and sometimes by encouraging smuggling, frequently afford a smaller revenue to government than what might be drawn from more modest taxes.*[5]

What might surprise some of our friends who resist these ideas is that even John Maynard Keynes, whose economic theories, which favored government expansion, reigned as the established doctrine for much of the twentieth century, showed that he understood the dynamics of the Laffer Curve when he weighed in on the subject in 1931 with his usual rhetorical flare:

> Taxation may be so high as to defeat its object, and . . . given sufficient time to gather the fruits, a reduction of taxation will run a better chance than an increase of balancing the budget. For to take the opposite view today is to resemble a manufacturer who, running at a loss, decides to raise his price, and when his declining sales increase the loss, wrapping himself in the rectitude of plain arithmetic, decides that prudence requires him to raise the price still more.[6]

Even America's founding fathers, perhaps the greatest group of thinkers gathered in one place at one time in history, saw the wisdom of keeping taxes low. Thomas Jefferson was also a supply-sider. He argued that "a wise and frugal government, which shall leave men free to regulate their own pursuits of industry and improvement, and shall not take from the mouth of labor the bread it has earned—this is the sum of good government."[7]

For this reason the founding fathers resisted an income tax (the Constitution banned "direct taxation" on labor), and for the first hundred or so years of our nation's history, there was no income tax and the overall tax burden rarely rose above 10 percent. But as the income tax rose to 70 percent, 80 percent, and even above 90 percent during and after World War II, the economic harm of this tax was greatly magnified. These high tax rates reduced the incentive to produce. To understand why, consider the story of Robinson Crusoe and three other poor souls stranded on a desert island.

Our four friends are in dire straits. They are hungry, cold, and ill-clothed, and have nowhere to sleep but on the cold beach or in damp caves. They are living in a depression economy, because there is no production of goods and services. They want and need housing, food, clothes, fresh water—and will give up nearly everything to get these necessities. They have a supply-side problem, not a demand-side problem.

Surely, the key to their survival is for them to start producing things: to find and gather food, to turn bamboo sticks into housing, to hunt wild animals for food. Of the four people on the island, one, Robinson Crusoe, is hyperproductive, and he gets up early in the morning before sunrise and trudges off to gather the fruit, hunt for meat, and build a fire, and then he spends the rest of the day carving bamboo shoots to build huts. He shares some of his output with his friends—but he also takes a lot for himself. He is the entrepreneur of the foursome. The other three are unmotivated, lazy, and fatalistic about their fortunes. They sleep in, hang out at the beach, and complain about their unhappy predicament.

One day the three slouches huddle together in the hut that their colleague built, and they decide that this island will operate as a democracy and the "ruling council" has decided that there will be a 90 percent tax on everything that is produced: fire, fruits and nuts, huts, meat, coconut milk, and so on. This is justified, they say, because it is the only "equitable" way to prevent a growing income gap on the island between the rich (Robinson) and the poor (them)—the haves and the have-nots. Why should Robinson have so much and the other three of us so little, they complain indignantly, as they munch on some of the nuts and drink some of the coconut milk he supplied them?

But now Robinson isn't feeling so motivated anymore under these new rules. He decides that being assessed a 90 percent tax so that the other three get nine-tenths of what he produces isn't so fair at all. So Robinson goes on strike and decides that he, too, will lounge around all day. But then he realizes that he has to work or he will starve and get cold at night. So he decides to move to the other side of the island to avoid the high taxes imposed by the council. He moves into the "underground economy." He finds fruits, nuts, and vegetables, but he quickly eats them all himself and doesn't report to the other three that he found food—90 percent of which he would have to turn over to them. In other words, he engages in tax evasion. He underreports his income to the other three. They see their own plight becoming more desperate, so they decide to raise the tax rate to 95 percent so they don't starve. Six months later a ship arrives on the island only to find three corpses on one side and one healthy, thriving survivor on the other side.

We can see from this tale of Robinson Crusoe that a 90 percent tax does not lead to a fairer distribution of the output of the economy. Rather, it leads to less output and in this case even deprivation, as everyone cuts back on his production.

Mick Jagger: Supply-Sider

Now let's turn to some real life examples of the Laffer Curve. Those who don't believe that taxes affect behavior might want to recall the story of the Beatles and the Rolling Stones. In 1965 George Harrison of the Beatles wrote a famous anthem to supply-side economics called "The Taxman." The first line of the song goes like this: "Let me tell you how it will be, here's one for you nineteen for me."[8]

The four Beatles were furious about British tax rates and felt unfairly punished for their success. In the mid-1960s, when this song was written, the English government imposed a 95 percent tax rate on very rich people . . . like the Beatles. A 95 percent tax rate meant that for every twenty pounds the Beatles earned, the British tax collector took nineteen and the Beatles kept one. And then they even had to split their earnings with Ringo. (Just kidding!)

It should not be too surprising that many British pop stars in that era, including Mick Jagger, moved their income "offshore" or quit writing hit songs to avoid these confiscatory tax rates. Thank goodness Mick, who, by the way, attended the London School of Economics, chose the former.

Rock stars and celebrities are still engaging in tax minimization

28

strategies even today, much to the consternation of their home countries. In 2006, U2's Bono, a humanitarian renowned for fighting AIDS in Africa, was said to be "furious that Ireland is doing away with its law exempting artists and authors from taxation," according to the *Irish Examiner*. The story continues, the group has begun to move parts of its business interests to the Netherlands. U2 pays "virtually no tax on royalties" in Holland.[9] There are evidently limits to how much taxes even great humanitarians are willing to pay.

The Logic of the Laffer Curve

It would seem to be a matter of simple arithmetic that if you raise tax rates, the immediate effect will be that revenues from taxes will increase. A doubling of the tax rate should cause revenues to double; a halving of the tax rates should cause tax receipts to fall by 50 percent. That is indeed the expected effect. But a pattern has been observed over the years, or rather the ages, that calls into question this truism. Instead, history has documented an alternative truism: Politicians have tended to overestimate the expected gains from an increase in tax rates, and they have tended to overestimate the loss in tax revenue from a decrease in rates.

What explains this conundrum? Well, to start, the real-world effect of a tax increase is to take away some of the incentive to work—as George Harrison, Mick Jagger, and Hollywood actor Ronald Reagan discovered. Why should workers or entrepreneurs break their backs if the government is going to take half or more of what they make? Moreover, higher taxes cause high income earners to hire expensive accountants and lawyers to find tax shelters and other means to reduce their tax burden. And high rates can also induce people to move from high-tax places to low-tax places. Conversely, lower tax rates have the reverse effect: a greater incentive to both workers and entrepreneurs to create wealth (and a smaller incentive to engage in tax sheltering). This wealth creation process provides more jobs and more profits, which in turn often spins off more tax revenues than expected—just as Henry George explained the process at the beginning of the chapter.

Here's what the Laffer Curve looks like (Figure 2-1):

Figure 2-1: **The Laffer Curve**

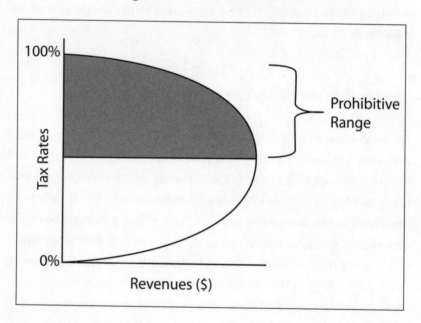

The central insight of the Laffer Curve is that there are always two tax rates that produce zero revenue. This is obvious when one thinks about it. It is clear that 0 percent taxes produces zero revenues. No surprise there! But there is another tax rate that produces zero revenues, and that's a tax rate of 100 percent. If the government takes everything you earn you don't work. (Actually, people would work to sustain themselves, but they would not report the income to the tax collector and thus the government would get nothing.)

Another insight of the Laffer Curve, as shown in the figure, is that between these two extremes of 0 percent and 100 percent rates of tax, there are two tax rates that will collect the same amount of revenue: a high tax rate on a small tax base and a low tax rate on a large tax base.

The Laffer Curve doesn't say whether a tax cut will raise or lower revenues. Revenue responses to a tax rate change will depend upon the tax system in place, the time period being considered, the ease of moving into underground activities, and the prevalence of legal loopholes. As you follow the shape of the curve, notice that when you get most of the way up the line on the left, tax revenues start to go down. The theory is simply saying that at these higher tax rates (in the "prohibitive range"), there is a disincentive to make more money, which will result in lower revenues from taxes. In the end, it's really all about incentives to work, invest, take risks, and earn money.

Incentives matter in life. They guide our behavior, sometimes even subconsciously. Remember the famous case of Pavlov's dog that we all learned in biology? Pavlov would ring the bell and the dog would then immediately be given a treat. After just a few iterations of this experiment, the ringing of the bell would cause the dog to salivate. We are, whether we like it or not, Pavlovian creatures. A stimulus generates a response. In much the same way, rewards for work generate more work. If you pay people not to work (through welfare programs or other income transfers) or put a hefty tax penalty on them if they do work, it's human nature that they won't work.

Most of us strive to help our fellow man, but human beings are not saints. We are public-spirited and charitable creatures, but almost all of us are first and foremost interested in our own welfare and that of our family. People do not work so they can pay taxes. If people were motivated entirely to help other people and sought to pay as much in taxes as possible, there would be no need for mandatory taxes. But we know from thousands of years of experience that people try to avoid the taxman, and they often do everything possible to minimize their payments. There is a voluntary program that the federal government runs in which tax filers can donate *more* than their tax liability to the government to help pay down the national debt. That fund collects less than $3 million, or less than three cents a year from the 130 million Americans who file a tax form.

Supply-side economics is also resisted because it poses a central challenge to the orthodoxy of Keynesian economics. That theory is based on the premise developed by the famous British economist John Maynard Keynes, that in a recession government should help stimulate demand for goods and services to put idle resources back to work.[10] By contrast, the supply-side tax theory argues that the economic problem is not one of insufficient demand for goods and services, but insufficient production. After all, poor nations such as Bangladesh and those in Africa do not have insufficient demand. Their problem is an inability to produce enough goods and services—a lack of supply.

Laffer Curve Lessons

So what does the Laffer Curve teach us about what governments should and shouldn't do when they establish tax policies? Here are a few of the most important lessons we wish the politicians would commit to memory:

Principle 1. When you tax something you get less of it and when you tax something less, you get more of it.
Most lawmakers know instinctively that taxes reduce the activity being taxed—even if they don't care to admit it. Governments routinely tax things that are "bad"—like cigarettes and alcohol, and gambling and prostitution (by banning it, which is the equivalent of a 100 percent

tax)—to discourage an activity. We reduce or in some cases entirely eliminate taxes on behavior that we want to *encourage*, such as buying a home, going to college, saving money for retirement, investing in energy-efficient appliances, and giving money to charity.

This explains why it is wise to keep taxes on work, savings, and investment as low as possible in order not to deter these activities.

Principle 2. The best tax system helps make poor people rich, not rich people poor.
Again, this does not seem a controversial statement, but sometimes we wonder if lawmakers simply want to punish the wealthy with high tax rates regardless of whether more money is raised to fund the government. When the government tries to redistribute income through high tax rates, it seldom succeeds. But it does succeed in slowing the economy and reducing the volume of income which makes everyone poorer.

Principle 3. The higher the tax rate, the more damage to the economy and the greater the economic gain from reducing the tax rate.
This is best explained with an example: A 90 percent tax rate means workers get to keep just 10 cents for every additional dollar they earn. Cutting that tax rate by just ten percentage points to 80 percent allows workers to keep 20 cents on what they earn, thus doubling their take-home salary. But now let us say that the tax rate is 20 percent, meaning the worker keeps 80 cents on the dollar. Now if that rate is cut by the same ten percentage points as in the first example, the worker now keeps 90 cents on the dollar. But his increase in after-tax pay is only 12.5 percent (from 80 cents to 90 cents). Economic output and the tax base are increased more by lowering the higher rate than the lower rate.

Principle 4. If tax rates get too high, they may lead to a reduction in tax receipts—as demonstrated by the Laffer Curve.
This is the principle that gives some of our friends on the left heartburn. But history proves there is a prohibitive range in which tax rates

are so high that cutting them can produce more, not less revenues. This is what we learned in the 1920s, 1960s, and 1980s. Tax rates went down but tax revenues went way up, as we will document in Chapter 3.

Principle 5. An efficient tax system has a broad tax base and a low tax rate.

Taxes are undoubtedly needed to fund government. But the ideal tax system of a state, city, or nation will raise this revenue in a way that minimally distorts or retards economic activity. High tax rates make the value of tax deductions, tax evasion, smuggling, and other tax avoidance techniques much greater and thus reward unproductive lobbying activities. If the tax base is broad, tax rates can be kept as low and non-confiscatory as possible. This is one reason we favor a flat tax with minimal deductions and loopholes. It is also why at last count twenty-four nations around the world had adopted the flat tax. Russia gets more revenues with its 13 percent flat tax than it did under the old tax system when tax rates were well over 50 percent.

Principle 6. People, businesses, and capital move from high-tax to low-tax areas.

We don't have a Berlin Wall around our cities, states, or nation—thank God. This means people and economic resources can move freely from one jurisdiction to another. We have powerful evidence from cities, states, and countries that businesses and people flee high-tax areas in favor of low-tax areas. In Chapter 8 we show this to be true of states (i.e., low-tax states attract more productive people than high-tax states).

So is there any recent evidence to confirm our thesis that excessive taxes on production can reduce jobs, incomes, and business creation? In this book we put plenty of evidence on display, but we have been struck by the number of studies published in recent years confirming the Laffer Curve. For example, one recent study done by Nobel Prize–winner Edward Prescott and published by the

National Bureau of Economic Research (NBER) found that people work more when tax rates are lowered. "Americans now work 50% more than do Germans, French and Italians." Lower marginal tax rates on income account for "the large change in relative labor supply [in the U.S.] over time."[11]

We were not surprised to see research findings from another NBER study detecting a big behavior effect from the reduction in the dividend tax by George W. Bush. "The individual income tax burden on dividends was lowered sharply in 2003 from a maximum rate of 35% to 15%," reports the study. "The surge in regular dividend payments after the 2003 reform is unprecedented in recent years."[12]

And finally a 2007 study by Christina Romer and David Romer, which was financed by the National Science Foundation, examined tax policy changes in the United States from 1947 through today. It found that "tax increases are highly contractionary. The effects are strongly significant, highly robust, and much larger than those obtained [in earlier studies]. The large effect stems in considerable part from a powerful negative effect [from tax increases] on investment."[13] We hope that gets the politicians' attention.

Is There a Laffer Curve Effect from Taxing Beer?

Can taxes on alcohol get so high that raising them at the state level reduces tax revenues? A 2004 Tax Foundation study documents that there is competition among the states for beer purchases and that beer drinkers make more purchases in low-beer-tax states than in high-beer-tax states. In 2000, for example, states lost $40 million in sales and excise tax revenues due to cross-border beer shopping. The study found that "the greater the price differential, the more likely it is that individuals living in border areas of high-tax jurisdictions will shop in a low-tax jurisdiction." The biggest loser in this cross-border drinking was Illinois, which lost 4.5 percent of its revenues due to its residents' purchasing beer out of state. The state lost $8 million in revenues because Illinois residents bought 4.8 million cases of beer outside their home state. Meanwhile, 15 percent of beer purchases in Delaware, which has one of the lowest beer taxes in the Northeast, were to out-of-staters. Delaware's windfall from the low taxes: $338,000 in revenues. And of course that doesn't include the extra business for its retail stores.[14]

So Illinois: This Bud's for you.

Supply-Side Economics 101

To be sure, the supply-side school preaches more than the deleterious effects of high tax rates, as shown in the Laffer Curve. In fact the Left likes to parody supply-side economists as believing that "tax cuts are the solution to every problem in the world." Wrong. Taxes are important, but supply-side economics is about expanding the supply of goods and services produced in an economy through all sorts of incentives (and by knocking down negative incentives).

Supply-side theory is based on a series of policy imperatives beyond tax cuts:

- Free trade.
- Stable prices and sound money.
- Light and efficient regulation of industry.
- Reform of welfare policies to encourage work.
- A generous immigration policy.
- Less costly and more efficient government.

We describe in the following chapters how these policy principles were violated in the 1930s during the Great Depression and again in the 1970s during the era of stagflation—i.e., rising prices with falling output. The result was an impoverishment of our own

36

workers and the destruction of the means of production, which are among the most immoral acts that a government can perpetrate on the citizenry.

Uncle Sam Versus the Laffer Curve

And yet many of our policymakers just don't get it. One of our frustrations over the past thirty years has been that the number crunchers in Washington who are in charge of telling us in advance how much tax cuts will "cost" in lost revenue and how much tax increases will "gain" in extra tax receipts seem genetically incapable of learning the Laffer Curve. The modelers slavishly employ the simple arithmetic model we described above: Double the tax rates and you will get twice as much revenue.

If you think we are exaggerating how detached from the real world tax policy has become in Washington, consider this extraordinary occurrence on Capitol Hill back in 1989. Senator Bob Packwood of Oregon asked the crystal ball gazers at the Joint Committee on Taxation to estimate the revenues that would be raised from a 100 percent income tax rate on all Americans with earnings above $200,000. You don't have to have a Ph.D. in math from MIT to know that the answer to that question is zero. But the geniuses at the JTC ran the numbers through their computer model and here is what it told them. In the first year the 100 percent tax rate would raise $104 billion, in the second year, $204 billion, and in the third year $232 billion. This was more than enough to balance the budget! Mr. Packwood was flabbergasted by this revelation. "Our models assume people will work if they have to pay all of their money to the government," he protested. "They will work forever and pay all of their money to the government. Clearly anyone in their right mind will not."[15]

The same people who say that a 100 percent tax on the rich will raise more than $200 billion a year also say that Senator Barack

Obama's plan to raise tax rates to more than 50 percent will raise boatloads of money without any offsetting negative economic effects. And because of the clear fallacy of these predictions, we are on the verge of making a very big mistake that could cost many millions of Americans their jobs and their income. We might soon learn firsthand the wisdom of Chief Justice John Marshall, who wrote in the landmark Supreme Court case *McCulloch* v. *Maryland*: "The power to tax is the power to destroy." [16]

Onslaught from the Left

The Laffer Curve has proven enormously controversial over the years, and the notion that reducing taxes can result in higher revenues sends some liberals into a hissy fit of vitriol and name calling. We have been called "greedy," "ideological zealots," and purveyors of "the great lie of supply-side economics." Why? We don't really know why a provable economic theory might provoke the emotional responses supply-side economics does. We will leave it to those better versed in psychology to figure it out.

In case you think we are exaggerating the tone of the critics, here's the title of an article penned by Jonathan Chait, senior editor of the *New Republic*: "Feast of the Wingnuts: How Economic Crackpots Devoured American Politics." Mr. Chait calls supply-siders a "cultlike fringe" and "right-wing extremists." [17] Does he put JFK in that grouping? How about more modern tax cutters like Germany's Angela Merkel or New Mexico Governor Bill Richardson, or California's Jerry Brown, who ran for president in 1992 on the flat tax? A few years ago Chait wrote a column called "Less Is Moore" in which he accused Steve Moore of having a small brain— but fortunately Moore has thick skin. [18] Paul Krugman of the *New York Times* snidely lashes out at supply-side economics every few weeks and discards the ideas of simpleminded "frustrated academics" who have scant support from the learned class. "There is one important thing that the supply-side movement has not gotten and still desperately wants," writes Mr. Krugman. "Intellectual vindication." [19]

He's wrong actually. We much prefer to have the real-world evidence on our side than the approval of the intellectuals.

"Trickle Down" Economics

"Trickle down" is the term applied to supply-side economics by some critics of the supply-side theories. The critics' view is that supply-side economics is really based on a theory that if you give enough tax advantages to the rich, i.e., the creative and the hardworking, some of the benefits of their higher wealth will eventually "trickle down" to the less fortunate workers at the bottom of the social and economic ladder.

Experts debate the topic of class warfare and income distribution ad nauseum. Without getting into a long debate, let's instead look at the IRS data on income over the past thirty years. Some of these statistics should be adjusted to reflect various changes over this time, including the fact that the average number of people per tax return has been declining over the years, so the average income per tax return understates the trend in income per capita. Also, the IRS data don't include transfer payments (such as Social Security), which have increased dramatically over time and which benefit the bottom 50 percent of income earners to a greater extent than they do the wealthy. Table 2-1 shows the share of the total income captured by the top 1 percent of taxpayers has more than doubled from 9 percent in 1980 to 21 percent today. The share of the income to the bottom 50 percent of taxpayers has fallen from roughly 18 to 13 percent. So income distribution is becoming more skewed. The rich are indeed becoming a lot richer, especially after the adoption of supply-side economic policies such as sound money, low taxes, free trade, freer immigration, fewer unions, less regulation—

the list goes on. The reality of less equal distribution of income is hard to deny, and we don't deny it. This is happening not just in the United States but around the globe.

Table 2-1: **Share of Income Earned**

	1980	2005
Top 1%	8.5%	21.0%
Top 5%	21.0%	33.0%
Top 10%	32.1%	44.4%
Top 25%	56.7%	66.1%
Bottom 50%	17.7%	13.4%

Source: Internal Revenue Service (September 2006 update).

But here is a crucial point: The increasingly unequal distribution of income during the era of supply-side economics was the result of many millions of Americans' becoming fantastically, unthinkably rich, not a result of the poor getting poorer. In fact the vast, vast majority of the people who got rich over the last twenty-five years were not rich at the start of this period, and a good number of these people were lower middle class or poor.[20] America cleared away the speed bumps on the path to prosperity and became an economic opportunity society. Enterprising people in huge numbers took advantage of the opportunity to amass fortunes. That's the American way.

Another point: In the era of supply-side economics, the tax rate cuts on the highest earners have resulted in the highest income earners paying a *greater share of total taxes* than before. What is striking about this history of tax rates since the late 1970s is that as tax rates have generally fallen by half, taxes paid by the wealthy have *increased.* Lower tax rates have made the tax system more progressive, not less so (see Figure 2-2).

Figure 2-2: The Rich Pay More

**Top Marginal Income Tax Rates and
Income Tax Share for the Top 1% of Earners 1980–2005**

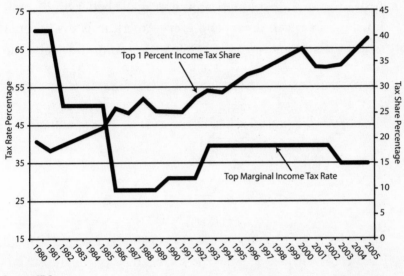

Source: IRS.

There is a loud clique of critics on the left who are united in a plan to redistribute income from the rich to the poor through high tax rates. Robert H. Frank, an economist at Cornell, wrote in a *New York Times* op-ed piece:

> *Progressive taxation is not about envy. Top earners have captured the big share of all income and wealth gains during the last three decades. They're where the money is. If we're to pay for public services they and others want, they must carry a disproportionate share of the tax burden.*[21]

Um, Professor Frank: They already are paying a disproportionate share of the tax burden. If the top 50 percent are paying 97 percent of the income taxes, how high does he want the tax burden to go on the rich? You can't go over 100 percent.

We prefer a different strategy, one not based on greed or envy or pulling down the rich, but one premised on making the vast majority of our citizens more prosperous. We agree with President Kennedy, who said: "No American is ever made better off by pulling a fellow American down, and every American is made better off whenever any one of us is better off. A rising tide raises all boats." [22]

3

"WE CAN DO BETTAH":

TAX-CUTTING LESSONS FROM THE

TWENTIETH CENTURY

A LETTER TO SENATOR TED KENNEDY AND CAROLINE KENNEDY

Back in 2004, when two of us (Moore and Laffer) were on the board of a political group called the Club for Growth, we ran a series of political TV ads noting that the Bush tax cuts were part of the legacy of Presidents John F. Kennedy and Ronald Reagan. Both of these presidents had argued that tax rate cuts would stimulate economic growth and might even generate more tax revenue for the government.

We were surprised to receive a letter a few weeks later from President Kennedy's brother, Senator Ted Kennedy, and his daughter Caroline, asking us to cease and desist. The two of them argued that the TV ads were "politically irresponsible and grossly inaccurate."

Huh? We hold President Kennedy and his accomplishments in high regard and it was certainly not our intention to in any way tarnish the Kennedy presidential record or his family's legacy. In fact, the ads trumpeted the economic achievements of President

Kennedy and the success of his tax reduction policies, which were enacted into law shortly after his tragic assassination.

Out of respect to Ted and Caroline Kennedy, we reviewed the ads carefully, but discovered there was nothing factually inaccurate in them, and independent watchdog groups that monitor the veracity of political TV ads agreed that they were truthful. The TV networks also did a round of fact checking and found nothing objectionable or misleading. The ads included the following factually accurate statements:

- President Kennedy sponsored legislation to cut income tax rates by 30 percent.
- Those tax cuts spurred economic growth and job creation. Total national employment grew by more than 1 million jobs in the four years after the enactment of the Kennedy tax cuts. The economic growth rate climbed from 4.3 to 6.6 percent.
- Those tax cuts generated an increase in tax revenues, which helped balance the budget. Figure 3-1 shows that total income tax receipts grew from $48.7 billion in 1964 to $68.7 billion by 1968. This was a faster rate of growth of tax revenues than had been achieved in the five years before the tax cuts were enacted.
- After tax rates were cut, Americans increased their work effort, businesses increased their investment spending, and the economy accelerated into a higher gear of economic growth, in very much the same way that President Kennedy and his economic advisers predicted they would.

Those basic facts of the supply-side successes of President Kennedy's tax cuts (more of which we will discuss later) are incontrovertible.

Senator Kennedy's main objection to the TV ads was that the Kennedy tax cut was, as he and his niece put it in their letter, "responsible," and the Bush tax cut was not. By this they meant that the Kennedy tax cut would not blow a hole in the budget deficit.

Figure 3-1: Kennedy Tax Cuts Boosted Revenue

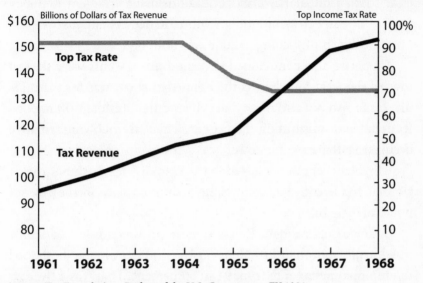

Sources: Tax Foundation, *Budget of the U.S. Government, FY 1991.*

But this cannot have been true, because the Kennedy tax cut was much larger than the tax cut President Bush proposed in 2003. The Tax Foundation compared both tax cuts and found that the Bush tax cut was about one-third as large as the Kennedy tax cut when measured as a share of national income and as a share of the budget.[1] How could the much larger tax cut under President Kennedy have been "responsible," if the Bush tax cut was not?

The letter from the Kennedys further argued that one reason the Bush tax cut was unwise was that the deficit and the national debt (the sum of all deficits in the past) were larger in 2003 than forty years earlier when President Kennedy was enacting his tax cut. Here again, the data paint a different story. In 1963 the federal debt was 42 percent of GDP, compared to 36 percent in 2003. They wrote in their letter that "it is not responsible for President Bush to propose a tax cut when the budget is in deficit." But the federal government was running a deficit in 1963 of 1 percent of GDP when the Kennedy tax plan was unveiled. It is true that in 2003 we were running a budget deficit of roughly 2.5 percent of GDP, but it is clear that an unbalanced budget did not deter President Kennedy from endorsing an economic-growth-oriented tax cut, just as President Bush was proposing in 2003.

The letter also complained that the Bush tax cuts were skewed toward the wealthy, whereas the Kennedy tax cut was for the middle class. We would note that in reading President Kennedy's speeches and writings on the tax cut, which are richly informative in making the case for lower tax rates as an engine for higher growth, he never once resorted to the kind of "rich-bashing" rhetoric that has become so distressingly commonplace in the current political dialogue.

In any case, President Kennedy's tax cut was not less favorably tilted to the rich than President Bush's. President Kennedy slashed the top income tax rate from 91 to 70 percent. That was a twenty-one-percentage-point decline in the tax rates on the rich. The Bush plan, by contrast, cut the top income tax rate from 39.6 to 35 percent, which is a 4.6-percentage-point reduction in rates. It seems obvious to us from these numbers that the Kennedy plan gave a larger tax break to the rich than either the Reagan or the Bush tax cuts.

The Kennedys' letter ends by noting correctly that the JFK tax cuts increased jobs, wages, and economic growth. No argument from us on that score, except to note that 8 million new jobs were created in the four years after the Bush tax cut. But then Senator Kennedy writes something that bears repeating. He says that back in the 1960s the tax rates of 90 percent or more were "effectively confiscatory." Bravo. We should all agree that in our free market capitalist system in America, tax rates of 90 percent are punitive and unjust.

In our response to Senator Kennedy we asked him the same question we would ask Barack Obama and all modern Democrats: "Where do you draw the line between a fair tax rate and a confiscatory one? For example, could we not all agree that tax rates above

70 percent are excessive?" If the answer is yes then we should sharply reduce (or better yet, eliminate) all the multiple taxes on savings, the income tax, plus the capital gains tax, plus the corporate tax, plus the estate tax, plus the myriad state and local levies that can raise the tax rate to or above 70 percent.

Senator Kennedy never responded to that question in our letter, so we are still wondering what liberals believe is a nonconfiscatory tax rate—40 percent, 50 percent, 70 percent? Most Americans, according to public opinion polls, don't think that a tax rate of more than 25 percent is fair.

Whither the JFK Democrats

We recount this incident because it illustrates an irony of modern-day partisan politics. Back in the 1960s it was Republicans who complained that President Kennedy's tax cuts were "fiscally irresponsible" and would increase the budget deficit to intolerable levels and Democrats who argued for the sanity of lower tax rates to grow the economy.[2] Amazingly, it was Republican icons and future presidential candidates Barry Goldwater and Bob Dole who in 1964 voted *against* reducing the tax rate from 91 to 70 percent. It was President Kennedy himself who was the most eloquent in dismissing the tax cut naysayers when he pronounced:

> "Our true choice is not between tax reduction, on the one hand, and the avoidance of large federal deficits on the other. . . . It is between two kinds of deficits—a chronic deficit of inertia, as the unwanted result of inadequate revenues and a restricted economy—or a temporary deficit of transition, resulting from a tax cut designed to boost the economy, produce revenues, and achieve a future budget surplus. The first type of deficit is a sign of waste and weakness—the second reflects an investment in the future."[3]

Well said and still quite true today.

But in the intervening forty-some years, partisan politics has been turned completely on its head. In 2003 Senator Ted Kennedy led the charge *against* the Bush tax cuts, just as he did against the Reagan tax cuts in 1981, lobbing the same grenades that Republicans once tossed at his brother's plan. The Reagan tax cuts of 1981 were nearly a mirror image of the Kennedy across-the-board tax cuts. Our nonpartisan conclusion from these economic policy fights, based on the subsequent evidence, is simply this:

1. The Republicans were wrong back then to oppose President Kennedy's tax plan as unaffordable and risky.
2. Liberal Democrats starting with Ted Kennedy are wrong now to oppose tax rate cuts and to try to raise the capital gains, dividend, and personal income tax rates.

It's striking that the Kennedy tax-cutting legacy has become an embarrassment not only to the Kennedy family, but to all liberals—even those who trumpet the Camelot years, the success of the Kennedy presidency, and the resiliency of his ideas. Liberals can change their positions, but they can't whitewash history. John F. Kennedy was a supply-sider. The best way to grow the economy, he argued, "is to reduce the burden on private income and the deterrents to private initiative which are imposed by our present tax system—and this administration is pledged to an across-the-board reduction in personal and corporate income tax cuts."[4] Republicans starting with Reagan stole that line in 1980. President Bush, too, made that argument forty years later, but it was heresy then, while it was applauded by liberals and Keneseian economists in the 1960s.

So in this chapter we will put aside partisan and ideological spears and begin to examine the real record of supply-side tax cuts. Let's look at "just the facts, ma'am."

Laffer Curve History Lessons

Since the U.S. income tax was not constitutionally permitted until 1913, with the passage of the Sixteenth Amendment, our nation's experience with differing tax rates on income began in the twentieth century. In the last century there have been four episodes of significant tax rate reductions. These reductions occurred in the 1920s under Presidents Warren Harding and Calvin Coolidge; in the 1960s under President John F. Kennedy; in the 1980s under President Reagan; and in the early 2000s under George W. Bush. In each case the tax cuts were predicted to lose revenue, but instead federal revenue increased after the tax rates were cut, because the economy responded positively to the lower tax rate regime.

Harding-Coolidge Tax Cuts

Although the United States briefly instituted an income tax during the Civil War, the Supreme Court struck down this act and other income taxes throughout the nineteenth century. It was not until 1913, with the passage of the Sixteenth Amendment to the Constitution, that the income tax became a permanent fixture of government in America. This was a black chapter in American history. The *New York Times*, yes the *NEW YORK TIMES*, long opposed an income tax, writing in 1894 when Congress tried to enact one that this would be a "vicious, inequitable, unpopular, impolitic, and socialist act." The tax, argued the *Times*, was "the most unreasoning and un-American movement in the politics of the last quarter century."[5]

Then in 1909 the *Times* reiterated its firm opposition by prophetically noting, "When men get in the habit of helping themselves to the property of others, they cannot easily be cured of it."[6]

And even the *Washington Post* saw the negative effects on work and effort from a graduated income tax. "It is an abhorrent and calamitous monstrosity," the *Post* editorial board seethed. "It punishes everyone who rises above the rank of mediocrity. The fewer additional yokes put around the neck of labor the better."[7]

The tax was supposed to be capped at no higher than 10 percent, and it was only supposed to apply to the very richest Americans: the Rockefellers and the Vanderbilts. But by World War I the income tax rate had soared to 73 percent, and those high tax rates caused the U.S. economy to crumble a few years later.

The first president to recognize the debilitating impact of high income tax rates was Calvin Coolidge. Since then, presidents of both political parties have relied on tax rate reductions to help strengthen the economy and put unemployed Americans back to work. And in most cases, this economic game plan has worked quite successfully.

The first income tax was a progressive rate system with rates from 1 to 7 percent. When the income tax amendment was debated, some of its opponents in Congress argued that there should be a constitutional cap on the income tax at 10 percent. But the income tax supporters assured voters that there would never be an income tax rate that high, so this protection was not necessary. They couldn't have been more wrong.

Within just eight years of the first income tax, the top tax rate cascaded from 7 percent to 73 percent by 1921 during Woodrow Wilson's presidency. The tax rate increases were justified as a means of raising the revenue needed to fight the Germans in World War I. In the 1920 presidential election the Republicans promised a "return to normalcy," and Warren Harding was elected in a landslide.[8] The country was suffering a postwar recession, and unemployment soared. Harding and, after he died in office, his successor, Calvin Coolidge, promoted a steep reduction in tax rates to get the U.S. economy moving again.

The Harding-Coolidge tax rate reductions brought the top income tax rate down in stages from the wartime high of 73 percent in 1921 to 25 percent in 1925. This was the largest reduction in tax rates on the wealthy in American history. Coolidge argued for the reductions in his 1924 State of the Union address by reminding the public that his plan "would actually yield more revenues to the government if the basis of taxation were scientifically revised downward."[9]

He was proven remarkably correct. The economy roared back to life in the mid-1920s, and the nation's greatest period of prosperity up until that time replaced recession. Happy days were here again and America's industrial production surged back to full throttle. These were the roaring twenties, when America reached levels of affluence never seen before. Babe Ruth made a salary of $100,000 a year—for playing baseball and for achieving the unthinkable: swatting sixty home runs in a single season. It was indeed a gilded age, the era of the Great Gatsby. The rich got unbelievably rich, but as per capita income soared, a joyful prosperity spread like a gale-force wind across the nation. More and more middle-class Americans gained a level of affluence that was unthinkable in earlier times. The middle class and even many of the poor could, for the first time ever, afford radios and plumbing and hot water and trips to the movies.

How much of this prosperity was a direct result of tax cuts is not exactly clear, and to this day is still a subject of debate. But what is undeniably true is that tax revenues increased even as tax rates fell. Between 1923 and 1928 real tax collections nearly doubled as the economy surged.[10] As the tax rates were chopped by almost two-thirds, the share of taxes paid by those earning over $50,000 (the rich back then) rose from 45 percent in 1921, when the rate was 73 percent, to 62 percent in 1925, when the rate was 25 percent. Those who made more than $100,000 a year saw their tax share rise from 28 percent to 51 percent. As figure 3-2 shows, total tax revenues rose from $720 million in 1921 to $1.15 billion by 1928. There was no long-term loss of revenue from the tax rate cut.

President Calvin Coolidge—"keep cool with Cal"—pushed hard for the tax cuts and made eloquent speeches on how tax rate

Figure 3-2: Lower Tax Rates in the 1920s
Meant More Tax Revenue

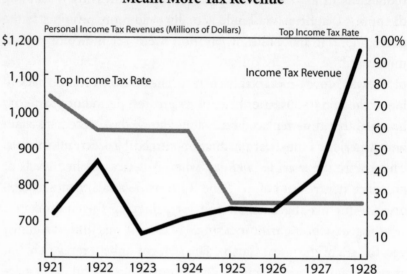

Personal Income Tax Revenues (Millions of Dollars)   Top Income Tax Rate

Sources: Tax Foundation: Joint Economic Committee, "The Mellon and Kennedy Tax Cuts: A Review and Analysis." Staff Study, June 18, 1982.

cuts would spur greater output and employment. Sounding much like Reagan and Kennedy to come, he said in 1924,

> *Experience does not show that the higher [tax] rate produces the larger revenue. Experience is all the other way. There is no escaping that when the taxation of large incomes is excessive, they tend to disappear.*
>
> *I agree with those who wish to relieve the small taxpayer by getting the largest possible contribution from the people with large incomes. But if the rates on large incomes are so high that they disappear, the small taxpayer will be left with the entire burden. If, on the other hand, the rates are placed where they will produce the most revenue from large incomes, then the small taxpayer will be relieved.[11]*

One of the main architects of this first American supply-side tax cut was Secretary of the Treasury Andrew Mellon. (Sometimes the twenties tax plan is called the "Mellon tax cuts.") Mellon, arguably the greatest Treasury secretary of the twentieth century, was one of the few people in Washington or on Wall Street who predicted that lowering the tax rates would produce more growth and even more revenue. "It seems difficult for people to understand," he said of the tax cuts, "that high rates of taxation do not necessarily mean large revenues to the government and that more revenue may often be obtained by lower tax rates." He observed that when tax rates were as high as they were in the early 1920s, "a decrease in taxes causes an inspiration to trade and commerce, which increases the prosperity of the country so that revenues of the government, even on a lower basis of tax, are increased." [12]

In other words, Mellon espoused the ideas behind what later became known as the Laffer Curve, and the tax cut he helped design proved the theory. He was perhaps the first heralded proponent of a flat tax. He argued that "it is not too much to hope that some day we may get back on a tax basis of 10 percent, the Hebrew tithe, which was always considered a fairly heavy tax." [13]

Crash!

In the fall of 1929, the stock market crashed and the economy toppled as wealth evaporated. A troika of catastrophic policy mistakes plunged the economy deeper and deeper into a ditch. The first was an overly restrictive monetary policy by the Federal Reserve which caused prices to fall and smothered growth. This was chronicled famously by Milton Friedman (the father of free market economics) and Anna Schwarz, in their classic *A Monetary History of the United States.* The second was a rising tide of trade protectionism in the United States (specifically, the Smoot-Hawley Act—see Chapter 12), which was then copied abroad, causing the shut-down of the global trading system.

And the third factor was the compounding impact of higher

tax rates, which reversed the Coolidge tax rate cuts. In Herbert Hoover's last year in office, as the economy continued to sag, the federal government faced a $2 billion budget deficit.[14] Hoover called for a tax increase, much to the displeasure of workers. In 1932 a tax revolt erupted in cities across the country.[15] But that didn't stop Hoover and the Republicans from enacting the Revenue Act of 1932. The tax hike shattered all hopes of recovery. The budget deficit actually grew to nearly $3 billion the next year. The budget deficit would have been lower in 1933, based on the original forecasts, if the tax increase had never been enacted into law. This was the swan song of the Hoover administration.

Franklin Roosevelt's New Deal programs were mostly a bust as the Depression rolled on through his first two terms in office. The U.S. unemployment rate *averaged* more than 12 percent for the entire decade 1931–41 with an ungodly 24.9 percent peak under Hoover in 1931. Even after nearly two presidential terms of New Dealism to put Americans back to work through massive public works programs, the unemployment rate in 1940 was still 14.6 percent.[16] As the economy worsened, Roosevelt raised tax rates repeatedly in the 1930s, so that by the onset of World War II the highest income tax rate reached 81 percent. The 1920s tax cuts were fully wiped out. The GNP reached $203 billion in 1929 (1958 dollars), but a decade later it had barely grown at all and came in at $209 billion. The U.S. industrial system under the weight of the parade of grand policy mistakes had shut down its mighty engines, and it wasn't until 1941, when the nation mobilized for World War II, that they were revved up again.

Americans in the 1940s—the greatest generation—shrugged off the consequences of high tax rates (which rose to an unfathomable 94 percent) as the nation united in a great and patriotic crusade to win the war against global fascism. The New Deal was over. Funding of domestic government programs was dramatically reduced as the nation shifted priorities almost overnight after December 7, 1941, toward rapid wartime mobilization. The United States also borrowed $186 billion (about $2 trillion in today's dollars) to help finance the war as Americans patriotically snapped up war bonds to pay the bills of the mightiest military arsenal in the history of mankind.[17] After VJ Day in 1945 the U.S. national debt was nearly 100 percent of our nation's GDP. (To put that number in perspective, today our national debt is only one-third as high, or about 35 percent of GDP.)

But even after VJ Day the tax rates stayed stratospheric in the United States for many more years. In 1945 the top rate was cut from 94 to 85 percent. In 1950 Harry Truman signed into law a bill reraising the tax rates to 92 percent. When Eisenhower was elected, the Republican party was conflicted. Conservatives like Senator Robert A. Taft shepherded through Congress a supply-side tax cut that reduced these tax rates substantially. But, incredibly, Ike vetoed the tax cut, and the rates remained above 90 percent on the rich. He and his chief economist, Arthur Burns, who later headed the Federal Reserve System, said we needed high tax rates to balance the budget.

Enter JFK.

The Kennedy Tax Cuts

America's high tax rates took a toll. The economy grew in the 1950s, but in fits and starts, and by the end of the Eisenhower presidency, the economy was stalled again. A young but successful actor of that era, Ronald Reagan, would later recall while campaigning for president that with tax rates of 90 percent, once you were in that highest tax bracket you stopped working; stopped making movies; stopped activity that would give ninety cents of every dollar earned to the government.

John F. Kennedy ran for president promising to spend more money on defense to close "the missile gap," and to get the economy growing faster. "We can do bettah," was the famous catch-phrase from the young and charismatic Massachusetts senator.[18] In 1960 the Democratic Party's theme was growth and more growth. The 1960 Democratic national platform called for the achievement of 5 percent real economic growth rates—something we wish either party today would strive for.[19]

When John Kennedy took office in 1961, the highest federal tax rate at the margin was 91 percent. The lowest was 20 percent.[20] Imagine: If you were paid a high salary or otherwise earned a high income, you gave ninety-one cents out of the last dollar you earned to the government, and you kept only nine cents of that dollar. So why would you make any effort to earn more money? Many of Kennedy's advisers, including John Kenneth Galbraith, argued for a massive government spending program to induce more demand and create more jobs.[21] But Kennedy was ultimately his own counselor on economics, and he understood human nature and the lessons of history. He decided that the way to shift the American economy into a higher gear was through reductions in taxation. "It is a paradoxical truth," Kennedy proclaimed in 1963 at the Economics Club of New York, "that tax rates are too high today, and tax revenues are too low and the soundest way to raise the revenues in the long run is to cut the tax rates." He continued by stating that "an economy constrained by high tax rates will never produce enough revenue to balance the budget, just as it will never create enough jobs or enough profits." He also insisted on a cut in the capital gains tax on stocks.[22]

Kennedy made it very clear early on that he had an innate understanding of the policies that nurture and reward growth. He was the first modern-day supply-side president. Tragically, he was assassinated a few months before his tax cut package was enacted into law in early 1964. The tax cuts reduced the maximum marginal personal income tax rate from 91 to 70 percent by 1965, and the lower rates were chopped as well.[23]

By the way, when an economist refers to the "tax rate at the margin," or "marginal tax rate," he or she means the amount of tax you pay on the *last* dollar you earn. Our income tax is progressive, which means that it starts low and gets higher as your income goes up. A worker earning $25,000 a year pays a lower tax rate than an executive who makes $250,000 a year. The lower rate may start at, say, 20 percent on the first $50,000, then rises to 35 percent on the next $50,000, and so on.

The Kennedy tax cut was debated for months in the halls of Congress—and ironically, as noted earlier, this tax cut agenda was almost universally opposed by Republicans and almost universally favored by Democrats. One of the most vocal supporters of the policy was House Ways and Means Committee chairman Wilbur Mills. His speech on the floor of the House is worth repeating, because here was one of the most prominent and economically respected Democrats arguing that this tax cut would *raise revenue.*

> *Mr. Chairman, there is no doubt in my mind that this tax reduction bill, in and of itself, can bring about an increase in the gross national product of approximately $50 billion in the next few years. If it does, these lower rates of taxation will bring in at least $12 billion in additional revenue.*[24]

Then Mr. Mills prophesied that because of additional economic growth from the tax cut, "the larger revenues derived from this additional income will result in the federal budget being balanced sooner than would be the case in the absence of the tax cut."[25]

Both Kennedy and Mills were proven correct in their predictions that the American economic engines would roar to life if taxes were less oppressive. The economy grew rapidly in 1964, 1965, and 1966. The unemployment rate fell to its lowest peacetime level in more than thirty years.[26] "The unusual budget spectacle of sharply rising revenues following the biggest tax cut in history," announced a 1966 *U.S. News & World Report* article, "is beginning to astonish even those who pushed hardest for tax cuts in the first place."[27] No kidding. Arthur Okun, President Lyndon Johnson's chief economic adviser, calculated a massive stimulus from the plan: "The tax cuts of 1964 are credited with a $25 billion contribution to our GNP by mid-1965, a $30 billion effect by the end of 1965, and an ultimate $36 billion increment."[28] Remember: This was 1966, when the U.S. economy was about one-fifth as large as today, so $36 billion was more than a 10 percent addition to national output.

Even more shocking was the impact on the distribution of taxes paid. Lower tax rates on the rich led to these income classes' paying a much larger share of the tax burden. Americans earning over $50,000 per year (the equivalent of about $200,000 today) increased their taxes by nearly 40 percent after the rate cut. Their tax share rose from 12 percent of the total in 1963 to almost 15 percent in 1966 (see Figure 3-3). Americans with an income of more than $1 million nearly doubled their tax payments, from $311 million in

Figure 3-3: Rich Paid More Under Kennedy Tax Cuts

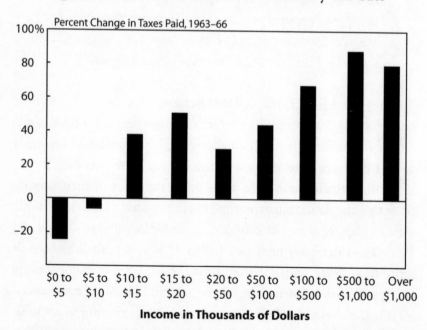

Income in Thousands of Dollars

Source: Joint Economic Committee, "The Mellon and Kennedy Tax Cuts: A Review and Analysis." Staff Study, June 18, 1982.

1962 when the tax rate was 91 percent to $603 million in 1965 when the tax rate was 70 percent.[29]

The Age of Affluence

To determine the effect of Kennedy's tax cut, one has only to look at what the IRS collected in periods before and after the tax cut (Table 3-1).

Table 3-1: Income Tax Revenue *Before* and *After* Kennedy Tax Cut (Personal and Corporate) in Billions, Adjusted for Inflation

Before Tax Cut			*After Tax Cut*		
Fiscal Year	Revenue	% Change	Fiscal Year	Revenue	% Change
1961	$63.5	0.5%	1965	$75.1	9.2%
1962	$67.5	6.2%	1966	$82.0	9.2%
1963	$71.2	5.5%	1967	$83.7	2.1%
1964	$68.8	−3.4%	1968	$95.7	14.3%
4-Year Average		**2.1%**	**4-Year Average**		**8.6%**

Walter Heller, who had served as President Kennedy's chairman of the Council of Economic Advisers, summed it all up neatly in his testimony before Congress in 1977:

What happened to the tax cut in 1965 is difficult to pin down, but insofar as we are able to isolate it, it did seem to have a tremendously stimulative effect, a multiplied effect on the economy. It was the major factor that led to our running a $3 billion surplus by the middle of 1965 before escalation in Vietnam struck us. It was a $12 billion tax cut,

which would be about $33 or $34 billion in today's terms,
and within one year the revenues into the Federal Treasury
were already above what they had been before the tax cut.
    Did the tax cut pay for itself in increased revenues? I
think the evidence is very strong that it did.[30]

Before we examine the two most recent episodes of tax rate reductions under Presidents Reagan and George W. Bush, we need to
review what went wrong with the American economy in the late
1960s and the 1970s.

4

HONEY, WE SHRUNK THE ECONOMY: *THE AWFUL 1970S*

We are all Keynesians now.
                    —RICHARD NIXON, DECEMBER 1971

Within the first few months of the Carter Administration I sold every stock I owned and I wouldn't buy stocks right now with your money.
                    —FORMER TREASURY SECRETARY WILLIAM SIMON, 1978[1]

THE DESTRUCTIVE LEGACY OF LBJ, RICHARD NIXON, GERRY FORD, AND JIMMY CARTER

In the summer of 1979 a popular Chicago radio DJ announced that he would host "Disco Demolition Night" at old Comiskey Park between games of a White Sox doubleheader. The idea behind the promotional gimmick was that fans could enter the park for ninety-eight cents if they brought a disco record that they would burn in a giant bonfire to be set ablaze in the middle of center field. For weeks before the big night, listeners were reminded: Show your disdain for Disco Fever by bringing your Bee Gees and Gloria Gaynor and Earth Wind and Fire plastic forty-five records. Bring

61

such late seventies, er, "classics" as "Disco Duck," "Love Machine," "Saturday Night Fever," "Play that Funky Music White Boy," and "Do You Think I'm Sexy." People were requested to bring along strobe lights, polyester suits, bell-bottom pants, platform shoes, and John Travolta posters to toss into the bonfire as well.

What happened that night was a spontaneous revolt against much of what had gone wrong with American culture in the 1970s. Some fifty thousand fans turned out, armed with twenty thousand disco albums, and they stormed over the walls and spilled onto the field while they screamed: "Disco sucks, disco sucks." The blaze at second base got larger and larger as more debris and relics of the disco era were joyously tossed into the fire and charred to a crisp. The outfield grass caught fire and huge patches turned ashen black. The security guards and the Chicago cops tried to restrain the crowd of young people running amok, but they were totally out-manned by the manic crowd. The second game of the double-header that night had to be canceled because of the damage to the field, and it was one of the most notorious black eyes for major league baseball in the league's history.[2]

In many ways that single event abruptly brought to a close the era of disco music in America. But it was also a symbolic rebellion against a decade that Americans would soon want to forget (al-though today disco is back big-time on retro nights across the country, and it doesn't sound so bad anymore—in small doses).

It could be that the music—as music so often does—reminded people of the era. And Americans were sick of the seventies—all that had gone wrong. As John Lennon put it in 1980 shortly before he was murdered: "Weren't the seventies a drag?"[3] Yes, they assur-edly were.

Before we can appreciate the twenty-five-year boom that began in the 1980s, we need to dissect why the economy turned so coyote ugly in the late 1960s and in the 1970s. What caused the economic "malaise" that Jimmy Carter admitted to in the summer of 1979?

The Four Stooges of the American Presidency

The story of what went wrong starts in 1966. That was the year America hit a gold-plated economic milestone that was well celebrated as a symbol of post–World War II industrial might and productivity. What happened on that red-letter day of January 18 was this: the Dow Jones Industrial Average briefly climbed over 1,000 for the first time in American history. The theme of the nation at that time when the nation's potential seemed limitless was: "We're in the money."

The Kennedy tax cuts of the 1960s had helped fuel this stock market rally. The Vietnam War had not yet fully escalated or become unpopular, American manufacturing was at its zenith, firing on all eight cylinders. Smokestack industries—autos, trucks, steel, chemicals, apparel—were global leaders. The "Made in Japan" label was a tipoff that you were buying an inferior product. Cities like Cleveland, Detroit, and even Newark and Gary, Indiana, were prosperous places and beehives of economic activity. All was good in America. The American middle class was buying up Zenith and Motorola color TVs (this was still an era where TVs were made in America), dishwashers, washing machines, electric garage door openers, and air-conditioners for the first time—because they could finally afford such luxuries. This was the era, as John Kenneth Galbraith wrote, of "The Affluent Society."[4] And no society had ever experienced such affluence for the great preponderance of the population.

On that celebrated day, when growth seemed to be unlimited, no one would have predicted what would happen to stocks and the value of all U.S. assets over the next fifteen years. No one would have predicted how the U.S. economy would malfunction in the years ahead.

In 1982, America was sinking in economic quicksand, and the rest of the world was catching up to us—and worse, exceeding the United States. The era of America's post–World War II economic and military preeminence seemed to have vanished overnight. All you had to do was go to the cities of Cleveland, Detroit, and Pittsburgh to see the devastation—the boarded-up houses, the closed factories, the panhandlers, the public housing war zones, the unemployment lines, the drug use, and the poverty. Perhaps the low point was reached in 1969 when the Cuyahoga River, which funnels into Lake Erie, and which had been used for recreation and fishing, caught fire due to residue of industrial waste—much to the delight of late-night comedians.[5] It was because of this incident that Cleveland (Arthur Laffer's hometown) became known as "the mistake on the lake."

If any one picture can summarize the awful downward drift of the country it would be the decline of the stock market in these years (shown in Figure 4-1). From 1966 until that terrible summer of 1982, the fifteen years preceding the advent of Reaganomics, the Dow Jones Industrial Average suffered one of its blackest bear markets in history, falling not just 20 percent in nominal terms from

Figure 4-1: **How to Kill a Bull Market**

Source: Global Financial Data, http://www.globalfindata.com/freesm.htm.

1,000 to 800, but more than 70 percent in after-inflation terms.[6] Over this period of decline stocks lost 8 percent per year after inflation for sixteen years. Yikes.

In this period, our nation's wealth was evaporating right before our eyes. This was the worst stock market performance since the Great Depression. We need to investigate why.

We call the era 1966–82 the period of the Four Stooges of the American Presidency. Let's see: Lyndon Johnson, Richard Nixon, Gerry Ford, and Jimmy Carter. Two Democrats, two Republicans. Four presidents emitting one dimwitted economic policy after another in what was the largest assemblage of bipartisan ignorance ever. We'd say that from an economic policy perspective, it just doesn't get a lot worse than these four. Laffer tells the story of meeting with President Reagan in the mid-1980s and telling him: "Sir, you were blessed by the incompetence of your predecessors." That's true. Ronald Reagan's star shines a lot brighter due to the litany of failures of those who preceded him.

If that seems unkind, let's review their assaults on the economy.

LBJ and the Great Society

After being elected in a landslide as the slain JFK's natural successor, LBJ deepened America's involvement in the Vietnam War—one of the most unpopular foreign conflicts in American history. He instituted the military draft in 1967 for all men between the ages of eighteen and twenty-six. The wartime budget grew from $51 billion in 1965 to $82 billion in 1969.[7] Students protested on college campuses and in Washington, D.C., with chants of "Hell no, we won't go," and, "One, two, three, four, what are we fighting for?"[8]

But the real economic poison pill was that for the first time in American history, at the same time we were spending more money for guns to win in Vietnam, LBJ unleashed a huge new spending barrage on butter, i.e., domestic programs. In 1965 LBJ launched the Great Society social welfare state "to end poverty in America." The grand failure of the welfare state would plague America for the next thirty years—not just in the $5.4 trillion in budget costs that were poured down this rat hole, according to the Heritage Foundation's cost estimate, but also in ill-designed programs that depreciated the value of work and family cohesion and created several generations of a permanent American underclass who were sucked into a cycle of welfare dependency. Poor families on welfare were pushed into 100 percent plus effective tax rates, because they could lose more money in government benefits from working than they could earn on the job.[9]

Walter Williams, an economist from George Mason University and our esteemed friend and colleague, said it best: "The black family in America survived intact the horrors of slavery, the Ku Klux Klan, Jim Crow laws, and 'separate but equal' segregation laws. What it could not survive was the welfare state." By 1980 more black children were born into homes without fathers than with fathers, and in cities like Detroit, as many as two in three black children were born out of wedlock—what we would soon learn first-hand and catastrophically was a prescription for social disaster in urban America for a quarter century.[10]

Supply-side economics, we would note once again, is predicated on the idea that incentives matter. People respond to financial incentives, both positive and negative. The wreckage caused by the welfare state is the greatest single validation of this idea in the last century. We paid people not to work and paid them to have children out of wedlock. We trained teenagers to gain financial independence by dropping out of school and getting pregnant, by getting the father out of the home, and by keeping any earnings from work hidden from the government. These policies gave birth to a massive underclass which responded to each of these incentives by engaging in each of these dysfunctional patterns of behavior.

A study in 1976 by Martin Feldstein documented the extent of the work disincentives of LBJ's welfare state. Feldstein found that benefits were so high relative to the income that could be gained by work that untaxed unemployment compensation was just about as generous as a paycheck for many low-income workers. Feldstein quantified the insipid impact of these programs: By making unemployment pay about as much as working forty hours a week, these programs raised the unemployment rate by 1.25 percentage points and reduced economic output and the tax base by the amount of lost production of roughly one million workers.[11]

Common sense could have predicted that this would happen, but none of the social engineers of the sixties and seventies saw it coming.

In addition to launching the $2 trillion welfare state, LBJ began to reverse the supply-side effects of the Kennedy tax cut legacy. In 1968 he signed an income tax surcharge to finance the growing cost of the war in Vietnam. Yet revenues grew more slowly after the tax increase than they did after Kennedy's tax cut.

The 10 percent income tax surcharge was the first stage of a succession of tax hikes on rich and middle-class Americans over the next decade. The top tax rate went back up to 77 percent.

At the end of the LBJ presidency came the infamous alternative minimum tax. The Johnson Treasury Department discovered in 1968 that 155 tax filers with adjusted gross income of $200,000 ($1.2 million in today's dollars) were exploiting loopholes in the tax code to avoid paying any income tax. This became a national outrage, and instead of lowering tax rates and closing the loopholes, the Democrat-dominated Congress passed a new shadow tax system called the AMT.[12] This meant that after completing all the tax forms, the rich would also have to calculate an alternative minimum tax and pay the greater of the two. (We've always said the alternative minimum tax should really be called the Mandatory Maximum Tax—because this tax is not a voluntary alternative, and you pay the maximum of the two, not the minimum.) The effect of the AMT was to further raise effective tax rates in the United States on high income earners.[13]

Lyndon Johnson was elected president in 1964 against Republican Barry Goldwater with one of the largest margins of victory in American history. At the time of his election it seemed that America's military and economic potential were boundless. By the time he left office four years later, Americans were starting to lose confidence in those lofty ambitions. Things were starting to unravel—and the Great Society he had tried to build wasn't feeling so great.

The Nixon Years

Overwhelmed and exhausted by the failures of the Vietnam War, LBJ chose not to run for re-election in 1968 and was replaced by Richard Nixon. Nixon was despised by the Left because of his foreign policy, his hatred of the media, his raging paranoia, and his abuses of power. What is not well known is how catastrophic his economic policies were. Nixon launched the modern era of the regulatory state with the passage of the Clean Air and Clean Water statutes, which were well intentioned but heavy-handed blows to the solar plexus of American industry, imposing costs far exceeding benefits from the cleanup legislation. The statutes gave super-regulatory powers to the Environmental Protection Agency, which would cripple many blue-collar industries over the next decade. Nixon also launched an ABC of other regulatory agencies. The 1970s was to be the era of economic strangulation by regulation. Pages of legal gobbledygook in the *Federal Register* more than tripled, from twenty thousand in 1970 to seventy-two thousand in 1980. In constant 2000 dollars, spending by federal regulatory agencies rocketed from $5.2 billion to $10.2 billion over Nixon's tenure. By 1979 the spending had zoomed to $13.5 billion. The federal government's army of snoopers was now regulating everything from the width of doorway entrances to speed limits on state highways to the flush capacity of toilets.[14]

In 1971 Nixon made a fateful decision that would profoundly

affect the economy for years to come. He closed the gold window—meaning that the U.S. was now officially off the gold standard. This was a monumentally important change in American monetary policy, so it is worth reviewing the events surrounding this decision.[15]

In July 1944, as World War II wound to its conclusion, more than seven hundred delegates from all forty-four Allied nations gathered in Bretton Woods, New Hampshire, to reconstruct the international economic system. The only currency strong enough to meet the rising demand for international liquidity was the U.S. dollar, which, at the time, was the only currency backed by gold. To maintain confidence in the dollar, the U.S. agreed to link the dollar to gold at the rate of $35 per ounce of gold. At this rate, foreign governments and central banks were able to exchange dollars for gold.

The logic here was correct. When there is too much money in circulation, prices rise and investors turn to gold. The very fact that gold was purchased from the U.S. Treasury would technically bring the quantity of money down and thus restore its value. The process was simple, automatic, elegant, and it worked for more than two decades.

Other countries were required to keep their currencies from either appreciating or depreciating against the U.S. dollar. But foreign governments' inability to keep inflation in check with their paper currencies and their mischievous shenanigans of selling off their dollars for gold led Nixon and his advisers to believe the gold standard was no longer sustainable. Nixon administration economists Paul Volcker and Arthur Laffer argued strenuously against this policy change, but Nixon proceeded to close the gold window. The dollar was no longer hinged to a hard commodity. The price of gold and the value of the dollar would now float with supply and demand.

Laffer immediately warned that this would cause a great inflation. In 1972 he wrote a famous *Wall Street Journal* editorial entitled "The Bitter Fruits of Devaluation," which argued that a depreciating dollar and other currencies would lead to worldwide inflation of double digits by the end of the decade.[16] Unfortunately, he was exactly right.

The dollar's value, relative to gold, melted down over the course of the next ten years. In 1971 gold was at $35 an ounce. By 1980 gold was selling at $850 an ounce—twenty-five times higher. The end of the gold standard was the start of the era of hyperinflation.

Then in August 1971 Nixon imposed one of the most radical and arguably unconstitutional interventions into the American free market system in American peacetime history: a ninety-day freeze on wages and prices—which was eventually extended for one thousand days. In addition, a 10 percent tariff was imposed on all U.S. imports in blatant violation of our trade agreements.

The freeze on salaries and prices of goods and services seemed to be an admission that inflation, which was raging at 6 percent, was uncontrollable and that since the market wouldn't hold down prices, the iron fist of the government would accomplish the goal through command and control. The intervention by the government seemed to be the kind of goofy state directive lampooned in Ayn Rand's novel *Atlas Shrugged*.[17] But these controls weren't fiction; they were real.

To impose wage and price controls so that prices of individual goods and services could not rise exposed a fundamental lack of understanding of how the pricing system in a free market operates to allocate and place value on output. If prices aren't allowed to fluctuate up and down when the market dictates they should, shortfalls and waiting lines occur, and producers have an incentive to produce less, not more. If prices are held too high, the economy produces too much of the product. We had seen in the Soviet Union for decades the result of central-planning pricing, yet this is what America had adopted. Price controls remained in place off and on through 1973, when Nixon replaced them with "voluntary restraints."

Wage and price controls also created immense inequities. Consider, for example, the case of a star major league pitcher named Vida Blue. He was signed by the Oakland Athletics at the age of nineteen. Two years later, Blue had one of the greatest seasons in baseball history. He won twenty-four games, struck out 301 batters, and tossed eight shutouts. He won not only the Cy Young Award, but also the MVP. And for all this brilliance—the near-perfect season—he was paid a paltry $14,700.

Wage and price controls meant that it was illegal in many cases for someone who was a top performer to get a raise even if it was deserved. The penny-pinching owner of the Athletics gave Blue a $10,000 Cadillac at the end of the season instead.[18]

When the price controls were lifted, nine months of pent-up inflation exploded like the cork released from a shaken Dom Perignon champagne bottle. Clerks stood at ready position prepared to put new sticker prices on nearly everything once the clock struck midnight and the price freeze was officially over. At this time, Mr. Nixon and his economic team didn't understand that inflation was a result of too much money and a falling dollar, not insufficient government mandates.

Next came Nixon's big spending proclivities—the budget ran wild during his tenure, much of this facilitated and urged by a spendthrift Congress. In 1970 the federal budget stood at $196 billion. By 1974 the budget had increased to $269 billion, an increase of almost 30 percent.[19] Nixon saw federal spending as stimulatory for the economy, and that is when he declared himself a Keynesian. As economist Paul Craig Roberts has noted about that era: "The standard remedy was for government to increase total spending by incurring a deficit in its budget. GDP, it was believed, would then rise by some multiple of the increase in spending."[20]

This was a formal surrender in the fight to control government expenditures. The combination of easy money, increased federal spending, and budget deficits was supposed to be the ultimate solution to slow growth and unemployment. Oops. Unemployment doubled on Nixon's watch from 3.5 percent to 7 percent.

Again, Nixon's domestic policy failings were not well understood at the time and are not much covered by historians, who tend to be liberal and have tended to concentrate on Nixon's Vietnam War and Cold War strategies, on his policies toward China and the Soviet Union, and, later, on his downfall in the Watergate saga. Conservatives have tended to defend Nixon because he was so vigorously attacked by the Left and the media. But there was little in Nixon's presidency on the economic front to commend him.

We once asked the economist Milton Friedman who the worst president on economics was during his lifetime, and he pointed to Nixon for the myriad state intrusions into the market we have mentioned above. (Reagan, Milton Friedman said, was the best president of his lifetime.)

Whip Inflation Now

Gerry Ford entered the White House in August 1974 as the first unelected president to sit in the Oval Office. He was dealt a bad hand, to say the least. The presidency was at its lowest ebb of prestige after Nixon's disgrace, and liberal Democrats in Congress were ready to steamroller over Ford and launch a new era of the Imperial Congress.

After the midterm elections in November 1974, Ford faced a Democratic majority whose numbers were staggeringly large, the number of Democrats having increased by 49 in the House and 5 in the Senate. To his credit, Ford vetoed more than two dozen of the Democrats' more left-leaning spending and regulatory measures, but many of those vetoes were overridden by Congress.

One of the worst acts of this new Congress was the 1974 Budget Act. This empowered Congress with broad new spending authority over the federal budget process and stripped the president of his historical impoundment power to not spend money when the expenditure was not necessary. The reputed purpose of the 1974

Budget Act was to insure a balanced budget. Just the opposite occurred. Congress ran budget deficits in thirty-two of the next thirty-five years.[21] The federal budget climbed in nominal terms from $250 billion to $3.0 trillion. In short, the 1974 Budget Act was a license to spend for Congress.

President Ford had no strategy for dealing with rising oil prices in the mid-1970s; instead he did mostly the wrong things. In his 1975 State of the Union address he called for a windfall profits tax on oil companies. In December of that year he signed that tax into law as well as an energy bill with price controls and the first-ever fuel efficiency standards on cars. As we will show, none of these policies worked, and the main effect of the bill was to curtail domestic production, which played into the hands of the Middle East oil cartel, OPEC.

Ford's biggest failing was in misunderstanding how to combat inflation, which was still raging. Ford asked the nation in October 1975 to be "energy savers" and to wear Whip Inflation Now (WIN) buttons to try to slay the inflation beast, as if inflation were a state of mind, rather than a result of monetary policy run amok.[22] On taxes, Ford and Congress refused to cut the high rates of the era, and offered up impotent tax rebates instead. The unemployment rate and inflation rate hit 7 percent each in 1976, and the nation wanted a change.

The Carter Catastrophe

Ford lost his bid for re-election, narrowly, to Georgian Jimmy Carter, who had run on an appealing anti-Washington, anti–big government, pro–balanced budget message. He was to be a new-era Democrat. It was a brilliantly crafted slogan for the times, yet once Carter was in the White House it became clear he had no idea how to lead the nation out of its deepening economic troubles. The Democrats in Congress, led by Speaker of the House Tip O'Neill of

Massachusetts, had their own left-wing agenda to pursue, and they expected Carter to fall in line—which mostly he did. Carter had promised to restrain the federal budget, but it stampeded on his watch. The budget deficit skyrocketed from $40 billion in 1979 to $74 billion in 1980.[23]

Lacking a core pillar of ideology, Carter proved to be a micromanager and a constant vacillator on policy. In his one term he launched seven major economic programs, none of which worked and some of which contradicted each other. As American Enterprise Institute historian Steve Hayward writes in his biography of Carter, *The Real Jimmy Carter*, "Both the policies and their articulation were characterized by vacillation, indecision, inconsistency and confusion."[24]

For example, in Carter's first year in office he lobbied for a tax rebate to help the middle class and to stimulate the economy. But in the later years of his presidency he attacked tax cuts as unaffordable. He opposed the Proposition 13 property tax revolt by the middle class in California, erroneously predicting that "there's no doubt unemployment will go up" if it passed.[25] It did pass, and California had a jobs boom over the next decade.

The supply-side tax revolution was just getting started in the late 1970s but Carter and his Treasury secretary, Michael Blumenthal, did everything they could to block it. The bipartisan Steiger-Hansen capital gains tax cut (see Chapter 10) was denounced by Carter as "the greatest hoax ever perpetrated on the American people." This was really the birth of the Left's class warfare rhetoric. The bill passed by such huge, veto-proof majorities that Carter grudgingly signed it into law.[26]

One side effect of the stifling inflationary spiral of the 1970s was that Americans were steadily plowed into higher tax brackets due to inflation. This was called inflation bracket creep: Americans' real incomes weren't rising, and the taxman was automatically taking a larger share of their income.

Making matters worse, since the 1964 Kennedy tax cuts, most of the taxes at the federal, state, and city levels had been relentlessly climbing. The payroll tax for Social Security had been rising due to scheduled rate increases, and the combination of bracket creep and payroll tax increases resulted in a shrinking after-tax paycheck. This was explained well by James Gwartney, an economist at Florida State University, who examined the impact of taxes on the middle class in this period. According to Gwartney's research:

> The major sources of rising tax rates were legislated increases in Social Security taxes and higher personal income taxes as a result of inflation and the "bracket creep" it generates. In 1965 the employee's share of the Social Security tax was 3.625% on the first $4,800 of income. The maximum tax on the employee was $174. By 1982 they were paying 6.7% on the first $32,700 of income for a maximum tax bite of $2,191.
>
> Between 1965 and 1978 taxes as a share of the taxpayer's adjustable gross income increased from 19.4% to 29.5%.
>
> By 1980 the average tax rate of a typical working couple with two children had risen to 20.9% compared with only 13.7% in 1965. More importantly for incentives, the couple's marginal tax rate jumped from 23.6% in 1965 to 35.13% in 1980. There has been a substantial increase in tax rates since the mid-1960s [through 1980] in the United States.[27]

Supply-siders were just starting to make their case for tax cuts. A leading voice for this economic strategy was the *Wall Street Journal*, which published an editorial called "Tax The Rich" in 1977. The *Journal* advised: "It stands to reason that the U.S. economy would benefit enormously if the rich paid more taxes. We have been arguing this, at least implicitly, for years. What we have not been able to get the politicians to understand, though, is that you can't get rich people to pay more in tax revenues by raising their tax rate."[28]

President Carter would have none of this. He opposed almost all efforts to alleviate the tax bite.

Washington Creates an Energy Crisis

One of Carter's biggest blunders was his energy policy, even though it was his top domestic policy concern. Carter had declared that ending the energy crisis was for the nation "the moral equivalent of war." We need to explain why Carter's energy strategy failed, because many of these same flawed prescriptions for high prices are now being resurrected to deal with high energy costs and to punish "big oil."

The three of us were living in different parts of the country in the 1970s, but we all remember vividly the miserable experience of gasoline lines. Motorists would start lining up at 6:00 A.M. on frigid winter mornings to be first in line to fill up the tank. The joke was that there was a natural limit on how long the lines could get. Their length couldn't exceed the amount of gas necessary to get from the end of the line to the front of the line. These gas lines were one of the most enduring symbols of America's decline in the 1970s. Americans aren't the kind of people who like to wait in lines, so the gas lines incited much rage and hand wringing.

Jimmy Carter was elected in 1976 in part by promising to end the energy crisis and put a muzzle on OPEC. But the Carter energy policies were one botched intervention after another that only made the crisis worse and drove prices at the pump higher.

Let's start by setting the dreary scene: Throughout the 1970s, under Nixon, Ford, and Carter, OPEC severely restricted production of oil, contributing to a big spike in the price of heating oil and gasoline. The fall in the value of the dollar—and the loss of its purchasing power—also played a key and underappreciated role here. By the late 1970s the price of a barrel of oil had more than tripled, from ten dollars to thirty-two dollars a barrel.[29]

When it came to energy policy Carter was thoroughly Malthusian, and he even gloomily predicted in 1977 that "we could use up all of the proven reserves of oil in the entire world by the end of the next decade." [30] In a nationally televised speech he told the nation: "We must face the fact that the energy shortage is permanent." [31]

Political panic during his administration spawned a potpourri of crackpot policy responses, including gas rationing; wellhead price controls; a "gas guzzler tax" on cars; an odd-even license plate system for rotating the days of the week that Americans could fill-er-up; a voluntary policy urging stores and public buildings to turn the thermostat to a chilly sixty-five degrees in the winter and no lower than a sweaty eighty in summer; a windfall profits tax imposed on producers of domestic oil, so that drillers could not "profit" from the OPEC price spikes; and a $2 billion "investment" in something called the Synthetic Fuels Corporation, an alternative renewable energy boondoggle that produced not a kilowatt of electricity by the time it was closed down in 1982.

The single policy change that was desperately needed was decontrol of the oil and natural gas prices—which Ronald Reagan was calling for on the 1980 presidential campaign trail. But Carter fought the idea and denounced proposed natural gas price decontrols as "immoral and obscene." [32]

At the 1980 Democratic National Convention in August the debate on energy policy was between the Ted Kennedy faction, which favored gas rationing coupons, and the Carter team, which wanted to stick with price controls. It was a debate, in short, between Tweedledee and Tweedledum.

What was the market response in the late 1970s to price caps? Here's a quick review, and a useful economics lesson too:

1. *Price controls reduced domestic oil production.* U.S. oil production fell from 11 to 9 million barrels a day from 1971 to 1980 (incredibly, even as the retail price at the pump for gasoline more than tripled). Price controls brought new drilling in the

United States to a standstill because the price that producers
could legally charge was well below what it cost to produce
the next marginal barrel of oil. This was a policy that only
Jimmy Carter and Saudi oil sheiks could love.

2. *Price controls increased U.S. oil consumption.* Oil consumption
by U.S. households and industry increased from 15 to 19 million barrels of oil a day from 1970 through 1978, because the
price controls kept oil prices lower than they would have otherwise been. This discouraged conservation. Artificially low
prices contributed directly to the wrenching 1978 to 1981 energy shortage.

3. *Price controls increased reliance on foreign oil.* U.S. imports of
foreign oil rose from 4 to 8.5 million barrels of oil a day from
1970 to 1977, as demand for oil rose and domestic production
fell. This was at a time when OPEC was holding back supply!

What Jimmy Carter would not do was allow the free market
pricing system to work to alleviate the crisis. By the end of his administration he had decontrolled some of the energy market. But
Reagan was the one who wisely scrapped the whole system. The
first official act of the Reagan presidency was an executive order
repealing all remaining price controls on oil and natural gas. With
a stroke of the pen, the oil crisis ended.

Two years after the elimination of energy price controls domes-
tic production surged, prices fell in half, and OPEC had been
crushed. A *Time* magazine caption in the early eighties proclaimed:
"Down, Down, Down: OPEC Finds That It Is a Crude, Crude,
World." *Newsweek* was even more to the point, writing: "OPEC:
From Cartel to Chaos!" (see Figure 4-2).[33]

Like busing, nuclear-free zones, and Whip Inflation Now buttons, price controls should be viewed as one of those discredited
1970s experiments that deserves to be forever banished from public policy discussions. We despair that they are now being seriously
debated in the current energy policy discussion in Washington.

Figure 4-2: The Dollar Price of a Barrel of Oil

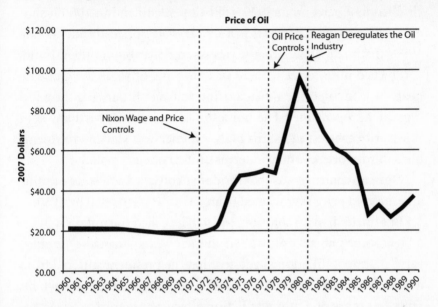

Barack Obama and many other leading Democrats favor a windfall profits tax on oil companies and anti-price-gouging laws. UGHH! The lessons of Carter's failures still haven't been learned.

Carter's Inflation

It wasn't just high energy prices that flummoxed Jimmy Carter—but the rise in all prices seemed an irresistible force of nature during his presidency. He was a convert to the Phillips-Curve religion that high inflation had to be tolerated to put people to work, so even with the money supply rising by 11 percent a year in 1977, he and his cadre of economists urged the Federal Reserve Bank to lower interest rates and quicken the pace of the printing presses to push more dollars into the economy. One of his chief economic advisers, Lawrence Klein, said "We need faster monetary growth," even as inflation raged and monetarist economists argued just the opposite.[34]

79

In 1978 inflation was an intolerable 7 percent. Later that year it climbed to 9 percent; in 1979 it hit 12 percent; and in 1980 it shot up further to 14.5 percent. Price rises were so steady in the late 1970s that the joke was that if you saw a dollar bill on the ground, you picked it up to see if there was anything of value lying underneath it.[35] In 1980 the mortgage interest rate hit an astronomical high of 21.5 percent.[36] The home-building industry virtually shut down with interest rates this high. America was starting to resemble a third-world country in terms of its monetary policy.

One consequence was that the dollar collapsed as a store of value and the gold price skyrocketed from $35 in 1970 to $850 by 1980.

But Carter had no solution. In 1978 he called the inflation bulge a "temporary aberration." Then in later years when the "temporary" nature of inflation suggested that the president suffered from a detachment from reality, Carter said that inflation wasn't his fault, but more of a moral affliction affecting American society because we had lost our capacity to "sacrifice for the common good." He declared in one speech, "It is a myth that the government can stop inflation."[37] Americans scratched their heads and wondered, If the Fed and Congress and the president couldn't stop inflation, who could?

Losing the Cold War

America's military might also disintegrated to a post–World War II low by the late 1970s, thanks to Carter's naïve ambivalence about using military force or funding the armed forces. When the Soviets flexed their military muscle and invaded Afghanistan, his feckless response was to pull America out of the Summer Olympics, which were held in Moscow. When the Iranians invaded the U.S. embassy on November 4, 1979, and took Americans hostage, he did nothing for months, then launched a half-baked rescue operation that was an embarrassing failure—demonstrating to Americans how far U.S. military prowess had declined.

In 1980 one of the biggest concerns of the public, according to Gallup polls, was "global thermonuclear war." Americans had come to think the Cold War would not have a happy ending—that we were losing. And we were.

Carter's Malaise

Worst of all, by the late 1970s Carter was a doomsday prophet who believed that the world was heading toward ecological catastrophe. The Carter administration's magnum opus: *The Global 2000 Report*, a five-hundred-plus-page multiagency assessment of the earth's future, opened with the following famous dreary forecast: "By the year 2000 the world will be more crowded, more polluted, and less stable ecologically and the world's people will be poorer in many ways than today."[38]

Then came Carter's infamous nationally televised "malaise" speech in summer 1979. In that speech Carter told Americans that they suffered from a crisis "that strikes at the very heart and soul and spirit of our national will. We can see this crisis in the growing doubt about the meaning of our lives and in the loss of unity of purpose for our nation. The erosion of confidence in the future is threatening to destroy the social and political fabric of America."

He continued in this mournful vein, stating that "for the first time in the history of our country a majority of our people believe that the next five years will be worse than the past five years."[39] The biggest pessimist in America was sitting right there in the Oval Office.

The Misery President

In the 1980 campaign Reagan skewered Carter by traveling across America asking workers, "Are you better off than you were four years ago?" Hell no, most Americans responded.

And they were right: They weren't better off. From 1978 through 1981 average real family income for the middle class fell from $32,319 to $30,916.[40] The Carter years were among the worst for family incomes in post–World War II history. Americans were getting *poorer*.

Reagan used a clever line in the 1980 election campaign that resonated well with these agitated voters. He said that "the definition of a recession is when your neighbor is out of work. The definition of a depression is when you are out of work. The definition of recovery is when Jimmy Carter is out of work."

At about this time a new term crept into the American lexicon: stagflation. This was the deadly combination of high inflation and high unemployment. When Jimmy Carter ran against Gerald Ford for president in 1976 he cited something called the misery index, a statistic invented by economist Robert Okun of the Brookings Institute. This was the inflation rate added to the unemployment rate.[41] In 1976 the index was at 14 percent (7 percent inflation and

Table 4-1: **Years of "Misery"**

	Unemployment	Inflation	Misery Index
1975	8.5%	9.2%	17.7%
1976	7.7%	5.8%	13.5%
1977	7.1%	6.5%	13.6%
1978	6.1%	7.6%	13.7%
1979	5.9%	11.2%	17.1%
1980	7.2%	13.6%	20.8%

Source: Bureau of Labor Statistics.

7 percent unemployment rate)—and Carter quite correctly told voters that a president presiding over this dismal performance hardly deserved to mismanage the economy for four more years. By 1980 the misery index had climbed to 21 percent (13.6 percent inflation and 7.2 percent unemployment—see Table 4-1).

By his own standard of performance, Carter didn't deserve four more years—and fortunately voters agreed.

5

THE TWENTY-FIVE-YEAR BOOM:
THE REAGAN ECONOMIC REVOLUTION

Reagan changed the trajectory of America in a way that Richard Nixon did not and in a way that Bill Clinton did not. He put us on a fundamentally different path because the country was ready for it.[1]
—BARACK OBAMA, 2008

REAGAN'S RIVERBOAT GAMBLE

During the first few years of Ronald Reagan's presidency, Senator Bob Dole of Kansas, a Republican, but a stubborn tax cut skeptic, used to delight in telling and retelling a joke about supply-side economics. It went like this: I have good news and bad news. The good news is that a bus full of supply-siders drove off a cliff and all the people on board were killed. The bad news is that there were three empty seats. And the even worse news is that Arthur Laffer was not on board. Ha. Ha.

We were never convinced that he was kidding.

The point is that supply-side economics was resisted by both parties in the early 1980s. Ronald Reagan faced major challenges in persuading stodgy old bulls in Congress and academia that his new economic policies would work. Almost all the conventional economists said they would not. But one thing Reagan had going for him was that Jimmy Carter had left the country in such wreckage that people were willing to try a radically new economic game plan. In 1980 inflation hit double digits. Mortgage interest rates soared to 21 percent, creating a moribund housing industry.[2] Inflation-induced middle-class bracket creep was pushing Americans into higher tax brackets and eroding take-home pay. How could things get much worse?

This economic crisis helped grease the wheels for the passage of the Reagan tax cuts in August 1981. But even at the time the tax cuts were enacted, Republican Howard Baker, the Senate majority leader, memorably reflected the view of many in Congress by calling the fiscal plan a "riverboat gamble."[3]

Over the next year things went disastrously wrong, and it appeared the gamble had failed. The economy didn't get better, it slid into yet another deep recession, the worst since the Great Depression of the 1930s. The stock market sagged to its nadir in the dreary summer of 1982 as the Dow Jones slid to 777.[4]

The unemployment rate in the spring and summer of 1982 hit 10 percent in many states—and it was the middle class worker, the primary wage earner in the family, who was often out of work. College graduates were lucky to find a job even as a burger flipper.[5] Business bankruptcies rocketed to their highest level since the height of the Great Depression in 1933. The real estate market cratered from mid-1981 to the summer of 1982, with new home sales falling by 10 percent in less than twelve months.[6]

This was about the time that Billy Joel captured the public mood with his chilling song "Allentown," about the troubles in the steel towns of Pennsylvania where they were "closing all the factories down" and wondering what happened to the American dream. The record was an ode to this era of industrial retrenchment.

Even many of the Gipper's closest advisers were losing faith and calling for a total reversal of course, starting with higher taxes. Budget Director David Stockman, once the most devoted supply-sider in Reagan's cabinet, had fretted to William Greider of *The Atlantic* that the deficits were spiraling out of control, the tax cuts were too large, and no one in the White House had any idea how to stem the tidal wave of debt that was coming. "The whole thing is based on faith," Stockman was quoted as saying in the famous *Atlantic* article.[7] Stockman was the whiz kid of the administration, the brainiac, and now he was confessing that Emperor Reagan wore no clothes. It was a public relations disaster for the new administration.

It was also about this time that academic economists like Lester Thurow of MIT and Nobel Prize winner Lawrence Klein of the University of Pennsylvania began to peddle a new "industrial planning" model, as had been showcased over the past decade in Asian countries, such as Japan.[8] This mercantilist strategy revolved around government-directed investment to key strategic industries—semiconductors, aerospace, computer software, manufacturing, and the like. This idea was the diametric opposite to the laissez-faire philosophy of Ronald Reagan, who had told voters in 1980, "Big government is the problem, not the solution."[9] But Democrats in the House of Representatives found this "new industrial policy" formulation highly alluring—as did the labor unions—and legislation was drawn up to spend tens of billions of dollars to allow industries such as steel, airlines, electronics, and semiconductors to compete against the government-subsidized industries of Japan and Europe. This all sounded like a giant "corporate welfare" giveaway scheme to big industries—a Chrysler bailout for any failing company that was considered "too big to fail."[10]

Stay the Course

To his credit, Reagan himself rejected all of this talk of government activism in the economy and told the nation again and again, "Stay the course." His advisers—Stockman and chief of staff Jim Baker, as well as congressional Republicans like Bob Dole—persuaded him to agree to a tax increase in 1982, just eighteen months after he took office. This snatched away some of the corporate tax incentives that had been part of the 1981 tax bill the year before. For years afterward Reagan believed that he was snookered into accepting that tax increase compromise in exchange for false promises of fiscal discipline from Congress. Reagan was promised three dollars of spending cuts for every dollar of tax increase, and during the rest of his presidency, whenever new taxes were proposed to reduce the deficit, he would shut down the discussion by announcing: "I'm still waiting for those three dollars of spending cuts I was promised from Congress."[11]

Shortly after the 1981 Reagan tax cut was enacted, Arthur Laffer warned the Gipper that the slow phase-in of the tax rate cuts was a critical mistake that would delay an economic recovery. Most of the tax cuts would not arrive until 1983. Laffer explained the folly of delaying the implementation of the tax cuts to Reagan by telling him: "If you know a store is going to hold a sale tomorrow you don't rush off to the store today." Mr. Reagan's original plan would have cut income tax rates 20 percent in his first year in office, but instead American families received only a 1.25 percent tax cut in 1981 and a 10 percent cut in 1982.[12] No wonder there was no recovery; there was no tax cut to speak of.

In January 1983 the *Wall Street Journal* editorial page pronounced in big bold lettering: "Finally a Tax Cut."[13] Reagan's critics were nonetheless busy declaring supply-side economics a failure. Alan Blinder, who would become a Clinton administration economist, rejoiced in the *New York Times*: "The failed supply-side experiment has restored faith in Keynesian economics in a way that scholarly debate never can."[14] Lester Thurow added, "The engines of economic growth have shut down here and across the globe, and they are likely to stay that way for years to come."[15] So at just the time that critics were writing obituaries for supply-side policies (the *Washington Post* exulted at about this time: "Reaganomics is a failure for all to see"), the U.S. economy finally roared back to life—

and with a mightier eruption than even Reagan probably thought possible.[16]

In 1983 the economy expanded by 3.5 percent, and in 1984 by a gravity-defying 6.8 percent, after inflation—the highest single-year growth rate in fifty years. Inflation was down by two-thirds.[17] Reagan with his usual wit noted in October 1983 that "I knew the program was working when they stopped calling it Reaganomics."[18]

But the terrible recession, along with a big defense buildup, ballooned the budget deficit to unthinkable levels: $100 billion, then $200 billion. It seemed that George Bush, Sr., was right when he warned in a 1980 Republican presidential debate that supply-side economics was "voodoo economics."

So in 1984 Democrats selected Walter Mondale to take on Reagan in the presidential race. Mondale ran by berating the Reagan budget deficits and his "tax cuts for the rich," and he even promised the voters that he would raise their taxes to stop the red ink. The result was that the Gipper won an overwhelming victory, carrying all but one state, in one of the biggest electoral landslides in American history. When Reagan asked in 1984 if Americans were better off than they had been four years earlier, now they overwhelmingly said hell yes. Reagan promised to keep taxes low. In 1986 he worked with the Democrats to enact the admirable 1986 Tax Reform Act, which broadened the tax base and flattened the tax rates down to just two: 15 percent and 28 percent.[19]

The economy continued to grow throughout the decade at a 3.5 percent real rate and didn't slip into a recession until late 1990. The National Bureau of Economic Research in 1999 declared the period 1982–99 one continuous megaeconomic expansion, "the longest sustained period of prosperity in the twentieth century."[20] Despite another very brief eight-month contraction in 2001, the economic spurt continued through 2007, though in 2008 it was teetering on the brink of recession.

We call this period, 1982–2007, the twenty-five-year boom— the greatest period of wealth creation in the history of the planet.

In 1980 the net wealth—assets minus liabilities—of all U.S households and businesses, according to the Federal Reserve Board, was $25 trillion in today's dollars. By 2007, the Fed calculated, net wealth was just shy of $57 trillion. Adjusting for inflation, more wealth was created in America in the twenty-five-year boom than in the previous two hundred years.

Reagan was particularly proud of another economic accomplishment: He took the misery out of the "misery index" (see Figure 5-1). When he took office inflation plus the unemployment rate stood at a post–World War II high of 20.6 percent. By 1986 that was down to 8.8 percent. When's the last time anyone has even talked about the misery index?

The Left now tries to look back and explain away the boom of the 1980s as a natural "business cycle" bounce back following a

Figure 5-1: **Ending the Misery**

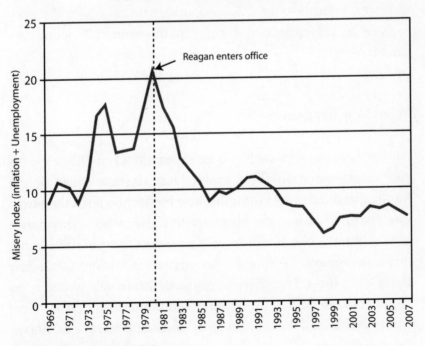

Source: Bureau of Labor Statistics.

particularly severe economic retrenchment. These same critics had nearly guaranteed before the Reagan fiscal and monetary policies were implemented that this agenda would surely make things *worse.* For example, Walter Heller, who had earlier endorsed the Kennedy tax cuts, was not so enthusiastic about Reagan's plan. "A $114-billion tax cut over three years," he predicted, "would simply overwhelm our existing productive capacity with a tidal wave of demand and sweep away all hope of curbing deficits and containing inflation." [21] But once the Reagan expansion gained steam they began to recite a new story: The recovery was inevitable. Some Reagan critics even pouted that Reagan was "lucky."

We take a different view. This was no normal recovery. The expansion was improbably resilient and powerful because economic policy was radically realigned to reward risk taking and entrepreneurship and unleash the gale-wind forces of technology, information, and the new digital age. As Robert Bartley aptly summarized in his book on the era, *The Seven Fat Years,* "It was like we added another California to the U.S. economy." [22]

Now let's investigate how and why this economic boom happened.

What Was Reaganomics?

During Reagan's first cabinet meeting in the Oval Office shortly after his inauguration, the assembled Reagan team waited eagerly for the marching orders from this new president—an actor—from California. What was the blueprint to repair a broken nation— militarily and economically? As the story goes, Reagan waited until there was complete silence in the Cabinet Room. You could have heard a pin drop. Then Reagan rose and theatrically waited a few moments to build the anticipation and then finally spoke. "Gentlemen and ladies," he told his team, "I hate inflation; I hate taxes;

and I hate the Soviets. Do something about it." Then he exited the room.

No one will ever accuse Reagan of being a president who sweated the details. Reagan from day one in the White House pursued three simple but desperately important national priorities: wring inflation out of the economy; cut taxes on American businesses and families to make the economy competitive again; and win the Cold War.[23]

That's all.

A point of clarification: Reaganomics and supply-side economics were not just about cutting tax rates. In fact Robert Bartley recounts in *The Seven Fat Years*[24] that from the beginning the supply-siders believed that fighting inflation was as high a priority as cutting tax rates. At a series of dinners held at the Michael 1 restaurant near Wall Street a group that included Laffer, Wanniski, and 1999 Nobel Prize winner Robert Mundell plotted an overthrow of the economic orthodoxy of the time. "We realized," wrote Bartley, that "to fight inflation you needed one lever, and to fight stagflation you needed a second one. To the diners at Michael 1, the answer was clear—you fight inflation with monetary policy, preferably with a commodity link, but in any event with tight money. And you fight stagflation by stimulating the economy with incentive-directed tax cuts. You find the highest marginal rates and you cut them."[25]

So Reagan's economic revolution included a more complete arsenal of ideas than just tax cuts, though tax cuts were the centerpiece. But on a broader scale, Reaganomics was a wholesale repudiation of the orthodox governing philosophy of the 1970s. It was a dismissal of Keynesian economics, which had ruled, more or less, since the Roosevelt years. This was a frontal assault against big government. Reagan had said repeatedly during the campaign that "a government big enough to give you everything you want is a government big enough to take everything you've got."

So the Gipper came into office armed with the following six-plank economic program that became the creed of Reaganomics:

1. Reduce personal income tax rates.
2. Eliminate inflation and restore a strong dollar.
3. Downsize the government and balance the budget.
4. Deregulate key industries like energy, financial services, and transportation.
5. Expand free trade and embrace globalization.
6. Win the Cold War by rebuilding the military.

Reagan was backed by a board of outside trusted economic advisers who met with him about once a month over a long lunch to advise him on policy and to reassure him of the rightness of the course he had set out. This group consisted of William Simon, Milton Friedman, Alan Greenspan, George Schultz, and Arthur Laffer, with a few others. They continually pushed Reagan to cut the budget and not to give up on the tax cuts, which were under pressure as the deficit rose in the early 1980s. Reagan's eyes twinkled whenever he met with this group, which constantly praised him for his steely determination to restore growth.

We will now discuss each key plank of the program and how it all worked.

The Kemp-Roth Tax Cut

The crown jewel of the Reagan economic program was the reduction in income tax rates to spur savings, investment, work, and economic efficiency. This was the tax bill that Congressman Jack Kemp of Buffalo and Senator Bill Roth of Delaware had been trying to enact for five years. It was the largest tax cut in American history and was signed into law in August 1981, eight months after Reagan's inauguration.

In the 1970s the highest income tax rate reached 70 percent on unearned income—such as dividends and other investment income. This meant that for every additional dollar invested for high-income individuals, the government kept seventy cents and the investor pocketed just thirty cents. The end result of this high tax penalty was that investors demanded a very high rate of return on their financial activities in the United States to offset the tax premium. Paul Craig Roberts of the Treasury Department explained the problem this way:

> Keynesians do not realize that investment is crowded out by taxation. Suppose that a 10 percent rate of return must be earned if an investment is to be undertaken. In the event that the government imposes a 50 percent tax rate on investment income, investments earning 10 percent will no longer be undertaken. Only investments earning 20 percent before tax will earn 10 percent after tax. When tax rates are reduced, after-tax rates of return are raised, and the number of profitable investments increases.[26]

The Broadhead Amendment to Kemp-Roth slashed the highest tax rate to 50 percent. Later in 1986 the highest rate came down to 28 percent. This meant that at the start of the decade investors kept thirty cents of the dollar, but by the end of the decade they kept seventy-two cents on each marginal dollar of earnings. The after-tax rate of return on investment was thus increased by a gigantic 140 percent after the tax rate cuts were enacted. No wonder there was a boom.

One consequence of the high tax rates of the late 1970s was the United States was a net capital exporter. Americans invested more abroad than foreigners invested here. That turned around with the Reagan tax cuts; America became a massive net importer of capital, as shown in Figure 5-2. Over the course of the 1981–2007 expansion, the United States was a net importer of $5.2 trillion (2007 dollars) in capital.[27] The high tax rates of the 1970s had also en-

Figure 5-2: Tax Cuts Attract Capital

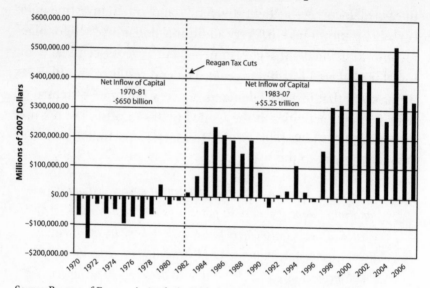

Source: Bureau of Economic Analysis, Table 1.1: International Transactions.

couraged inefficient investment patterns, in which Americans poured their money into tax shelters—ranging from municipal bonds to sham real estate trusts to wind farms to bull sperm. Yes, bull semen received a preferential tax treatment in the 1970s, and it became a popular "investment." That all ended in the eighties as well.

A second major component of the Reagan tax cuts was to lower the capital gains tax rate from 28 to 20 percent. Three years earlier the tax on capital gains had been slashed under the Steiger Bill from 49 to 28 percent. These two tax cuts caused an explosion of venture capital funding for start-ups. Brent Rider, president of the Small Business Investment Council, told the Joint Economic Committee in 1982 that the capital gains cut was critical for unleashing venture capital pools and that "almost every new business in high tech fields during the past twenty years, including Teledyne, Apple Computers, Atari, Intel, American Microsystems, and Data General, received backing from one or more venture companies." [28]

Perhaps the tax cut provision that most immediately benefited the middle class was the indexation of the tax brackets for inflation, something that a friend, economist Steve Entin, then of the Treasury Department, helped convince President Reagan to include in the tax package. In the 1970s the thief of inflation pushed Americans into paying higher tax rates even as their real incomes stagnated or fell. The IRS was one of the biggest winners from the high inflationary seventies. This inflation bracket creep infuriated voters and contributed to the massive tax revolt in the late 1970s. Those who say the Reagan tax cuts benefited almost exclusively the rich often ignore the cost savings to the middle class from ending inflationary tax bracket creep.

One other vitally important tax change happened in Reagan's second term: the Tax Reform Act of 1986. This was the bipartisan tax bill that consolidated and reduced tax brackets to 15 percent for lower- and middle-income workers and to 28 percent for higher-income Americans. That bill was "revenue neutral" because it widely broadened the tax base by eliminating many of the tax deductions, loopholes, and carveouts that K Street corporate lobbyists had chiseled out of the tax code over the previous two decades. The tax code had so many loopholes it had come to resemble a piece of Swiss cheese. Dan Rostenkowski, a Democrat in the House, and Bob Packwood, a Republican from Oregon in the Senate, deserve great credit for this victory over the Gucci-loafered special interests.

Dale Jorgenson, an economist at Harvard, estimated that the Tax Reform Act was "a major contribution to the future growth rate of the U.S. economy." [29] He calculated that the discounted present value of the TRA was between $775 billion and $999.4 billion, or "more than the entire federal budget in 1986." We argue in Chapter 15 that if we could move all the way to a flat tax, the gains would be similarly large.

Shortly after Reagan left office, the late great economic journalist Warren Brookes examined how much more in taxes Americans would have paid in 1990 if the Reagan tax cuts had not happened

THE END OF PROSPERITY

at all. He found that the average filer with an income of less than $10,000 would have paid roughly $500 a year more, or 134 percent more than their actual liability that year. People with an income of between $10,000 and $30,000 would have paid roughly $2,000 a year more, or a 79 percent increase. And a family with an income of $60,000 a year would have paid $6,000 a year more.[30] These were *not* tax cuts that benefited only the rich.

Harvard economics professor Lawrence Lindsey showed that taxes paid by the wealthy were substantially higher than they would have been if the top tax rate had remained at 70 percent. In a famous study published in the *Journal of Public Economics* he found that for *all* of Reagan's income tax cuts, between one-sixth and one-quarter of the expected revenue loss was "recouped by changes in taxpayer behavior." But what was most remarkable about Lindsey's findings was that the tax cuts for the richest Americans *raised* revenues. He found that about $17.8 billion more was collected from these wealthy individuals than had been predicted. Lindsey concluded, "Some of the more extreme supply-side hypotheses were proven false. But the core supply-side tenet—that tax rates powerfully affect the willingness of taxpayers to work, save and invest, and thereby also affect the health of the economy—won as stunning a vindication as has been seen in at least a half-century of economics."[31]

Taming the Hydra-Headed Monster of Inflation

If taxes were one of the killers of prosperity in the 1970s, the twin assassin was inflation. A major plank of Reaganomics, often now forgotten by the critics, was the restoration of sound money. By sound money, we mean a currency that retains value over time, one that the politicians are not permitted to devalue or inflate away. A stable currency policy had not been followed since the late 1960s.

As discussed in Chapter 4, in the late 1970s and early 1980s the

Left was entirely confused about what to do about inflation. Jimmy Carter's anti-inflation policy included credit controls, oil price caps, and gas rationing. Many of the top Nobel Prize–winning economists were equally confounded by inflation. "Two-digit price inflation is a distinct possibility for much of the decade of the 1980s," Paul Samuelson, one of the most famous economists of the day and the man who wrote the Economics 101 textbook that a generation of college students across the country read, somberly suggested in his 1980 *Newsweek* column.[32] He also wrote that "five to ten years of austerity, in which the unemployment rate rises toward an 8 or 9 percent average and real output inches upward at barely 1 or 2 percent per year, might accomplish a gradual taming of U.S. inflation." Gardner Ackley of the University of Michigan, a former chairman of the Council of Economic Advisers, told Congress: "I am ready to predict and to promise that the effect of the president's program will not be—as he so confidently predicts—to cut the present inflation rate in half. Whatever effects it would have on the inflation rate surely would work in the opposite direction. The administration's projection is that inflation in the CPI will decline from 11.1 percent in 1981 to 4.2 percent in 1986. That, I think, would surely be a miracle."[33]

Reagan and the supply-siders knew better. What was needed, argued Laffer, Robert Mundell of Columbia University, and Milton Friedman, among others, was to regain control of a money supply run amok. Reagan instinctively understood what the Keynesians had forgotten: that inflation was a result of too many dollars chasing too few goods. Monetary restraint was accomplished in 1981 and 1982 by Federal Reserve Board chairman Paul Volcker. Reagan gave Volcker the green light to take the corrective action after the years of disastrous easy money policy in the seventies under his Fed predecessor William Miller.

In 1982 Volcker slammed the brakes on the money supply, with the rate of growth of new dollars into the economy slowing to a crawl of 2 percent for the year after double-digit annual growth in the late seventies. Some, including supply-sider Paul Craig Roberts, fume that Volker tightened too much too quickly and this deepened the trough of the 1981–82 recession. Perhaps. But what is certain is that the economy could not withstand more years of stampeding inflation. (We also believe the economy was hurt by the slow phase-in of the tax cuts.)

The strategy worked. Inflation was tamed much faster than any Keynesian thought possible. The inflation rate tumbled from 14.5 percent to 4 percent in two years.

But the success of taming inflation does not rest only with the Volcker tight-money policy. The supply of dollars declined in the early 1980s, but meanwhile the supply of goods and services—economic output—increased, thanks to the tax cuts. The combination caused prices to fall, just as the supply-side model had predicted would happen. As Robert Mundell assessed the nation's inflation ills as early as in 1974: "It is simply absurd to argue that increasing unemployment will stop inflation. To stop inflation, you need more goods, not less."[34] That is a big part of the story behind the licking of inflation in the 1980s: increased output.

Larry Lindsey, a Federal Reserve governor and later an economist in the Bush administration, has noted that monetary policy alone cannot explain the disinflation of the eighties. By the mid-1980s as the economic output of the United States exploded and worldwide demand for dollars accelerated, the money supply increased at nearly the rate that it had in the late 1970s, but the inflation rate remained temperate because the supply of goods and services increased. To use an analogy, producing more apples doesn't raise the price of apples, it lowers the price. The Keynesians believed, perversely, just the opposite. The critiques of the Reagan agenda in the early 1980s claimed that the tax cuts would cause "rampant inflation." In fact, by unleashing economic growth, the tax cuts helped cure inflation. One of our favorite cartoons of that era depicted Ronald Reagan in 1983 behind the wheel of a jalopy, sitting next to Mr. Volcker as they speed down the hill. And Reagan is yelling, Whee!!!

There are still some on the left who have tried to rewrite the history of this era by asserting that Reagan and supply-siders had nothing to do with the disinflation of the 1980s. In 1986, the *New Republic* ran an astoundingly revisionist editorial whose argument is still heard to this day:

> *One man is more responsible for the political success of the Reagan presidency than any other, and his name is not Ronald Reagan. It is Paul Volcker, the man Jimmy Carter appointed as chairman of the Federal Reserve Board. A relatively stable currency has been the basis . . . for the economic boom of recent years. . . .*
>
> *Volcker did it. In October 1979 he persuaded his colleagues to starve inflation of the dollars it feeds on. President Reagan did little to help. In fact, his deficits worked against Volcker's efforts.*[35]

This was fanciful rewriting of history. Yes, it is true that Paul Volcker was a Jimmy Carter appointee. But the necessary monetary tightening of the screws never happened under Carter because there was not the political will to do it, and in any case none of his economists understood why there was inflation or how to tame it—which was through the interplay of tight money and lower tax rates.

The conquering of inflation was one of the great accomplishments of Ronald Reagan and supply-side economics. In 1980 inflation registered as one of the five greatest concerns of Americans in the Gallup poll. By 1985 inflation was listed by just 2 percent of voters as a problem.

The Plunge in Interest Rates

A related benefit to the Reagan-Volcker disinflation policy of the early 1980s was the steady decline in interest rates. In early 1981 the prime interest rate was at 21.5 percent, but incredibly it fell to 8.2 percent by 1987. As inflationary expectations continued to decline in the 1980s and 1990s, the prime rate hit its twenty-year low in 1993 at 6.0 percent.[36] The Treasury Note rate also fell dramatically in the 1980s, from 14 percent in 1981 to 7 percent in 1988 as shown in Figure 5-3. Remember: The Left had predicted in the early 1980s that the supply-side tax cuts would *raise* interest rates.

In the 1980s the budget deficit exploded, and throughout the decade the adversaries of Reaganomics continued to predict high interest rates from budget deficits. Clearly that didn't happen. In fact one of the few economists to admit that the Reagan debt did not have the corrosive impact that many had predicted was Robert Heilbroner. Here is what he wrote in 1988 in a *New York Times* article called "How I Learned to Love the Deficit": "In 1982 when the

Figure 5-3: **Reaganomics Reduces Interest Rates**

10 Year Treasury Note Yield
October 1955 to January 2008

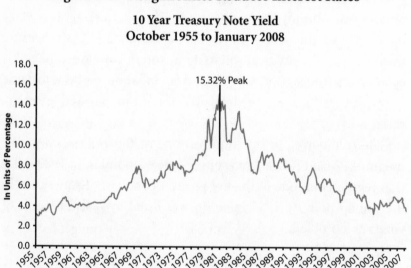

Source: Treasury Department.

deficit first climbed into triple digits (that year it came to $120 billion), interest rates on high grade corporate bonds average 13.79%. By the end of 1987 after five years of deficits that totaled $1 trillion, corporate interest rates had actually fallen to 9.38%. So much for crowding out."[37]

We couldn't have said it better ourselves.

Commodity prices also plunged after the Reagan-Volcker monetary policy was implemented. The gold price, which had hit $850 an ounce under Carter, fell to $300 an ounce under Reagan. The diamond market also collapsed. A one-carat white flawless gem, the benchmark jewel, cost $64,000 in 1980 but by the end of 1982 that same gem cost $21,000. This was disinflation.

Get Government Off Our Backs

In the campaign of 1980, Ronald Reagan relentlessly attacked Jimmy Carter for his fiscal mismanagement. He believed that Washington's unquenchable spending appetite was devouring the private capacity to create wealth. One of Reagan's economists, Martin Feldstein, said it well in 1981: "As long as the government's role in the economy was sill relatively small, it was intellectually fashionable among economists to identify failures of the free market system and to theorize that government policies could cure them. The experience of living with large-scale government activity in the 1960s and 1970s showed that much of that theory was wishful thinking." The actual data confirmed Feldstein (and Reagan's) observations about the steady encroachment of government. In 1960 the government consumed 18 percent of GDP, with half of that for defense. In 1970 the government share was 20 percent, and by 1980 it was up to 22 percent, even though the military budget had been plundered over these years.[38]

In the late 1970s the spending onslaught and the battered economy caused the deficit to grow to a new high of $77 billion. The

Reagan team labeled that a disgrace. Reagan pledged to balance the budget. This was also one of the most controversial of Reaganomics' promises. Reagan's opponents said it would be impossible to increase the military budget, cut taxes by $500 billion, and cut the domestic budget enough to close a $50 billion deficit. In a 1980 Republican presidential debate, Reagan's rival for the nomination, George Bush, Sr., described this combination of events as "voodoo economics."

Whether or not the critics were right in saying that it was impossible, what is unquestionably true is that the budget was never balanced under Reagan; in fact, the deficit quadrupled from 1980 to 1984 and the national debt tripled over Reagan's two terms, from $1 trillion to $3 trillion. But he did manage to substantially slow the growth rate of the budget from the previous dozen years, and domestic spending actually fell in real terms in his first two years in office.

In 1981 Reagan signed into law the Gramm-Latta spending reduction bill, which the *Washington Post* described as containing "Ronald Reagan's giant catalog of spending cuts." This 1981 budget was one of the leanest spending blueprints to pass Congress in the last thirty years, to be sure. But many of Reagan's spending cuts were not cuts at all. Most conspicuously, Reagan had campaigned on eliminating the Departments of Education and Energy, which Carter had created as a favor to special interests. (The Teachers Unions crowed after the Education Department was created that "we're the only special interest group in Washington with our own cabinet agency.") But each of these agencies survived the Reagan budget knife and today they have bigger budgets than ever.

But Reagan made a very shrewd and fateful decision in 1981. He gave the tax cut highest priority; then the defense build-up, then the budget cuts—in that order. The balanced-budget crowd in both parties had tried to insist that the spending cuts should come first, and only then the tax cut. If Reagan had agreed to that trap door strategy we'd still be waiting for the tax cut today, more than a quarter century later, because the deep budget cuts necessary for a balanced budget were never made.

So what's the final verdict on Reagan's budget policies? First, the pace of federal spending was cut in the 1980s, but not the overall *level* of spending. In fact, for all the talk about heartless Reagan budget cuts, the federal budget was 69 percent larger when Reagan left office than when he entered it—22 percent larger in real terms. As a share of GDP, federal outlays declined by less than one percentage point. That decline happened even though the Reagan military buildup doubled Pentagon expenditures over the years 1981–89 from $158 billion to $304 billion. The years of the greatest spending hike in the military budget were 1978–87, when the Pentagon's expenditures rose from $180 billion to $280 billion in real 1987 dollars.

Domestic spending under President Reagan grew at a slower pace than it had under any American president in the post–World War II era.

What most Americans remember about the 1980s is those large budget deficits, which are pointed to as a refutation of the claims for the success of the Reagan program. But the story of the Reagan deficits was the Sherlock Holmes mystery solved by the dog that didn't bark. The very large increase in the debt had virtually no negative effects on the economy.[39] As we showed in the section above, the inflation rate fell, and more important, the interest rate fell by half even as deficits were climbing to 6 percent of GDP. Where was the evidence of deficits "crowding out" private investment, which soared in these years? Where was the financial panic?

Our explanation for this is not that government can spend and borrow ad infinitum with no negative short- or long-term consequences for the nation. Rather, there are two reasons the dog didn't bark. First, the debt as a share of our GDP grew, but not to unprecedented levels. By the end of the Reagan years the debt was a little more than 40 percent of GDP. In the 1950s the debt had been about 60 percent of GDP—because the country was still paying off the

World War II debt. But there was little evidence of restrained private investment or high interest rates.

More important, the Reagan critics had it all wrong in the 1980s and still do today. The crowding-out effect of government fiscal policy is not caused by government *borrowing*, but by government *spending*. Government deficits rose in the 1980s, but thanks to the tax cuts, the value of U.S. investments soared. This meant that foreigners were willing and able to finance U.S. growth. The savings rate of Americans—correctly defined as the increase in their wealth holdings—exploded, so government borrowing was financed through private sector savings.

The Regulatory Octopus

Reagan hated heavy-handed regulation, and for good reason. In the 1970s regulatory costs exploded and the noose around the neck of industry got ever tighter—leading to investment and jobs moving offshore. The proliferation of regulations and regulators help explain why Washington, D.C., had more lawyers in the early 1980s than there were in all of Japan.

In 1980 federal regulations cost the U.S. economy about $800 billion in today's dollars, costing the average family about $4,000—a massive invisible tax.[40] Yes, many regulations, for example, clean air and water statutes, have large societal benefits, but as with everything in Washington, we had long ago passed the point of negative marginal returns.

So it's not surprising that Reagan's first executive order, signed the day he was inaugurated, lifted all remaining oil and natural gas price controls. The free market in energy would finally reign supreme. As discussed in the previous chapter, with a stroke of the pen oil prices fell, and fell, and fell, and by the late 1980s the barrel price was less than half what it was in 1980.

From the late 1970s through the early 1980s one key industry after another was liberated from regulatory tentacles. Trucking, railroads, airlines, long-distance telephone service, and energy and financial services all were fully or partially deregulated. Some of this happened in the late Carter years—one of the few domestic policy issues Jimmy Carter got right. Here's a fact that may surprise readers. The architect of the airline price decontrols was none other than Ted Kennedy of Massachusetts.

In the 1980s the pages of the *Federal Register* fell from eighty thousand by half. This was a load off the back of industry and it was reflected in stock values. Economist James Bianco of Bianco Research has been tracking the relationship between federal regulations and the financial markets and has found that going back as far as the 1930s, a spurt of federal regulatory activity is strongly negatively correlated with the performance of the stock market.[41] When Washington went on a rulemaking blitzkrieg, in the 1970s, the stock market collapsed and long-term interest rates hit 15 percent. When the ankle chains were unlocked, it was liftoff for the stock market's twenty-five-year boom. The lesson here: Rules and rallies don't generally coexist.

Robert Crandall, an economist at the Brookings Institution, is the leading authority in the nation on the impact of deregulation in the 1970s and 1980s. His studies find a massive consumer benefit to the deregulation of this era. Prices in five industries—natural gas, telecom, airlines, railroads, and trucking—fell by between 25 percent and 60 percent from 1978 to 1995. The net gain to consumers from deregulating these industries was roughly $55 billion a year by 1995.[42] Not too shabby.

No discussion of the economic turnaround of the 1980s would be complete without a word about union policies. The union bosses had a vise grip around the neck of industry in the 1960s and 1970s. Labor unrest hit its high point with four hundred separate strikes involving one thousand workers or more.[43] These constant factory shutdowns and the explosive animus between labor and business further eroded the competitiveness of U.S. industry.

Strikes are instruments of mutual destruction that reduce the income of workers and the output of American firms.

One of Ronald Reagan's first acts as president, also often overlooked by historians, was the firing of the air traffic controllers, who illegally went on strike in the early days of the Gipper's presidency. It was a defining early moment for Reagan: It showed the American people, the unions, and even the Soviet Union that this was not a president who bluffed or backed down under pressure. The unions were shocked that for the first time in years a politician had stared them down. The firing seemed especially unlikely because the air traffic controllers union had endorsed Reagan for president in 1980. But this bold move helped break the back of the militant unions and blazed a course for twenty years of relative calm and peace between unions and industry. From four hundred strikes per year, on average, the number since the mid-1980s has fallen to fewer than fifty per year.[44]

Tear Down These Trade Walls

Reagan was a free-trader par excellence. He had a vision of creating not just a North American Free Trade Area, but a Western Hemispheric free trade region stretching from Alaska to Argentina. NAFTA was begun under Reagan and pushed by George Bush, Sr., then signed into law by Bill Clinton. Today the value of all U.S. imports and exports exceeds $2 trillion—almost double the real value of trade in 1980.[45] About one in four jobs in the United States is trade-dependent, and our ability to control inflation is highly related to the forces of international competition that hold prices down.

Alas, Reagan wasn't always a paragon of virtue on trade, and on more than one occasion he buckled under to political pressure, rather than doing what was right for the nation. One of Reagan's biggest policy mistakes was agreeing to "voluntary" auto import restrictions on Japan in the early 1980s. It was a sop to Detroit that infuriated many of the Gipper's most devoted followers. But Ronald Reagan was no saint, and he listened to pollsters and political pundits who told him wrongly these moves were essential to win the next election. Still the free trade agenda clearly advanced in the 1980s and 1990s, and import quotas and trade restrictions fell over this period. The Financial Services Forum estimates that today trade causes an aggregate gain to the U.S. economy of $1 trillion a year, or $10,000 per household. Ending trade tariffs between the U.S. and our trading partners would increase the size of the U.S. economy by an additional $500 billion.[46]

A Decade of Greed or Grandeur?

So this was the complete set of new economic policies installed in the 1980s, a radical departure from the economic regime of the 1970s under the Keynesians. How did they work? In this section we present the facts. Readers can decide for themselves if they believe the policies were effective.

The Reagan Bull Market

Exhibit A is the trend of the stock market, shown in Figure 5-4. This shows the unprecedented rise in the value of U.S. companies since the Reagan tax cuts. We also see the downturn in the 1970s and a clear point of inflection—the moment in time when the direction of the curve shifted course, or when the water started flowing in the other direction. Recall from the previous chapter that from 1966 to 1982, the fifteen years before Reaganomics, the Dow Jones Industrial Average suffered one of its blackest bear markets in history, falling 23 percent in nominal terms and nearly 8 percent per year in inflation-adjusted real terms. Stagflationary antimarket

Figure 5-4: Rising Stock Market
During the Twenty-Five-Year Boom

Real S&P 500, Log Scale

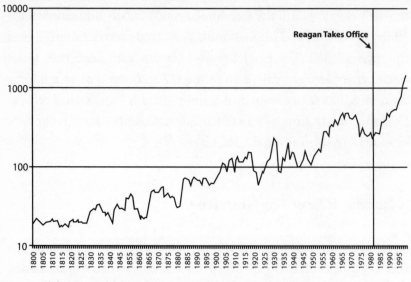

Source: Global Financial Data, http://www.globalfindata.com/freesm.htm.

Keynesian fine-tuning policies caused the wealth of American families to vanish before their very eyes.

The stock market more than tripled to 3,000 by the end of the Reagan years, then tripled again to 11,000 by the end of the Clinton years, and rose to 12,500 today.

During the 1982–2000 Reagan bull market stocks soared by 12 percent per year, raising the net worth of U.S. households by some $30 trillion. To match this performance over the next twenty years, the Dow Jones would have to soar to about 120,000 by 2020. If Washington politicians do no harm, and stay on Reagan's road, that could be accomplished.

A skeptic might ask: Why stress stock market performance, which benefits mostly the rich? There are three reasons. First, we're persuaded that the stock market is one of the best forward-looking indicators of how a national economy is performing. Stocks don't rise over the long term in nations with falling living standards or malfunctioning economic policies. The stock market is the collective bet of the global financial markets on how a nation's economy will grow over time. In the 1980s and 1990s global investors bet heavily on America, Inc., and they—and we—got a massive return on that investment.

Second, thanks to the creation of new vehicles for middle-class stock ownership in this era, the stock market was democratized in the 1980s and 1990s. The tax laws changed in the early 1980s to create IRAs and Keogh plans, which allowed tax-delayed accumulation of savings for retirement. This was an awesome public policy innovation: Nearly overnight, some 116 million Americans were qualified for tax-free savings accounts.[47] By 1983 $40 billion was invested in IRAs and Keoghs. In the early 1980s alone the money invested in money market funds tripled after these new savings vehicles were launched. At the same time, the financial markets created new products that made it easy for people to become investors: CDs, mutual funds, stock index funds, 401(k) plans, and the like expanded the investor class.[48] The entrepreneurial vision of Charles Schwab dramatically lowered the transaction costs for buying and selling stocks and meant that tens of millions of Americans could be at-home investors with Schwab accounts.

The result was a steady increase in the number and percentage of Americans who were converted into worker-capitalists. In 1980 about 16 percent—or one in six Americans—owned stock. In 1990 more than one in three owned stocks, and by 2000 one in two American households were stock owners—or 80 million adults (see Figure 5-5). Even more remarkable was the growth in mutual fund accounts. In 1980 there were 13 million such accounts. By the early 2000s there were 130 million.[49]

The emergence of this new investor class was the single most important demographic change in America in the last quarter of the twentieth century. Tens of millions of Americans owned Exxon, Microsoft, General Electric, Intel, and Google. It's estimated

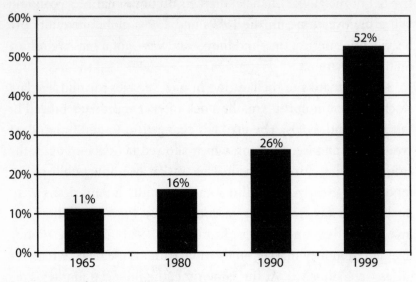

Figure 5-5: The Rise of Worker Capitalism

Percentage of All Workers Who Own Stock

Source: Survey of Consumer Finances.

that Bill Gates singlehandedly created some 10,000 millionaires in America.[50]

Finally, the soaring increase in the stock market value of U.S. firms is a measurement of the triumph of American business in virtually every high-value information-age industry—computer software, telecommunications, the internet, fiberoptics, semiconductors, biotechnology, and financial services. Even more breathtaking advances came in the late 1990s and early 2000s in areas like nanotechnology, molecular electronics, and cheap energy-creating fuel cells. Even many of America's more traditional "rust belt" industries, like the auto industry, industrial equipment, and steel—all of which were largely left for dead in the malaise decade of the 1970s—recorded productivity-enhanced comebacks, though they suffered through deep trenches.

Prosperity Rediscovered

What is impressive and underappreciated about the supply-side boom is not just that the economy more than doubled in size, but that the growth phases have been long stretches and the recessions have been short and shallow. Michael Cox, an economist at the Dallas Federal Reserve Bank and author of the brilliant book *The Myth of Rich and Poor*, calculated that between 1982 and 2007 the American economy was in a growth phase for 288 months of the 300-month period. That means the U.S. economy was advancing 96 percent of the time and in decline only 4 percent of the time. Simply awesome. From 1972 to 1982, the economy was constantly jerked into recession every time it began to dig out of the ditch it had slid into. The recoveries were short and the recessions were deep in the 1970s, just the opposite of the experience of the 1980s, 1990s, and early 2000s.[51] Throughout most of American history, the U.S. economy was in recession—or depression—nearly one-third of the time.

In the twenty-five-year boom launched by the Reagan policies, the average annual growth rate of real gross domestic product (GDP) from 1981 to 2005 was 3.4 percent per year. In Europe the growth rate over the 1981–2005 period was only a bit over 2.0 percent. By the end of the Reagan years, the American economy was almost one-third larger than it was when the 1980s began.

What War on the Middle Class?

Real median household income rose by $4,000 in the Reagan years, from $37,000 in 1981 to $41,000 in 1989.[52] This improvement was a stark reversal of the income trends in the 1970s (see Figure 5-6). Real median family income fell by $1,000 from 1973 to 1982. Me-

Figure 5-6: **Reversal of Fortune**

Real Median Income, 1970–88

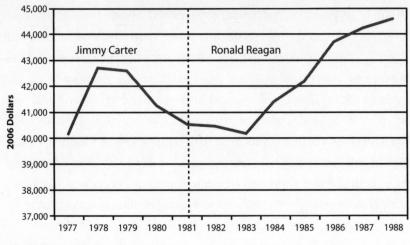

Source: Census Bureau.

dian household income was up 21 percent and per capita income was up 51 percent from 1981 to 2007.

The liberals like to play a trick with the income numbers by stating that from 1978 to 1989 real average income of poor households took a nosedive. But from 1979 to 1981 the Reagan tax cuts were not in effect. In those Carter years family income for the poorest fifth of households plummeted from $9,650 to $8,906. But after the Reagan tax cuts, the income of the poorest fifth rose to $9,431.[53] (All these numbers are adjusted for inflation.)

The Great American Jobs Machine

How is this for a testament to the success of Reaganomics? In 1989 Montgomery County, Maryland, established a commission on economic development in the region. One of its conclusions was, and we're not making this up: "We have to slow the FRANTIC PACE

112

OF NEW JOB CREATION."[54] Wow. What a wonderful complaint to have about prosperity. Too many jobs.

It certainly wasn't like that when Reagan took office in 1981, when the unemployment rate hit 7.6 percent. But the Montgomery commission was right: Over the Reagan years, job creation was "frantic." From 1981 through 1989 the U.S. economy produced 17 million new jobs, or roughly 2 million new jobs each year. Then in the 1990s another 26 million jobs were added.

Here we have solid evidence of the supply-side effects of the Reagan tax cuts. Hours worked per adult aged twenty to sixty-four grew much faster in the 1980s than in the pre-Reagan years. The tax cuts encouraged work, especially among married women, who tended to be the biggest victims of high tax rates because their earnings, which came on top of their husbands' earnings, were taxed at a high marginal rate.

Yes, some unionized factory jobs in industries like steel, autos, and textiles have been lost due to overseas competition, but for every job lost two or three have been gained in services, technology, and knowledge-based industries.

We're in the Money

Overall that's a record that's hard to rival. But this era of affluence was not without its loud critics, and the stories of the evils of the Reagan years persist to this day, so we thought we'd address some of the most common myths of these years.

Myth: Decade of Greed

In 1987 Oliver Stone made the movie *Wall Street* in which Michael Douglas, playing the part of Wall Street wheeler-dealer Gordon

113

Gekko, gives a speech to a crowded room of shareholders and declares: "Greed, for lack of a better word, is good. Greed works. Greed clarifies, cuts through and captures the essence of the evolutionary spirit."

For the Left, this became the symbol of the 1980s. The lust for money allegedly became a national obsession. No one bothered to pay attention to the AIDS epidemic, increased homelessness, and Wall Street corruption. People like Ivan Boesky (a criminal) and Michael Milken (the grandfather of the junk bond industry who in many ways was a great financial innovator) became the sinister poster children for the era in the media.

We happen to think that when people disparage the 1980s as a "decade of greed," it's an acknowledgment that the economic policies worked. In the 1970s Americans lost money and got poorer; no one called it an era of greed. If greed means more jobs, more prosperity, and more Americans enjoying a higher living standard, then, yes, this was a decade of greed.[55]

Myth: Trickle Down Economics

The poorest 20 percent of Americans experienced a 6 percent gain in real income in the 1980s after suffering a 5 percent decline in the 1970s. Black Americans saw their incomes grow at a slightly faster pace (11.0 percent) than whites (9.8 percent) in the Reagan years.

The middle class, whites and blacks, did a lot better, too, despite the "trickle down" economics claim. Table 5-1 shows that by 1989 there were 5.9 million more Americans whose salaries exceeded $50,000 a year than there were in 1981 (adjusting for inflation). Similarly, there were 2.5 million more Americans earning more than $75,000 a year, an 83 percent increase. And the number of Americans earning less than $10,000 a year fell by 3.4 million workers.

Table 5-1: Incomes Moved Up in the 1980s

Workers' Earnings (millions of workers and 1981 dollars)*

	less than $10,000	more than $50,000	more than $75,000
1981	66.0	9.9	3.0
1989	62.6	15.8	5.5
Difference	−3.4	5.9	2.5
%Change	−5%	60%	83%

Source: Cato Institute calculations, based on Bureau of the Census, *U.S. Statistical Abstract,* 1996, p. 478, Table 740.
* Earning levels are adjusted for inflation between 1981 and 1989.

Myth: The Era of Debt and Deficits

There is no doubt that the budget deficit and debt were way up in the 1980s, but it is factually untrue that the Reagan tax cuts were a major cause of the red ink. Real federal revenues grew by 24 percent.[56]

From 1950 to 2005, federal receipts averaged 18.4 percent of GDP. Throughout most of the Reagan years and clearly by the end (when taxes were 19 percent of GDP), taxes were above the post-war average. This was a point that even the *New York Times* had to acknowledge, and reporter David Rosenbaum conceded in 1992: "One popular misconception is that the Republican tax cuts caused the crippling federal budget deficit now approaching $300 billion a year. The fact is, the large deficit resulted because the government vastly expanded what it spent each year."[57]

Exactly right. Most of the deficit increase was a result of the defense spending buildup in the 1980s. The cumulative increase in defense spending from 1981 to 1989 ($806 billion) was larger than the entire cumulative increase in the budget deficit ($779 billion) in those years.[58]

But the vast majority of Americans now agree that the Reagan defense buildup had a major impact on the defeat of the Soviet empire and the liberating of hundreds of millions of people from the horrors of communism, and thus was well worth the cost. The issue then becomes: Was it appropriate to borrow for those large military expenditures? Was the Reagan administration justified in paying for this one-time increase in "public investment" spending through debt rather than taxes and asking our children and grandchildren to help defray the cost of defeating the Soviet menace?

Myth: The Rich Got Richer and the Poor Got Poorer

The *New York Times* published a front-page story on March 5, 1992, which screamed: "Even Among the Well-Off, the Richest Got Richer." It then pronounced that "the top 1% received 60% of the gain from the 80's boom."[59]

Not quite. From 1981 to 1989, every income group—from the richest to the poorest—gained income, according to the Census Bureau economic data (see Figure 5-7). The reason the wealthiest Americans saw their share of total income rise is that they gained income at a faster pace than did the middle class and the poor.[60] But Reaganomics did create a rising tide that lifted nearly all boats.

Colin Powell tells a wonderful story of Ronald Reagan's last day in the White House. As national security adviser he met with the president on that frigid January morning in 1989 and reported to Mr. Reagan: "Sir, here is my last security advisory to you: the state of the world is safe; there are no crises to report, and the nation's economy is healthy." It was short, snappy, and an entirely accurate assessment of the state of America at the end of the Reagan era. What a contrast to the world scene and the economic chaos that Reagan inherited exactly eight years before when he was first inaugurated.

Reagan noted in his farewell address to the nation in 1989, with his customary modesty, that "even though I was known as the Great

Figure 5-7: **Reaganomics: A Rising Tide Lifts All Boats**

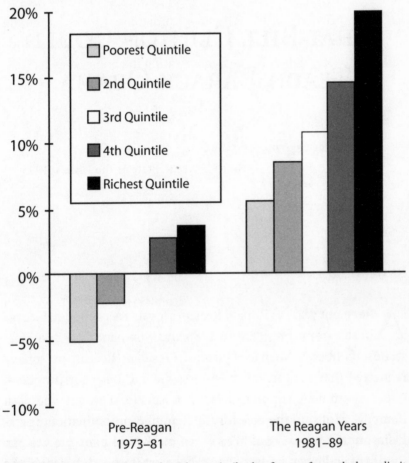

**Change in Real Family Incomes
(by upper limit of each quintile*)**

* Since there is no upper limit on the richest quintile, that figure refers to the lower limit of the top 5 percent.
Source: Cato Institute, based on data from the Bureau of the Census.

Communicator, it would be more accurate to say that I communicated great ideas."[61]

Yes, great ideas with great consequences, and we and our grandchildren are all the richer for it.

6

WHAT BILL CLINTON COULD
TEACH BARACK OBAMA

The era of big government is over.
—BILL CLINTON, State of the Union, 1995

READ MY LIPS

After eight years as Ronald Reagan's loyal vice president, George Bush ran for president in 1988 and won handily over a Massachusetts liberal, Michael Dukakis. President Reagan personally requested that Arthur Laffer endorse George Bush for president. Other prominent supply-siders, such as Pete DuPont and Jack Kemp, were also in the race for the Republican nomination, but as Laffer recalls: "I just couldn't say 'no' to the old man. He was my president and when he asked me to support Bush, I did." Laffer and other supply-siders had misgivings about whether Bush would actually carry on the Reagan legacy. When George Bush called for a "kinder, gentler nation," President Reagan was said to have asked: "Kinder and gentler than whom?"

These were prosperous times in 1988 as the Reagan expansion rolled on and Dukakis tried to run against the Reagan budget deficits just as Mondale had done four years earlier. The voters opted for what they hoped would be "Reagan's third term." Bush had run as a Reaganite and on no issue was he more forthright than on taxes. Bush said at the Republican convention in 1988 that the Democrats would push him and push him to raise taxes and he would finally turn to them and say: "Read my lips, no new taxes."

Some political analysts have said that the age of Reagan officially came to an end two years later in the fateful summer of 1990 when George H. W. Bush broke his "no new taxes" pledge and agreed to a tax increase budget deal with Democratic majority leader George Mitchell and other liberal Democrats in Congress. It is not clear why Bush was attracted to the tax hike option. One explanation is that he thought he could make history by slashing the budget deficit and balancing the budget—which had been in deficit since 1969. His budget director, Richard Darman, was clearly the instigator of the treachery. Mr. Darman had signaled in a speech in 1989 that a deal was coming. He sermonized that America had become a nation of "now-nowism" (which echoed the Left's complaint that the 1980s was the "me decade") and that we needed to overcome our "collective shortsightedness . . . to address the future."[1] These were code words for cutting the deficit with higher taxes.

When President Bush agreed to the tax hike, Newt Gingrich, who led the opposition to the Bush budget deal, decried the decision as a "supreme act of stupidity." Gingrich and other leading conservatives like Representative Dick Armey of Texas accurately predicted that this act would be the downfall of the Bush presidency. Conservatives abandoned Bush in droves. At the Republican National Convention in Houston two years later, many conservatives, wounded by the Bush betrayal, waved signs that read: "Read My Lips, No Second Term."

Crime of the Century

Over the last eighteen years a mythology has developed around the 1990 budget deal, which at the time was referred to as "the deal of the century." Bush is portrayed as having been persecuted by voters for doing the fiscally responsible thing. Bush himself later suggested as much, and predicted that history books would treat him kindly for raising taxes when he did.[2] But this is all historical revisionism, probably designed to try to persuade Republicans to raise taxes again—and destroy the party again.

The 1990 budget deal did not accomplish any of its goals. It didn't help the economy; in fact shortly after Bush agreed to the higher taxes, the economy slipped into the first recession in eight years. It didn't reduce the budget deficit: The deficit skyrocketed after the deal was consummated. And it increased, rather than reduced, government spending.[3]

When Reagan left office the budget deficit wasn't rising, it was falling. The deficit was $149 billion in Reagan's last year in office, or 2.9 percent of GDP.[4] Even if Bush had done nothing, the deficit was expected to drift down to less than 2 percent of GDP over the next four years. If Bush had enforced the budget rules under the Gramm-Rudman spending reductions bill, the budget would have been virtually balanced by the end of his term in office.[5] Instead, the budget deficit doubled to $290 billion in 1991, or twice what it was *before* the budget deal. From 1990 to 1994 the federal government borrowed $1 trillion. This was the worst four-year fiscal performance in forty years.[6] It was far worse than any four-year period under Reagan, but somehow the Reagan deficits were evil and the Bush deficits were benign. As Reagan economist Paul Craig Roberts concluded sarcastically: "Apparently there are two kinds of deficits. Reagan deficits deindustrialize America, force up interest rates, doom future generations, and soak up global savings. But Bush deficits resulting from the old routine of taxing, spending, and regulating, cause hardly a ripple in the economy."[7]

Meanwhile, rather than curtailing spending, the record is clear: The budget exploded during the presidency of George Bush, Sr. by 20 percent. "Notwithstanding all the budgeters' talk of pain," wrote Howard Gleckman of *Business Week* after the budget deal was consummated, "spending at home is in for a windfall."[8] Everything from Head Start to NASA to Medicaid to highway spending enjoyed beefy budget increases in this new "austere" budget environment.

Worst of all, the taxes didn't raise any revenues.[9] In 1989, without tax increases, federal revenues as a share of GDP were 19.3 percent. In 1991, after the tax hikes, revenues slipped to 19.1 percent. The *Wall Street Journal* editorial page ran the numbers and found that the rich actually paid *less* taxes when the rates were raised.[10] One *Journal* investigation noted in July of 1991 that "81 percent of the revenues expected from the 1990 budget deal's tax increase are failing to materialize." What a shock. Higher tax rates generated less revenues than anticipated. Pulitzer Prize winner Paul Gigot of the *Wall Street Journal* reported in January 1993 in a column entitled "Oops, Weren't We Going to Reduce the Deficit?" that the rich paid $6.5 billion *less* taxes in 1991, after the tax rate hike, than they did in 1990 before rates went up. "Rates had to go up, we were told, in order to produce a river of new revenues."[11]

Most embarrassing of all, and something that liberals who want to soak the rich at every turn would very much like everyone to forget, was the misbegotten "luxury tax" on the super rich. This was a 10 percent surcharge on yachts, jewelry, and private planes. Instead of wrenching more money out of the yacht owners, the tax drove yacht owners to stop buying yachts—at least in the United States. What Congress seemed to forget was that boats and planes are built by people whose last name is not Rockefeller or Trump. So in the first two years of the luxury tax, ninety-four hundred non-rich boatmakers lost their jobs. As one laid-off worker put it in disgust: "This Congress views jobs as a luxury."[12] In the ultimate political irony, it was liberal senator George Mitchell of Maine, one of the masterminds of the budget deal, who led the charge a year later to repeal the luxury tax, because the senator evidently had forgotten temporarily that a lot of boats are produced in Maine shipyards.[13]

The 1990 budget deal was the political equivalent of the Republican Party commiting hara-kiri. Throughout the last twenty-five years, Republicans have triumphed when they have taken a credible antitax stance; it has become the political brand of the party, and it wins elections. Amazingly, at one point George Bush, Sr., had a 91 percent approval rating, and Jay Leno joked on TV that Bush should run for the Republican and Democratic nominations for president in 1992.

But Mr. Bush's tax betrayal paved the way for the surprise election of Bill Clinton in 1992, as the economy was still weak from the 1991 recession, and Clinton made his famous claim to voters that "I feel your pain." In a three-man race—Bush, Clinton, and renegade billionaire Ross Perot of Texas—Mr. Bush won only 38 percent of the popular vote, one of the worst performances for an incumbent president in decades. Bush and his economic adviser, Dick Darman, had predicted that voters would forgive Mr. Bush this one transgression, but they were sadly mistaken. Bill Clinton was elected that year with 43 percent of the vote, hardly a mandate but an impressive victory from a man who grew up in humble surroundings in a small town in Arkansas. One person who voted for Bill Clinton, not once, but twice, was Arthur Laffer.

It's the Economy, Stupid

Mr. Clinton's elevation to the White House was seen at the time as the final voter repudiation of supply-side economics. Clinton had promised during the campaign to raise taxes on the rich, while offering a "middle-class tax cut." But he had also run as a "New Democrat," eschewing the liberal direction of the party in the past two decades and redefining the Democrats as the party of fiscal discipline, free trade, crime control, a strong dollar, and welfare reform.

The mastermind of the Clinton economics program was former Goldman Sachs CEO Robert Rubin, who was named Mr. Clinton's chief economic adviser in the White House and later became Treasury secretary. Mr. Rubin helped push the Democrats in a pro-growth direction on free trade, deficit reduction, and the need for a strong dollar. Fortunately, he was not a conventional tax-and-spend Keynesian Democrat from the 1960s and 1970s.

But at the core of Rubin's approach was the idea that supply-side tax cuts do not work. He argued that tax cuts lead to federal budget deficits; these budget deficits erode the pool of national savings available for investment; this shortage of savings raises the cost of borrowing through higher interest rates; and those higher interest rates crowd out private investment needed for long-term growth. According to this theory, raising taxes would increase national savings, reduce interest rates, and increase investment by businesses. This is a shorthand explanation of what became known as "Rubinomics." Hence a credible program for reducing the budget deficit would be rewarded with more domestic and international capital investment in the United States. Our problem with the argument is that if you leave out all the intermediate steps to the train of logic behind Rubinomics, it leads to the weird conclusion that raising taxes on investment will lead to more investment and reducing taxes on investment will lead to less investment. Nonetheless, the idea won Mr. Rubin the front cover of *Time* in the late 1990s as one of the men who saved the global economy.[14]

To this day, Mr. Rubin is regarded as one of the most influential economic public policy thinkers on the left. He is considered a guru on money and macroeconomic issues, and his advice and money-raising capabilities are sought by Democratic candidates for president, governor, and senator. He is also considered to be a front runner for the Federal Reserve Board chairman position under the next Democratic administration. Rubin and his protégé, Larry

Summers, who also later served as Mr. Clinton's Treasury secretary, are regarded as the architects of the new Democratic agenda that helped usher in the longest period of uninterrupted economic prosperity in modern American history. Since this new theory was seen as a rebuke to supply-side economics, let's see what worked and what didn't.

Once Bill Clinton was elected, on the theme that "it's the economy, stupid," dealing with domestic financial issues was his top priority. The United States was just coming out of recession—yes, the recession was over well before Mr. Clinton was inaugurated—but still the lingering effects continued to weigh heavily on the American psyche, and the initial recovery was slow. Mr. Clinton argued, only half persuasively, that the deficit was worse than he had been told, and this became the official excuse for him to cast aside the middle-class tax cut idea. Mr. Rubin and Clinton's first Treasury secretary, Lloyd Bentsen, the former conservative Texas senator (and, ironically, one of the original Democratic supply-siders in the late 1970s), insisted that deficit reduction had to be the top national priority in the early and mid-1990s.

Clinton's first budget in 1993, which was called Putting People First, included no tax cuts, but big tax increases on high-income individuals through higher income tax rates, a one-percentage-point rise in the corporate tax, a BTU energy tax, new taxes on Social Security benefits, a hike in the federal gasoline tax, and a $50 billion economic stimulus package of higher spending. When he announced the plan during his first State of the Union address, Federal Reserve Board chairman Alan Greenspan was sitting next to Hillary Clinton in the Senate Gallery. His presence was interpreted as a validation of the Clinton economic program.

The BTU tax, which had been supported by Clinton's vice president, Al Gore, as a measure that would raise revenues and be good for the environment by taxing greenhouse gases, was buried in the United States Senate after a furious lobbying campaign against it by taxpayer groups and the energy industry.[15] But the grand tax hike package—minus the BTU tax—was eventually passed in the House and Senate by one vote in each chamber. Not a single Republican in the House or the Senate voted for the tax package, and every Democrat who voted "yea" would later be pilloried for providing the deciding vote on the unpopular package.

The Clinton economic stimulus plan of new spending, a liberal wish list of social welfare programs—such as food stamps, aid to cities, and unemployment insurance—was also a casualty of the bitter budget fight. Republicans argued that if the agenda was to lower the deficit, then ordering up a $50 billion hot fudge sundae didn't seem consistent with the overall objective. It was defeated in the Senate. Mr. Clinton was said to be furious at how his liberal vision had been hijacked by the deficit hawks. In *The Agenda*, Bob Woodward's book about the Clinton economic program, Woodward relates that Bill Clinton was so angered by the defeat of his stimulus plan, and so tired of Mr. Rubin's explaining that the key to his success was maintaining credibility with financial markets, that the president pounded his fist on his desk in the Oval Office and fumed to his adviser Paul Begala, "You mean to tell me the success of the program and my re-election hinges on the Federal Reserve and a bunch of *(%@&(% bond traders?"[16] For the short term, the answer was yes.

How much of a repudiation of supply-side economics were the Bush and Clinton tax hikes? George Bush agreed to raise the top income tax rate from 28 percent in the late 1980s to 31 percent. Mr Clinton's plan raised that rate to 36 percent, then added a "millionaire income tax surcharge," of 10 percent, so that the effective top rate was now back up to 39.6 percent. So this was a rise in rates from 28 percent to nearly 40 percent. These rate hikes were clearly movements away from the tenets of supply-side economics, and many supply-siders predicted a recession if Mr. Clinton's plan were adopted. That didn't happen. The nearly 40 percent tax rate applied during the Clinton years was still a far cry from the 70 percent top marginal tax rate that had existed before the Reagan tax cuts of 1981. It was a victory of sorts for the supply-side ideas on taxes that even with Democrats holding every lever of power in Washington—the White House, the House, and the Senate—they did not propose raising the highest income tax rate on the wealthy back up to anywhere near the rates that had existed in the 1970s, and their highest rate was still slightly below 40 percent. The economic incentives to work, save, and invest at a 40 percent top tax rate are twice as high as the incentives with a 70 percent tax rate. At a 70 percent tax rate the investor or worker keeps thirty cents on the dollar earned, whereas under a 40 percent rate the worker or investor keeps sixty cents on the dollar.

Liberals, including Barack Obama, like to point to the success of the American economy in the 1990s as evidence that supply-side economics doesn't work after all and that tax rates are an afterthought to economic growth rates. By the late 1990s the unemployment rate was below 5 percent and the stock market was on a tear. In 1998, the federal budget was balanced for the first time since God performed his last miracle on earth with the Amazing Mets in 1969. Some said that a balanced budget under Bill Clinton was a miracle, but it happened.

In American politics the president gets the credit or the blame for whatever happens on his watch—and that's generally the way it should be, because the president guides the policies of the country while he is in the White House. Throughout the 1980s, however, liberals argued unpersuasively that Ronald Reagan and his policies deserved none of the credit for the prosperity or the national security triumphs of that decade. The writers at the *New Republic* and the *Nation* ranted about how "lucky" Reagan was. They sounded like sore losers.

Like Ronald Reagan, Bill Clinton wasn't lucky. Despite the tax hike of 1993, economic policies under his administration were mostly consistent with supply-side economic ideas.

What Bill Clinton Got Right

In his first two years in office, 1993 and 1994, Mr. Clinton governed from the left, and he lost control of a Democratic Congress run amok. His first policy act was the huge tax increase, one of the largest in American history. Americans might have swallowed that, but there were no budget cuts to go along with the new taxes, so conservatives argued persuasively that these higher taxes were going to be used to grow government, not to balance the budget. When Representatives Tim Penny and John Kasich proposed a bipartisan plan to cut hundreds of useless and obsolete agencies, the Clinton White House effectively pulled the plug on the project. Clinton wanted a balanced budget through higher taxes, not spending restraint.

During his first two years in office, policy missteps helped define Mr. Clinton as a liberal, not a moderate, when it came to governing. He got tripped up on the issue of gays in the military; his wife authored a health care plan that looked like a Rube Goldberg contraption and was designed as a government takeover of health care; the Democrats then tried to pass a multi-billion-dollar "crime bill," which was designed to create dozens of new social welfare programs, like midnight basketball leagues, to rehabilitate criminals. These and many other policy mishaps created a huge voter backlash in 1994 against the Democrats, who were wiped out in races across the country as Republicans took control of the Senate and the House, for the first time since the 1950s, and won a majority of the governorships and of many of the state legislatures.

Then Bill Clinton did a very smart thing for the country and his own political future. He re-embraced the "New Democrat" free market agenda that had gotten him elected in the first place.

Liberals point triumphantly to Clinton's world-record tax hike in 1993 as the turning point for the economy and the balanced budget. But they're dead wrong, and the numbers in Bill Clinton's own budget documents prove it. Two years after the Clinton tax hike, the deficit was still stubbornly above $200 billion for fiscal 1995. What's more, in early 1995 both the White House budget office and the nonpartisan Congressional Budget Office independently offered a long-term deficit prognosis under what we might call the "Clintonomics baseline." They both grimly announced that progress in reducing federal red ink was stalled: They predicted $200 billion deficits from now until kingdom come unless there were some radical readjustments to fiscal policy or improvements in economic conditions.[17] Again, this was two years *after* the Clinton-Gore tax hike.

What changed this bleak outlook? The answer is, in part, the election of a Republican Congress. The pivotal year in the deficit fight was not 1993. It was 1995. That was the year when the Republicans with their new majorities on Capitol Hill engaged in nine months of hand-to-hand combat with President Clinton over the budget, including a government shutdown. It's striking to us that the national media, when they dutifully report how successful Clinton's deficit reduction policies were, seem to be suffering from a collective amnesia about this entire period and the ferocious budget battles that ensued in 1995, 1996, and 1997.

The evidence confirms that Bill Clinton's tax hikes were not the major cause of the balanced budget. Let's compare the projected five-year Clinton baseline deficits right before Republicans implemented their new budgets with the actual record after Republicans implemented their budget cuts and reforms. In Table 6-1 we label the first column the Clinton baseline, that is; what the deficit would have been if Clinton's priorities had stayed in effect. The second column shows the actual budget deficits and surpluses after the GOP took control of Congress.

Over the period 1995–99 the deficits were $902 billion lower than under the Clintonomics baseline.[18]

Some of the factors that led to the balanced budgets of the late 1990s were set in motion long before Bill Clinton became president

Table 6-1: Clinton's Balanced Budget?

Federal Deficits (billions of dollars)

	Clinton Baseline*	Actual	Difference
1994	$203	$203	0
1995	175	164	11
1996	205	107	98
1997	210	22	188
1998	210	+69 (surplus)	279
1999	200	+126 (surplus)	326
Total	1,203	301	902

* Congressional Budget Office forecast, April 1995.

or the Republicans seized Congress in 1994. One was the U.S. victory in the Cold War. Today the military budget is almost $150 billion lower in real terms than it was at the height of the Cold War buildup in 1987. The peace dividend accounted for about one-third of the deficit reduction from 1995 to 2000.

By far the most powerful factor in attaining a balanced budget was the sizzling economy. In the 1980s Reagan, Jack Kemp, Art Laffer, and other supply-side tax-cutters were ridiculed—even by the old Rockefeller root canal Republicans in their own party—for believing in the "voodoo theory" that we could grow our way out of the deficit. But that's precisely what happened. The cumulative windfall of eighteen years of prosperity (1981–99) enabled the economy to finally outrace the federal budget. Tax receipts poured into the federal Treasury in tidal waves—an average of 10 percent growth during Clinton's second term.

The Clinton-Gore enthusiasts counter this conclusion by saying: Aha, but it was the 1993 tax hike that caused the prosperity and the surging revenues. Again, the historical facts don't corroborate this claim. The economy grew at nearly 4.5 percent real in the twelve months *before* Clinton and Gore were elected. After the tax hike was enacted, the economy actually slipped to a 2 to 3 percent growth trajectory in 1993 and 1994. The major economic rationale for the Clinton tax hike was to lower interest rates. Between November 1992 and November 1994 interest rates didn't fall; in fact, they *rose* by more than two full percentage points. Oops.

The economy boomed in the Clinton years, the stock market soared, and interest rates declined sharply, but Figure 6-1 shows that the turning point for interest rates and the stock market was November 1994. In fact, an analysis by Wall Street economist Larry Kudlow (now host of CNBC's *Kudlow & Company*) demonstrated that that day in 1994 when Republicans swept into power was the inflection point. It's not that markets predicted that Republicans would do Wall Street's bidding, but rather that a new check and balance would be placed on Mr. Clinton's agenda. He would no longer have free rein to raise taxes and spending, or to nationalize entire industries. If tax rates were going to change, it was now more likely that they would go down than up.

Critics of supply-side economics contend that the economy roared and tax revenues skyrocketed in the wake of the Clinton tax increases, thus poking big holes in the theory of the Laffer Curve. Hence, they conclude tax rates could be raised again with little if any lasting damage to the economy.

What this misses is the other offsetting positive trends in economic policy over these years. During Clinton's second term, one policy after another was bullish. In many ways, Clinton turned into an advocate of free market policies after 1994. Part of his strategy, as masterminded by Dick Morris, his political consultant, was to move back to the political center and "triangulate" the Republicans. This meant that Clinton would agree to many of the Republican policies but shave off the rough edges and make sure Republicans didn't carry things too far. This was the governing philosophy of Clinton's second term—and it worked.

From 1996 to 2000, Clinton increasingly began to validate,

Figure 6-1: GOP/Clinton Bull Market

Stock Market

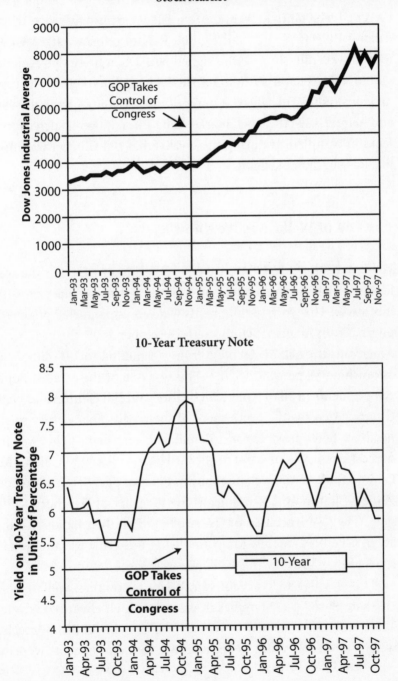

10-Year Treasury Note

rather than repudiate, the Reagan supply-side economic model by promoting free trade, tight-fisted budgets, signing a capital gains tax cut (reluctantly), reappointing Alan Greenspan twice to the Federal Reserve Board, and signing welfare reform (after two vetoes). It was Bill Clinton who signed NAFTA, arguing that America had to "compete rather than retreat" in global markets.[19] The capital gains reduction caused a burst of tax revenue in the late 1990s and helped stoke the stock market expansion. Liberals such as Jesse Jackson complained during these years that Bill Clinton was more like Reagan than like FDR.

The End of Welfare as We Know It

We believe that Mr. Clinton was also heroic in enacting the welfare reform bill, which had a profoundly positive impact on work incentives. The work requirements were an unparalleled policy triumph. From August 1996 through December 2005, the number of Americans on welfare declined from 4.4 million to 1.9 million, an astonishing 58 percent decline. This was one of the greatest policy achievements in all of American history, and Bill Clinton and Newt Gingrich deserve the lion's share of the credit. This victory might not have been possible for a Republican president. (This was the domestic policy equivalent to Richard Nixon's going to China.) Mr. Clinton took on the welfare lobby in his own party, some of whom vilified Clinton and Republicans for their act of treachery to the poor. They were accused of "having blood on their hands" for this act of cruelty.[20] We now know that what was cruel was the welfare state, not welfare reform (see Figure 6-2).[21]

This was also a victory for supply-side economics. Welfare policies had placed poor families in extremely high effective tax rates. Under the old system if a welfare mother with two children left welfare and took a job, as her earnings rose, her benefits were cut

Figure 6-2: Welfare Reform Worked

Number of Families Receiving TANF

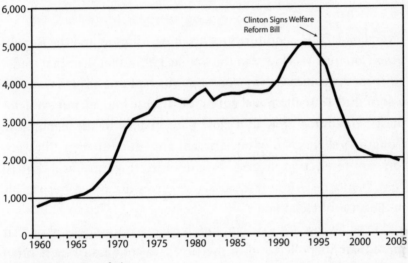

Source: Heritage Foundation.

back. Steve Moore published a widely cited study in 1995 by the Cato Institute showing that in high-welfare-benefit states, workers would have to earn up to twelve to fifteen dollars an hour to make up for the loss of AFDC, food stamps, Medicaid, public housing, and the array of other means-tested programs.[22] The *New York Post* reported on August 2, 1994, that in New York City a worker would have to find a job paying $45,000 a year to do as well financially as a person living on welfare benefits.[23] In other words, welfare recipients were facing more than 100 percent marginal tax rates. If they worked, they lost money. Was there ever a more preposterous, even immoral, set of policies?

And as for the assertion that the welfare reform would destroy the lives of low-income families, the evidence indicates just the opposite. From 1995 to 2004 the income of the lowest fifth of Americans grew faster than that of any other income group, thanks in part to the work mandates under welfare reform.[24] The experiment proved a supply-side economics maxim: The best antipoverty program is a job.

Overall federal expenditure growth under Clinton and the Republican Congress was lower in the period 1995–2000 than that under any president since Calvin Coolidge. Much of this growth was a result of the $100 billion real cut in the defense budget, but even domestic programs grew at a slow pace, thanks to the Republican Congress's skepticism of government growth. Even after Bill Clinton won re-election in 1996, he continued to govern as a centrist New Democrat. More trade deals were consummated—especially in the areas of technology.

We've always argued that supply-side economics is about far more than tax policy, and in the 1990s we got a lot of these other policies right, even though we moved in the wrong direction on taxes in 1990 and 1993. Our contention is that these positive policy developments helped cancel out the negative effects of higher tax rates.

The history books should get this story straight: Clinton with a Democratic Congress was a recipe for disaster, but Clinton with a Republican Congress produced a gravity-defying expansion. The Dow soared from 3,800 to 11,000 from November 1994 through summer 2000. The economy has expanded by 4 percent without inflation since then. The economic expansion in the 1990s was the longest in the post–World War II period and unemployment hit a twenty-five-year low. It was peace and prosperity and spending discipline that balanced the budget.[25]

Alas, the good times don't roll on forever. When the Clintonites boast about how well the economy performed in the 1990s and the budget surpluses that George W. Bush inherited when he was inaugurated in January 2001, they forget to mention that the technology bubble burst during Clinton's last year in office. If Bill Clinton deserves credit for the good times during his tenure—which we believe he does—it is only fair to note that he left office with the economy in a big hole. The stock market collapse of mid-2000 caused a massive reduction in tax revenues, and thus a return to deficits. Those problems were compounded by the terrorist attacks on September 11, 2001. The era of shortchanging our military and national security budgets was over. The new war against terrorism opened a new chapter of America's fiscal history.

7

How George W. Bush Soaked the Rich

We Democrats have to end our knee-jerk opposition to tax cuts. We have to be the party of growth and the American dream, not the party of redistribution.

—Democratic Governor Bill Richardson of New Mexico, who cut his state's capital gains tax and the top income tax rate in half.[1]

In January 2003, two of us (Laffer and Moore) were summoned to the White House with a small group of other free market economists to advise President George W. Bush on how to revive a moribund economy. We came armed with a new tax cut strategy. The group assembled for the meeting included former Federal Reserve Board member Wayne Angell, Larry Kudlow of CNBC, and David Malpass of Bear Stearns. We met with the president in the West Wing of the White House for more than an hour and a half. The consensus was that without a supply-side tax cut to provide some steroids for the economy, growth would continue to lag and Bush's chances of re-election seemed slim.

At the time, George W. Bush's presidency was in free fall. He looked like a "one-termer," in the famous words of his father. The first tax cuts enacted in 2001 had put dollars into consumers' pockets but were not aimed at increasing output and productivity, and had failed to pump much juice into an economy still hobbled by the 9/11 attacks and the tech bubble popping. The Clinton-era budget surpluses had quickly morphed into $400 billion of red ink.[2] Liberals were confident that Bush would surely be thrown out of office. We believe that the supply-side tax cut package President Bush agreed to in that meeting in the West Wing of the White House that morning helped airlift the economy out of the fire and helped assure his re-election less than two years later.

Our idea was for a new round of tax cuts designed to help revive the stock market and reverse the capital investment drought that was now entering its third year. If the rate of return on investment was increased, businesses would start spending again, stocks would start to regain value, and employers would start hiring again. As former Federal Reserve Board member Wayne Angell put it: "The economy isn't going to recover until the stock market does. This is unquestionably an investment recession that can't be solved through traditional Keynesian stimulus." Larry Kudlow added: "Mr. President, be as bold as you can and the politics will take care of itself."

This meeting was where the idea of eliminating the dividend tax was first hatched. Kudlow, Laffer, and Moore also urged a capital gains cut on the grounds that there would be little if any revenue lost by cutting the rate to 10 or 15 percent from 20 percent. What was clear was the need to stimulate investment, not consumption.

This was the precise opposite of what many in the Republican Party and most liberal Democrats and their think tank gurus were recommending. They wanted more Keynesian consumption-oriented sugar injections to get Americans buying again. The liberal deep thinkers wanted more money for states and localities—dollars that these entities would be sure to spend. A tax cut for investment would only lead to more saving, not more spending, they argued, thus making the recession worse.

Shortly after that White House meeting, President Bush officially became a supply-side president. He endorsed the full repeal of the dividend tax, arguing that it was an unfair double tax on investment because the same income is first taxed at the corporate tax rate of 35 percent. As his newly appointed Treasury secretary, John Snow, later told us: "Mr. Bush asked me if we should go for a 50 percent cut in the dividend tax or total repeal. I told him, 'Well, Mr. President, my economics training always told me that the capital should be taxed just once, not one and a half times.'" Good advice that the White House embraced. Although President Bush didn't get his full dividend tax cut, with the help of the wily House Ways and Means Committee chairman, Bill Thomas, the dividend tax was cut to 15 percent and the capital gains tax was also cut to 15 percent.

Many supply-side economists who cut their teeth in the Reagan era—such as Laffer, Kudlow, and investment advisor John Rutledge—publicly predicted that these tax cuts would have an immediate stimulus effect on the stock market. As Art Laffer put it: "If you cut the tax rate on stocks, they become more valuable. The after-tax rate of return rises, and that should be capitalized immediately into higher stock prices." The estimates of this effect ranged from 6 to 12 percent gains in stock values. We showed Secretary Snow a chart that illustrated the long-term trend of rising stock values triggered by Ronald Reagan's historic tax cuts, which reduced the cost of capital and snapped the markets out of a prolonged period of malaise.

President Bush conceded that he needed an economic boost midway through his first term. He had been dealt a bad hand to begin with as the economy was careening toward recession when he entered office. Thanks to the wealth implosion due to the stock market collapse, the economy slipped into recession during Bush's first months in office as stocks continued to slip. Even President Bush's severest critics cannot plausibly blame his economic policies for a downturn and a stock slide that happened *before* the policies were implemented. But they try.

In 2001 President Bush enacted a tax cut that was mostly aimed at lower- and middle-class workers and involved a $400 to $600 tax rebate to tax filers. We believe the overall impact of rebates may have been negative because they redistributed income from producers to non-producers.[3] This was not a supply-side tax reduction. The top tax rate was shaved by just one percentage point in the first years of that tax package, and although the death tax was being phased out, it wouldn't hit zero until nine years later, or 2010. And then all of these tax cuts would automatically expire at the start of 2011. In sum, the incentive effects for growth from these tax cuts was minimal. About half of the tax rebate dollars were saved, not spent, as the Keynesians had hoped, so the consumer demand side stimulus from the policy equivalent of dropping hundred-dollar bills out of helicopter windows over the United States was minuscule. Despite this evidence of its ineffectiveness, in early 2008 Congress and the Bush administration passed almost a replica of the 2001 tax rebate scheme to help juice the economy in the wake of the housing and mortgage crisis—hoping for a better outcome than the 2001 experiment delivered. It didn't work the second time either.

The economy limped out of recession in 2002, but the United States did not experience anything like the energetic burst of economic activity and job creation that usually occurs during the early phase of recovery. The job market was particularly lethargic, with payroll employment still down from its peak of 112 million jobs in early 2001 to 108 million jobs by early 2003.[4] Wages were also stuck in a rut and fell in real terms. The economy was shedding jobs through the middle of 2003 even though the recession officially ended in 2001.[5]

Bush Turns to the Supply Side

The 2003 investment tax cut was higher-grade fuel for the economy. After a five-month fight with the Democrats in Congress it passed in May 2003. President Bush didn't get the dividend tax down to zero, but he did win powerful supply-side incentives for growth:

- The dividend tax was cut from 39.6 to 15 percent.
- The capital gains tax was cut from 20 to 15 percent.
- The personal income tax (highest rate) fell from 39.6 to 35 percent.
- The tax on business investments in plant, machinery, and equipment was lowered.

While Ronald Reagan's tax cuts in 1981 had been mostly oriented toward trying to provide incentives for more output by increasing the rewards for work, the Bush supply-side tax cuts were more oriented toward increasing incentives for businesses to invest in the United States and for entrepreneurs to start new businesses because they could raise startup capital more easily with lower tax rates on the investment returns.

Right on cue the Left rebelled, with assurances that the package would not stimulate growth and would only worsen the deficit and the economy. Leading Democrats called it a "tax cut for "Joe Millionaire, not Joe Lunch Bucket."[6] Howard Dean, now the head of the Democratic National Committee, pouted that the Bush plan gives tax cuts to "those who need them least."[7] The *New York Times* editorial page wrote shortly thereafter that the Bush tax plan would surely not provide an "immediate stimulus for the economy."[8]

But here is what really happened. Just as supply-side economic theory predicted, lower tax rates incentivized wealth-creating activities in the business sector. It is surely no coincidence that the economy pivoted into recovery almost on a dime the very day when the 2003 Bush tax cut—particularly the reduction in the capital gains, dividend, and income tax rates—was signed into law.

The first and most immediate sign of expansion came from the stock market—as predicted. After years of stock market weakness following the collapse of the dot-com bubble, stocks climbed about 20 percent in the two years after the tax cuts (see Figure 7-1). The tech-heavy and battered NASDAQ was up about 25 percent. Over-all asset values rose by $6 trillion from 2003 to 2007.[9] That compares with a static price tag of about $600 billion for those tax cuts. A pretty good return on investment, we'd argue.

Clearly the dividend and capital gains tax cuts had the positive impact on the stock market that supply-siders anticipated. One of those economists was Donald Luskin of TrendMacrolytics. As Luskin puts it: "Cause and effect relationships are nearly impossi-

Figure 7-1: **Bush's Tax Cut Restores Reagan's Bull Market**

Household Net Worth, in Millions of Dollars

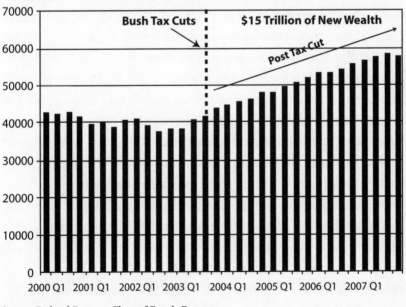

Source: Federal Reserve, Flow of Funds Report.

ble to conclusively prove when stock prices are involved. But considering that stock prices are so much higher since the tax cuts, the burden of proof is on the skeptics. We are satisfied we were right—because it happened."[10] Moreover, business capital spending which had declined by 4.8 percent in 2001 and 6.1 percent in 2002, surged by 7.4 percent in 2004 and an astonishing 9.5 percent in 2005. This was, in short, a classic supply-side recovery.[11]

Data collected by the Tax Foundation indicate that two out of every three Americans who are taxed at the highest income tax rate—the group that Dean, Obama, and other Democratic leaders now want to sock with a higher tax rate—are sole proprietors of businesses, large and small.[12] President Bush's tax rate reductions made it less expensive for the job-creating class to expand their businesses, to raise the capital for new plants and equipment, and to hire new workers. And the result was the job market shook off its lull of the early 2000s. Between 2003 and the end of 2007 some 8 million jobs were created, or about 150,000 new jobs a month as shown in figure 7-2.[13] The media give headlines to GM or Ford when they close a plant and lay off eight thousand workers, but that's what the great American job machine was churning out each business day during the Bush expansion.

Did this stock market and economic recovery enrich only gold cufflinked CEOs who are callously exporting jobs overseas, while shafting the middle-class assembly line worker, truck driver, or schoolteacher? Harold Meyerson of the *Washington Post* recently wrote that "the income tax cuts to most middle class families don't exceed a couple of hundred dollars."[14] Meanwhile, the rich got enough to purchase another yacht, or so the story goes.

Well, not exactly. Households increased their wealth by some $6 trillion between May 2003 and May 2007.[15] Since then, about $2 trillion of that wealth has been lost because of the housing crisis. Nonetheless, the median household has increased its wealth by almost $20,000 in real terms since the supply-side tax cuts took ef-

Figure 7-2: Investment Tax Cuts Create Jobs

Millions of Jobs, January 2000 to August 2007

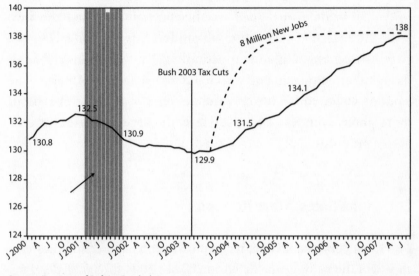

Source: Bureau of Labor Statistics.

fect in 2003. So much for the argument that only the rich benefited.

Moreover, the combined impact of the Bush tax cuts has been to make the tax system *more* progressive. As a result of the Bush tax cuts, the typical family of four with an income of $40,000 a year has seen its tax liability shrink by $1,000 a year, thanks to reductions in the lowest tax rate and an increase in the child credit.[16] Democrats condemn the Bush tax cuts as tilted toward the rich, but even after the Bush tax cut, the top 1 percent paid more income tax than the bottom 90 percent did, despite the fact that the bottom 90 percent had three times the income of the top 1 percent.[17]

Other areas of the economy rebounded smartly in the wake of the Bush investment tax cuts. Business profits surged from 2003–2007 causing corporate tax revenues to soar. Also, the Department of Labor reported that labor productivity in 2005 was up

5 percent in real terms. Just how good a number was this? Well, the DOL has been measuring productivity rates only since the late 1950s. The 2005 gain was the *highest* single-year increase ever recorded. The often-maligned manufacturing sector led the way. From 2003 to 2006 manufacturing productivity has had its largest-ever increase over a three-year period.[18] What this means is that although the manufacturing workforce is shrinking in America, the amount of production from each worker is rising. We churn out more goods with less labor, which is the very definition of economic progress.

Lower Tax Rates, More Revenue

The most remarkable chapter of this supply-side economics episode was the tax revenue explosion. From 2004 to 2007 federal tax revenue increased by an enormous $785 billion, the largest four-year increase in revenue in American history. The Treasury Department reported that federal tax receipts were up 11 percent in the 2006 fiscal year, which was the second-largest gain in revenues in twenty-five years. The biggest single-year gain came in 2005.[19]

Individual and corporate income tax receipts exploded like a cap let off a geyser, up 40 percent in the three years after the tax cut. Once again, tax rate cuts have created a virtual chain reaction of higher economic growth, more jobs, higher corporate profits, and finally more tax receipts. And the biggest gains in tax receipts have come from capital gains and dividend tax payments. These were precisely the tax rates that were cut the most severely. The latest data from the Congressional Budget Office finds a 70 percent increase in capital gains receipts and a 31 percent hike in dividend tax payments since 2003.[20] Observing these data, Larry Kudlow of CNBC recently declared that the Bush tax cuts "are the greatest vindication of the power of the Laffer Curve in American history."

144

Even the *New York Times* recently acknowledged on the front page that tax revenues in the mid-2000s were exploding and described the increase as a "surprise windfall."[21] The *Times* story notes "An unexpectedly steep rise in tax revenues from corporations and the wealthy is driving down the projected budget deficit this year, even though spending has climbed sharply because of the war in Iraq and the cost of hurricane relief." Yes, the ideas of the Laffer Curve still elude the Left.

What is truly remarkable about this story is just how much more in taxes the wealthy paid in the wake of the Bush investment tax cuts. The Obama campaign continues to maintain that the average family in America with an income of $10 million or more received a whopping half-million-dollar tax cut, but the middle class got crumbs, or less than $100 off their tax bill. If we examine the taxes paid in a static world, that is, assuming that there was no change in behavior and economic performance as a result of the tax code, then these numbers are accurate. Most of the tax cuts went to the super-wealthy.

But when we compare how much tax was paid under the old tax system with what was actually paid immediately after the Bush tax cuts, we see that the federal tax system became more tilted onto the backs of the wealthy. In part this was because lower tax rates reduce the incentive for tax avoidance schemes and therefore increased the amount of taxable income declared by tax filers. The latest IRS data through 2006 show a more than $120 billion increase in tax payments by the wealthy after the Bush tax cuts of 2003.[22]

Not only were there more Americans in each of these higher income categories, but also these rich people paid a lot more in taxes each year. Lower tax rates expanded the tax base and increased the amount of reported taxable income. For example, the new IRS data for 2005 show that the number of tax filers who have claimed taxable income of more than $1 million nearly doubled from 181,000 to 354,000 from 2003 to 2006. Or to put it differently, there was a

Table 7-1: More Taxes Paid by the Rich
Billions of Dollars

Adjusted Gross Income	Number of Returns			Taxes Paid		
	2003	2006	% Change	2003	2006	% Change
$1 million to $2 million	115,712	214,438	85%	$41	$71	73%
$2 million to $5 million	48,278	98,724	104%	$37	$72	95%
$5 million or more	17,294	40,931	137%	$54	$131	143%
$1 million or more	181,283	354,093	95%	$132	$273	107%

Source: IRS, Statistics of Income, Table 1.1.

95 percent increase in the number of "millionaires next door." The total taxes paid by millionaire households rose by 107 percent in two years, to $273 billion from $132 billion.

Even though the *New York Times* had to acknowledge that the biggest payment increases have been from the richest 10 percent of taxpayers who pay the bulk of American income taxes, this same paper, and its columnists, such as Paul Krugman, whine almost weekly about the unfairness of Bush's tax cuts for the super-wealthy.[23] How can Bush have cut taxes on the wealthy if their taxes have surged? The answer to this is a genuine mystery—well beyond our pay grade.

One other complaint also didn't pan out. The interest rates did not rise as a result of the Bush investment tax cuts; they fell. In early 2008 the federal interest rates on ten- and thirty-year bonds are as low as at any time in thirty years. So much for the argument that the Bush tax cuts would *raise* the cost of investment through higher deficits and higher costs of borrowing.

Finally, there is the issue of the Bush dividend tax cut. The idea here was to reward companies for paying dividends. Before the 2003 tax cut, most firms faced a strong disincentive to pay dividends because dividends were taxed as high as 40 percent, whereas the capital gains tax was 20 percent. Hence, rather than pay a dividend to shareholders, firms could retain the earnings and allow those earnings to be capitalized into the stock price. Shareholders could then sell shares and pay a tax of 20 percent on the gains, rather than the 40 percent dividend tax. For this reason, dividend payments fell out of favor in the corporate culture in the 1980s and 1990s. As Thomas Smith, president of Prescott Associates, a Connecticut investment firm, points out: "The tax code severely penalized a dividend payout, because the corporation pays a 35% tax on the profits and then the shareholder pays an additional punitive 40% tax rate if the profits are passed through in dividends."[24] Hence, paying a dividend under the old tax regime was not a "tax-rational option."

Reducing the dividend tax from 40 percent to the capital gains tax rate of 15 percent would eliminate this tax bias against dividends and, in theory at least, increase dividend payouts.

The evidence indicates that is precisely what firms did. Companies responded to the dividend tax cut as expected—by returning more cash to shareholders. After the first two years the total amount of increased dividends equaled nearly $80 billion. This increase in dividend payouts generate about $12 billion to $15 billion a year in additional tax revenues to the federal government.

One firm that responded to the tax cut was Microsoft. In 2004 Microsoft announced a plan to distribute $40 billion of its cash hoard in a massive special dividend of about three dollars per share. Before the Bush tax cut, Microsoft had never paid a dividend.[25] There were twenty-two other S&P 500 companies that didn't pay dividends before the tax cut that began paying them in 2003 and 2004. The list includes Viacom, with a payout of more than $400 million annually, Harrah's Entertainment, Staples, and Reebok. The twenty dividend initiations in 2003 marked the first annual increase since 1994. Even more significantly, the number of S&P 500 companies paying a dividend reversed a twenty-five-year decline.[26]

So with respect to the issue of whether the dividend tax cut would influence corporate behavior, the verdict is in and it is a resounding yes. Former Citigroup CEO Sandy Weill explained: "The recent change in the tax law levels the playing field between dividends and share repurchases as a means to return capital to shareholders. This substantial increase in our dividend will be part of our effort to reallocate capital to dividends and reduce share repurchases."

Other CEOs of Fortune 500 companies echoed this rationale for their dividend increases. Home Depot CEO Bob Nardelli said, "Given the recent changes in the tax law, the increased dividend is an effective way for the company to return capital to shareholders." Brad Anderson of Best Buy explained why that company, like dozens of others, chose to initiate dividend payments: "Changes in the federal tax code have made dividend payments more attractive to our investors." [27]

Drunken Sailor Spending

While George W. Bush's Tax policies were a success, his budget priorities were disastrous. In 2001 the budget was in $200 billion of surplus, but three years later the budget deficit was $400 billion. Democrats contend that all this red ink was another episode of supply-side tax cuts causing big deficits.

But as we have shown revenues increased after the tax cuts. The problem was that federal expenditures went up even faster. Under George Bush and a Republican Congress more money was spent at a faster pace than at any time since the 1970s. [28] A lot of that spending blitz was a result of the shopping spree triggered by big surpluses. Appropriators interpreted all that extra money lying around in the federal Treasury as an invitation to spend. If Congress had just held spending to the level of inflation and even taking into account the extra $200 billion annual cost for the war in Iraq, there would have been a $100 billion surplus in 2007 rather than a $162 billion deficit.[29]

It turns out that about half of the increased spending (over the 4 percent Congress had originally predicted) was a result of the military and homeland security expenditures required to fight the war on terrorism. But only half. As the *Congressional Quarterly* recently noted: "Although the need to respond to the September 11 terrorist attacks accounted for much of the increased spending, Congress was poised for a big spending boost even before then."[30]

Our friend Jeff Flake, a freshman Republican from Arizona, recently complained that every vote he has taken in Congress since 2001 has been for more government programs and more spending. "I'm still waiting," he says, "for a vote to cut the budget." He may have to wait for a long while. Despite a promise of new fiscal responsibility from the new Nancy Pelosi–led House of Representatives, the budget deficit has exploded from $190 billion to more than $400 billion in her first two years as Speaker.

The biggest outrage of all was the Republican addiction to earmark spending. When one of us (Moore) worked for the Republicans in Congress in 1994, Newt Gingrich said that it was an outrage to see that Democrats were passing out fifteen hundred pieces of bacon each year in the spending bills. These were such parochial projects as swimming pools, honey bee research, parking garages, and teapot museums. After twelve years of GOP control of Congress there were not fifteen hundred of these projects, but closer to fifteen thousand. These earmarks, said Senator Tom Coburn of Oklahoma, "are the gateway drug to bigger spending."[31] The biggest budget atrocity of all was the Bridge to Nowhere in Alaska. This bridge, recommended by Senator Ted Stevens of Alaska, had a $200 million price tag to service an island with fewer than fifty residents. It was going to be longer and larger than the Golden Gate Bridge in San Francisco. The *Wall Street Journal* reported that it would be cheaper for Congress to purchase a

Lear Jet for every person living on the island than to build the bridge.[32]

The Bridge to Nowhere became the symbol of Republican disregard for fiscal responsibility. The budget in six years of Republican control had gone from $1.9 trillion to nearly $2.9 trillion. Republicans suffered huge losses in the 2006 elections as both houses of Congress switched back to Democratic control. Most Republican voters felt that Republicans got what they deserved: a good whacking at the polls.

So the budget deficits of the Bush years were mostly a result of overspending, not undertaxing. Thanks to the tsunami of revenues from 2003 to 2007, the budget deficit fell in the wake of the Bush tax cuts from $401 billion to $158 billion by 2007. The deficit exploded in 2008 due to the housing crisis, tax rebates, and more unrestrained budgets, now passed by the Democratic Congress.

In his indispensable economic history book, *The Making of Modern Economics*, Mark Skousen notes that in the late nineteenth century some economists actually theorized that "the configuration of the stars and planets was the principal cause of commercial crises."[33] This superstitious belief in economic astrology is only slightly less bizarre than what today's Democratic leadership believes to be the solution to the current housing recession and economic slowdown. Many liberals continue to declare that the Bush tax cuts set off a chain reaction of higher deficits, greater income inequality, and greater turmoil in the financial markets, and therefore repealing those tax cuts will restore growth and equity to the U.S. economy. The Democrats are as militant as ever about letting the tax cuts die on the vine in 2010—if not before.

In reality, the capital gain and dividend tax cuts wrote another chapter of the supply-side experiment in America—added to the Coolidge, Kennedy, and Reagan successes. Lowering the hurdles of

Figure 7-3: **Rich Pay Highest Share of Taxes**

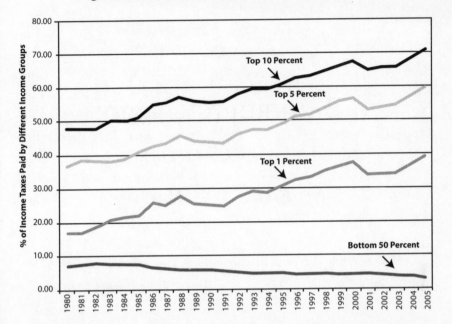

high taxes leads to prosperity and wealth gains, not just for the rich and famous but for the tens of millions in the middle and lower classes who are striving to get there. Perhaps most remarkable of all about the Bush tax cuts, the rich paid a larger share of the tax burden than at any time in forty years, and perhaps ever as shown in figure 7-3.[34] George Bush soaked the rich by lowering tax rates.

8

BANKRUPTCY 90210:

AS GOES CALIFORNIA,

SO GOES THE NATION

High tax rates don't redistribute income; they redistribute people.

—GEORGE GILDER

Back in 2003 two of us (Laffer and Moore) were asked by then candidate for governor Arnold Schwarzenegger to help construct an economic and budget revival program for California, or, as Arnold calls his home state, Kah-LEE-fornia.

Arnold had just recently completed filming his latest blockbuster movie hit, *Terminator 3*, and was now the highest-paid actor in Hollywood. One of the first rules in life is that you don't say "no" to the terminator, so we both volunteered to help. And we have to admit, it can be a lot of fun working with a movie star and a former Mr. Universe. The man has extraordinary charisma, talent, and intelligence—and a hearty sense of humor. At one of our first meetings Arnold excused himself to use the bathroom and while striding out of the room he turned around and declared: *"I'll be baaack."* It sounds schmaltzy, but we all rolled with laughter.

One time at a meeting at his house in Santa Monica, Arnold

turned to Laffer and said, "Arthur, what is it with you free market economists, that you are all so short. I met Milton Friedman and he is so short, too. You and Milton both remind me of Danny De-Vito, my sidekick in the movie *Twins*. Did you see that movie?" We all had.

One last story: When the governor called the Moore household to have a conversation with Steve about the budget calamity, on Halloween night, as fate would have it, nine-year-old Justin Moore came on the phone in the middle of the conversation and asked, "Hey, is this *really* Arnold Schwarzenegger?" And Arnold responded without skipping a beat and with an exaggerated thick accent: "Son, get off the phone or I'm going to have to *terminate* you." Young Justin Moore slammed the phone down shaking with fear. We have both worked with many governors and senators and presidents of the United States, but that never much impressed our kids. But *Arnold Schwarzenegger*, now that was really something.

Despite the glamour of advising a movie star (for Laffer this was his second opportunity to work up close and personal with a Hollywood actor—the first of course being Ronald Reagan), there was a more important reason why we couldn't say "no" to Arnold Schwarzenegger when he sought our help. California is the seventh-largest economy in the world. It is home to 38 million people and has a GDP of more than $1.7 trillion.[1] The California economy is larger than that of Canada and roughly the size of that of France. The U.S. economy can hardly grow if California is an anchor on productivity and progress. When California sneezes, New Yorkers say gesundheit. That's how dependent our national economy is on California's success.

What the two of us soon discovered when we got down to work was a punch to the solar plexus: Wow, did the state of California ever need help. California's $14 billion deficit was larger than the entire budget of twenty-six states. Arnold told us that even if he were to lay off every state trooper, every high school teacher, and every prison guard, Sacramento would still face a $5 billion deficit.

If ever a state needed a fiscal savior and a new economic course, it was California.[2]

We soon uncovered the chief reason for the state's monetary Armageddon. Tax revenues were falling because rich people were fleeing the state in record numbers. Next time you fly into Las Vegas just look at how expansive suburbia has become in that city, which was once a few blocks of concrete in the middle of a sun-drenched desert. Many of those housing developments and high-rent, high-rise condos are filled with disgruntled Californians.

Now here we are five years later and the state's arguably in worse shape than it was then. Now real estate values are plunging in California, much faster than in any other state. The median California home price fell by 32 percent in 2007 and 2008.[3] Americans are, for the first time in history, being repelled from the Golden State's sunshine, sandy beaches, scenic mountains, and those bikini-clad California girls that the Beach Boys sang about. The politicians in California have incredibly managed to transform this prime destination state into a place people want to leave, not enter.

Although Arnold took some of our advice (most importantly not raising taxes in 2003 to close the deficit), he moved to the left to get re-elected and has moved forward with liberal programs, such as a state-run health care system and draconian anti-global-warming regulations that make it increasingly difficult for industry to operate at a profit in this state. Worse yet, as soon as the state moved back into the black in 2005 thanks to the national expansion, Arnold and the legislators in Sacramento went on spending again. They had learned nothing from the previous meltdown. And now California is a fiscal mess again. Surprise, surprise.

Art Laffer finally got so fed up with the state's dysfunctional policies and hostility toward wealth and wealth creators that in 2006 he moved from Rancho Santa Fe, California, to Nashville, Tennessee. He took his business, with twelve employees, with him. Why? Here's one clue. California has a 10 percent income tax. Tennessee has no income tax. It was a no-brainer. In summer 2008, big employers like Toyota and AAA Auto Club announced they were leaving too, because of "the high cost of doing business in California."

For those who still don't believe taxes, regulation, overspending, and runaway debt can affect the economic fortunes of a nation, state, or city, we would hold up the tragedy of California as Exhibit A. California is always seen as a leading indicator of which way our nation is headed. A cascade of destructive economic policies and a deeply ingrained culture of liberalism have brought this state to the edge of the cliff. We wish to tell the tale of the Golden State's decline in the hope that it will serve as a warning of the rough waters ahead for the U.S. economy, if we repeat nationally the mistakes that California has made on the Left Coast.

The Tax Revolt Heard Round the World

If there is any silver lining to the California calamity, it is that this state has had to dig out of a Pacific Ocean of debt before. In the late 1970s the Golden State's government had gone on a similarly reckless tax-and-spend binge, which ended with the voters rising up in a thunderous revolt. On June 6, 1978, 60 percent of the voters in California approved the famous, and to some people infamous, Proposition 13, a ballot initiative that put a spending curfew on ill-behaved government officials in Sacramento and in localities throughout the state.[4] The parallels between then and now are quite striking. Thirty years ago, the chief problem was Californians' losing their homes, as is the case today. Then as now a big explanation for the housing crisis was an escalator of taxes that only went up, never down. Back in 1978 the biggest bite was property tax bills. Today the biggest drain on taxpayer wallets is a different levy: income taxes.

Proposition 13 has been called the most significant tax revolt in America since the Boston Tea Party—and by our reckoning, that's not so far off the mark, given the way it transformed the political landscape, not just in California, but around the nation. It has a special place in our hearts because in many ways this spontaneous tax rebellion was truly the first chapter of the supply-side revolution in America. It all was like a sneak preview movie trailer for the Reagan Revolution that was to follow two years later. We will take a moment to tell the story and its lessons for today—for California and the nation. Many of the recollections here come from Art Laffer, who was a pivotal player in the story.[5]

Two unheralded patriots led this tax revolt: Paul Gann and Howard Jarvis. The *Los Angeles Times* portrayed them rather unflatteringly at the time as "the chief agitators for this expanding group of angry and disgruntled taxpayers across the state, who believe they are paying too much for the cost of government." (The nerve of these people!) Whether the media liked it or not, and mostly they hated it, typical, middle-class Californians had come to believe that government was working against them, not for them. The Gann and Jarvis brainchild was a way for these disenchanted voters to collectively throw up their arms to the politicians and the bureaucrats and shout: *enough*.

And, they did so, for good reason. After a decade-long unrelenting expansion in the size of the Great Society welfare state coupled with years of double-digit inflation, taxes were getting excruciatingly heavy. Inflation was pushing Americans into higher tax brackets at the same time it was erasing the purchasing power of their pay checks. The popular slogan back then was: "My take-home pay won't take me home." Polls showed about two-thirds of Americans had come to believe that government wasn't giving them anything remotely close to their money's worth. In the 1970s tax bills grew faster than incomes in virtually every year.

Ground zero for the resentment over soaring taxes was California, where uncapped property tax assessments were driving thousands of residents out of their homes—particularly fixed-income seniors who had little capacity to pay the double-digit rates of increase in the taxes on their homes. But the politicians in Sacramento were arrogant and out of touch; they refused to pull in the reins. And that's when our two taxpayer superheroes, Messrs. Jarvis and Gann, put on their capes and rushed to the rescue with their remarkable and bold ballot measure.

At first no one took them seriously because Mr. Jarvis had failed with similar rabble-rousing initiatives before. Then when polls showed Proposition 13 to be a serious threat, almost everyone of consequence in both political parties (even Reagan was originally skeptical) and almost every organized interest group in the state condemned the measure as an economic wrecking ball. Big business not only stood opposed, it helped fund the "NO on 13" campaign. The opponents warned voters of the doom that awaited the state if Proposition 13 passed: San Francisco's schools and libraries would be closed, twenty-five hundred Los Angeles policemen would be laid off, the prisons would be opened up for lack of funds, and the UCLA Business School predicted a loss of 450,000 jobs in the state.

But on election day voters gave Proposition 13 a massive twenty-point victory—larger than any of the supporters had expected. Even unionized firefighters in Los Angeles voted two to one in favor of Proposition 13—even though the union bosses were spending their union dues trying to defeat it.

Proposition 13 limited property taxes by slashing property tax bills by more than half overnight. It limited assessments to 1 percent of a property's market value (down from the 3.5 percent rate that existed at the time) while capping annual growth in property tax bills at 2 percent (unless the property changed hands, at which point its market value was reassessed). Just as important, Proposition 13 mandated that any tax increases in the state must be passed by a two-thirds "supermajority" vote in both houses of the legislature, and it also limited the ability of local government to raise taxes without voter approval. The relief was felt immediately by California homeowners. The California tax burden had been $124.57 per

$1,000 of personal income, but fell one year later to $95 per $1,000 of income. For beleaguered taxpayers, it was blessed relief.[6]

One of the few academics in the state who would lend his name and his energy to the fight was Arthur Laffer. He became the economic defender of the measure. Shortly before the vote, Laffer wrote a famous pamphlet for the United Organization of Taxpayers. Laffer contradicted all the dire assessments of his colleagues and predicted that the static revenue forecasts vastly overstated the losses to the state treasury from Proposition 13, because those doomsday predictions ignored supply-side effects. Laffer wrote:

> Property tax revenues will fall by less than [the static forecast of] $7 billion because property values will rise and new construction activity will expand. Both of these effects will expand the tax base, and thus lead to less property tax revenue loss.[7]

Laffer predicted that a house worth $100,000 would rise in value to $125,000 if Proposition 13 passed, which meant that some of the predicted revenue losses would be recouped through the higher value of Californians' homes. He also predicted that higher home values would spur new housing construction and thus would mean more jobs and thus a further stimulus to tax revenues.

We are happy to report that history vindicated Laffer's analysis. In the ten years after the passage of Proposition 13 incomes in California grew 50 percent faster than incomes in the nation as a whole; jobs grew at twice the pace. California's unemployment rate was 1.2 percentage points higher than the U.S. rate in 1977; in 1980 the California rate was lower than the national rate by 0.4 percentage points. Housing prices in the state soared.

The boom was sustained by a 24 percent increase in California's population between 1978 and 1988, over twice the national increase of 10.7 percent. Over that same period, the number of jobs in California increased by 3 million, and many of them were in a brand-new industrial complex outside San Jose, called Silicon Valley.

But the critics still seethe over the impact of Proposition 13 and work endlessly to overturn it. So any time California gets into a budget hole, as it has today, the critics who objected to Proposition 13 in the first place and were wildly off base about what impact it would have, blame the measure for "starving the state and cities of revenues." Nonsense. In real dollars California's budget climbed from $55 billion in 1980 to more than $130 billion today. After inflation, tax revenues have more than doubled since Proposition 13 passed.[8]

For Californians, the legacy of Proposition 13 has been to save the average homeowner in California tens of thousands of dollars in property tax payments over the past twenty-five years. This is money that would have fueled an even more rapid escalation in California's state and local public bureaucracies if those dollars had been sent to Sacramento and city hall. Californians intuitively understand this. That is why every major poll has confirmed that a large majority or residents of California say that they would still vote for Proposition 13 again if it were on the ballot today—thirty years later.

Proposition 13 also taught us all an enduring civics lesson that we hope Americans will never forget: In America, yes, you really can fight city hall. And judging from California's dire financial straits and the not-so-benign neglect of the political class in the state, it may be high time for another tax revolt in the Golden State.

The Reverse California Gold Rush

So why is California back in the same financial crisis condition it found itself in back in 1978?

To explain, let us start by quoting from our friend Jack Cashill, who last year wrote a fabulous book called *What's the Matter with California?* Cashill notes that when you ask that question of life-long Golden State residents, you invariably get one of two answers.

First: "How much time have you got?"

Or, second: "Where oh where do I begin?"[9]

It wasn't always like this. For decades California was America's hippest and fastest-growing state. The future happened in California. The state was America's trend-setter: What people did in the Golden State, they would soon be doing everywhere else. And what's not to like about California? It has mountains, beaches, sunshine nearly every day, temperatures in the seventies and eighties. By some estimates, there is more oil and natural gas off the shores of California than in Saudi Arabia. In short, this state has perhaps the greatest natural endowments of any place on the face of the planet. To add to that there are the man-made attractions that have made California great and admirable: Silicon Valley, Hollywood, and some of the top world-class universities in the world.

Not so long ago Californians believed their state to be virtually recession-proof—naturally immune to business cycles and the repercussions of public policy folly. There were no natural limits here. During the high-flying 1980s and 1990s, and especially during the tech and dot.com boom years, Californians mocked slow-growing and more traditional and conservative midwestern America as "fly-over country."

But that was an era when California allowed free market forces and reasonable tax rates to prevail. Those were years when the economy sizzled. For at least twenty years after the passage of Proposition 13, the state's famous rollback of property taxes, California was the most dynamic place in the nation, if not the world, and it was a modern symbol of the American melting pot in action. The combination of the rich diversity of immigrant talent from around the world and California's homegrown brainpower converted the state into a trillion-dollar economy of high technology and international trade, and, of course, the entertainment capital of the world. The result of this economic dynamism and this culture of innovation in the 1980s and 1990s was a state economy that grew about 20 percent faster than did the economies of the other forty-nine states. The Golden State even enjoyed a $10 billion budget reserve by the mid-1990s.[10]

During the height of the technology boom surges in capital gains and stock option incomes caused flush reserves in Sacramento's coffers. It was reminiscent of the second California Gold Rush. Californians made billions just off the Google public offering, further swelling the fat times in the state capital. Some even called it the "Google surplus."[11]

It takes a lot of public policy bungling to screw this up but the politicians in Sacramento have proven themselves up to the task.

The latest Census Bureau data indicate that in 2005, 2006, and 2007 at least one-quarter million more Californians followed Tiger Woods's lead and left the state than moved in. More left than came in in 2003 and 2004, too.[12] The outmigration flows have become so systematic that the cost to rent a U-Haul trailer to move from Los Angeles to Boise, Idaho, is $2,090—or some eight times more than the cost of moving in the opposite direction.[13] It costs three times as much to go from L.A. to Austin, Texas, as does the reverse trip. That's because all the moves are going in one direction: eastbound. In all, nearly 1.5 million more Americans have left California than entered over the past decade.[14] Ouch.

So why are people suddenly streaming out of this little slice of heaven on the Left Coast? Why is the state, at the time of this writing, borrowing $30 million a day to pay its bills? Why is the housing market in a free fall, with 10, 20, and even 30 percent declines in home values? Well, there are a multiplicity of factors behind the state's decline, but at least we know where to begin this story. It's where all the trouble began: in the state capital, Sacramento, where the politicians hang out.

One of the first things that started to go wrong was the relentless rise of a tax and regulatory culture in Sacramento that began to treat rich people as if they were ATM machines. The cost to businesses of complying with California's rules, regulations, and paperwork is more than twice as high as that for businesses in other western states. In 2006 one of the leading companies that makes surfboards, a quintessentially California firm, closed operations in California in fear of fines, civil lawsuits, and even time in prison. When you can't even make surfboards in California any longer, the tide has shifted pretty decisively against business and wealth.

Making matters worse, in 2007 California passed the Godzilla of all economic regulations: carbon emissions restrictions on all power plants, cement producers, and oil refineries. According to a recent *New York Times* article, "Other states, particularly New York, are moving in some of the same directions, but no state is moving as aggressively on as many fronts. No state has been at it longer. No state is putting more at risk." [15]

Even if one believes that global warming is an ecological crisis with potentially hugely destructive long-term consequences, for any one state or city (or country, we would argue) to act unilaterally to reduce planetary greenhouse gases is the height of feel-good folly. The impact of one state's actions on total global CO_2 emissions is likely to be very, very close to zero. There are two reasons for this. First, even a state the size of California represents less than one-twentieth of world economic output. When one considers that even if all nations complied with the Kyoto Accord's CO_2 emission reduction mandates, the impact on global temperature change over the next fifty years would be less than one degree centigrade. [16] So California's unilateral contribution would be to lower the global temperature by at most 0.05 degrees. This is hardly going to save the earth.

But California's unilateral action is likely to have a tinier impact for another reason: because industry will relocate out of California and produce the goods and services somewhere else in the country or world where production costs are lower because that jurisdiction doesn't impose such restrictions. So all California has done is move economic activity out of the state and impoverish itself, with no impact on global warming. The latte drinkers in Sacramento with their designer sunglasses may want to sip on that dose of financial reality for a while as they watch the job base disappear before their very eyes.

As we write, Arnold Schwarzenegger and the legislature want to install a universal health care program in California as well. The cost of the program to taxpayers and businesses is $14 billion a year—coincidentally, the size of the state's current budget deficit. State Senate president Don Perata, a Democrat, advises that to launch this new health care entitlement now would be both "impractical and impolitic." [17] He's right, but the politicians are floating a two-dollar-per-pack increase in the state's cigarette tax to pay for it. So a shrinking number of smokers would be tapped to finance a growing number of citizens dependent on the state for health insurance. Brilliant.

Employers that don't provide health care to their employees would also be assessed a payroll tax under one of the leading plans. This is called "pay or play." The problem is, there is a third option, in some cases the most enticing of all for California's financially stressed businesses: Leave the state and you don't pay or play.

And then to cap things off, the legislature is pushing a huge increase in the state's minimum wage—and Arnold is an advocate. Here is what Arnold said in his State of the State address in 2006: "It is now time for those who often work the hardest and earn the least to benefit from California's growth. Let us increase the minimum wage by two dollars an hour, with half starting this year." [18] There are few policies that can torpedo small and retail businesses and their hiring plans more easily than a minimum wage hike. This is a state that *already* has an unemployment rate well above the national average, and the people in California who will be hurt the most by the mandatory wage hike are the least skilled workers in the Golden State—just the people that Arnold and the legislators say they want to help.

Here's another example of lawmaking ineptitude. The California legislature is one of few in the nation that has not conformed to the federal welfare reform law requiring a five-year time limit on welfare benefits. For all intents and purposes, California still offers a lifetime on the dole. This costs the state at least $1 billion to $2 billion a year in higher welfare costs. It also explains why California was one of the least successful states in the nation in reducing welfare caseloads in the 1990s. Worse yet, California has become a welfare magnet state: It repels those who add wealth and welcomes with open arms those who subtract from the state's wealth.

California political analyst Shawn Steel, the man who started the recall effort against then governor Gray Davis in 2003, isn't exaggerating when he says, "The politicians in Sacramento are the most left-wing collection of people ever to gather in one place at one time in North America." In 2004 in the midst of the state's financial woes, the state Senate actually passed a bill that would impose fines of up to $150,000 on employers (including the Boy Scouts) if they "refuse to hire individuals on the basis of gender or perceived gender, which could include cross dressers, and transsexuals."

Which brings us to the primary growth killer in California: a steeply "progressive" income tax with a 10.3 percent rate applied to high-income residents. That's the third-highest rate in the nation. So now the richest 10 percent of earners pay almost 75 percent of the income tax burden in the state.[19] And two of every three of these "evil rich" are small business owners, the people who create the jobs for the rest of the state's residents. Yet every two years or so a Hollywood liberal will join hands with environmentalists, union activists, and the poverty lobby to call for even higher taxes on the rich. Rob Reiner—yes "Meathead" on *All in the Family*—has launched and helped fund several of these ballot initiatives.[20]

The problem for Mr. Reiner and the politicians across the state who cheer him on is that California's high-income earners have made it clear they won't long tolerate these soak-the-rich policies. So they are buying up homes outside the state. If you don't believe us, consider some of the California fiscal statistics we confronted in 2003 while working to try to correct the problems. There were some 44,000 millionaires in California in 2000, and they contributed $15 billion to the state Treasury in that year. That is an unbelievable statistic when you think about it. It means that the richest 0.15 percent of Californians contributed roughly 20 percent of the state's income tax revenues! According to data provided to the audit committee by the State Board of Equalization, about 80 percent of the state's revenue loss between 2001 and 2003 was a result of disappearing millionaires. The number of reported millionaires in California astonishingly dropped from 44,000 in 2000 to 29,000 in 2002. These tax émigrés represented a loss of roughly $6 billion in annual tax revenue collections.[21]

Some of the loss of millionaires in this decade wasn't a result of people leaving but of people losing money in the dot-bomb bust that thrust many Californians into a horrific riches-to-rags spiral. But we also know from the Census Bureau data that high-wealth individuals have been leaving the state en masse. Figure 8-1 shows where these displaced Californians have been going.

We've heard some Californians shrug off this population loss and even cavalierly declare that fewer people is a good thing for the overcrowded and congested state. What this attitude fails to recognize is that the people who are leaving the state aren't the ones who couldn't make it in California, but the ones who did. Millionaires, business owners, and high-wealth individuals are disproportionately represented in the category of refugees from California. One California real estate financier who builds and owns upscale housing developments in Las Vegas told us in 2004 that of the 300 homes recently purchased in his latest Vegas property, 250 were purchased by tax refugees from California. Republican assemblyman Ray Haynes has noted that the average high-income individ-

Figure 8-1: Do You Know the Way Out of San Jose?

Net Domestic Outmigration by Destination, 1995–2000

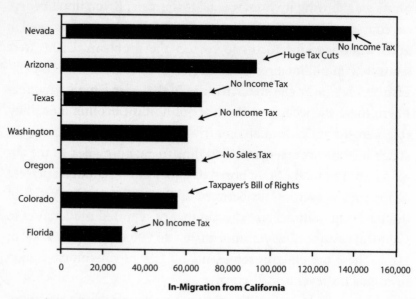

Source: Laffer Associates.

ual can buy a newly built house in neighboring Nevada and pay for it just from the money saved in a year of not paying California taxes.

Moving Up and Moving Out

We need to digress for a moment from the woes of the Golden State and make a broader point here.

California isn't the only example of how states that raise taxes lose people—not by a long shot. Americans vote every day on the economic policies of states by moving from one state to another. In the past decade a record number of Americans have moved across state lines, with 8 million packing their bags and relocating in 2007 alone. That's twenty thousand people every day who are on the move—mostly in search of greener pastures and greater opportunities. In the time it takes you to read this chapter, another five hundred people will have moved from one state to another. We agree with Rich Karlgaard, the publisher of *Forbes* magazine, who recently wrote: "The most valuable natural resource in the twenty-first century is brains. Smart people tend to be mobile. Watch where they go. Because where they go, robust economic activity will follow." [22]

The liberal-leaning northeastern states and to a lesser extent the old industrial unionized Midwestern states are being bled day after day of their most precious commodity: their human capital. The steady erosion in the power base of the northeastern states is a compelling illustration of what happens when politicians advance one reckless policy agenda item after another. The northeastern elites have been assuring their citizens for years that imposing some of the highest tax rates in the nation, forced union laws, and runaway government spending won't chase people out of the region. But over the past decade there are some 5 million Americans who have voted with their feet and abandoned this region who would beg to differ.

States with the highest income tax rates—California and New York, for example—are significantly outperformed by the nine states with no income tax, such as Texas and Florida. That is to say, these low-tax states have more economic activity and jobs than their higher-tax neighbors, as shown in Table 8-1. As a study from the Atlanta Federal Reserve Board put it not too long ago: "Relative marginal tax rates have a statistically significant negative relationship with relative state growth." [23] To put that in plain English: High taxes are like economic depressants. They slow you down.

The divergent experiences of America's four largest states illustrates that when it comes to growth, it is the quality of the economic policies that matters, not necessarily size. California and New York have little in common other than that they have been moving in a pro-government-intervention direction in recent years. They both stand out as flashing billboards for what states should *not* do if they want to gain income and wealth. See Figure 8-2 (page 170).

Some of the most compelling evidence comes from the moving van companies. The United Van Lines Company, for example, keeps meticulous track of the shipments it makes moving a family into and out of each state. Figure 8-3 (page 171) shows the geographical distribution of this internal migration for 2007. Take a good look at the winners and losers, because we think this highlights how the economic and political centers of gravity are shifting in America today. Throughout the last several years the one pattern that comes shining through is that the northeastern and Midwestern states are driving people away and the southeastern and western states are attracting new families and businesses.[24]

We hear from pollsters and political pundits that Americans are willing to pay more taxes to get more and better government services, but their migration patterns across state boundaries reveal just the opposite: that Americans don't like paying high taxes, no matter what they may tell the pollsters. This explains why the biggest population loser in 2007 was Michigan. Two families moved out of the state for every new family that moved in. Taxes are on the rise in the Wolverine State. In general, Americans are fleeing the entire industrial corridor, including New York, New Jersey, Pennsylvania, Ohio, and Illinois. Without interviewing the departed, it's impossible to know the reasons for this outward migration. But tax rates appear to play a very big role in this story because the states that are losing people generally have very high taxes. The nine states without an income tax are stealing talent and brainpower from other states. Those no-income-tax states are Alaska, Florida, Nevada, New Hampshire, South Dakota, Tennessee, Texas, Washington, and Wyoming, and each one gained in net domestic migrants. Each of them, except Florida, which has sky-high property taxes on new homesteaders, also ranked in the top twelve of destination states.

Table 8-1: The Nine States with the Lowest and the
Highest Marginal Personal Income Tax (PIT) Rates
(performance between 1997 and 2007 unless otherwise noted)

	Top Tax Rate	Personal Income Growth	Population Growth	Employment Growth
Alaska	0%	68%	12%	18%
Florida	0%	89%	20%	25%
Nevada	0%	119%	45%	45%
New Hampshire	0%	68%	11%	14%
South Dakota	0%	65%	7%	15%
Tennessee	0%	64%	12%	8%
Texas	0%	91%	21%	20%
Washington	0%	74%	14%	17%
Wyoming	0%	97%	7%	28%
9 States with no PIT*	**0%**	**82%**	**17%**	**21%**
9 States with Highest Marginal PIT Rate*	**9%**	**62%**	**7%**	**11%**
Kentucky	8%	60%	7%	9%
Hawaii	8%	62%	6%	17%
Maine	9%	60%	5%	11%
Ohio	9%	44%	2%	1%
New Jersey	9%	62%	6%	9%
Oregon	9%	61%	13%	13%
Vermont	10%	66%	4%	10%
California	10%	77%	13%	16%
New York	11%	64%	3%	8%
* Equal-weighted averages.				

Source: The Tax Foundation.

Or consider the contrasting economic fortunes of the Dakotas.
These two states are a wonderful laboratory experiment, because in
every way the states are identical twins: They have the same culture,
climate, economies (with a heavy dependence on agriculture), and
so on. All that divides these states is an arbitrary line through the

Figure 8-2: Low-Tax States Get Richer

Growth In Personal Income, 1990–2005

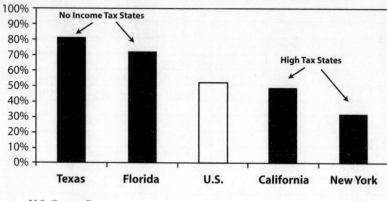

Source: U.S. Census Bureau.

dusty plains and the cavernous wheat fields. Yet, North Dakota ranked second worst in outmigration in 2007, while South Dakota ranked in the top ten as a destination place. We can think of only one possible explanation for why one of these states has been gaining people and the other has been losing them: North Dakota has an income tax and South Dakota doesn't. And Americans like to live in places without an income tax.

Some of our critics have pointed out that our analysis is far too simplistic and that there are, aha, exceptions to the rule. North Carolina has been one of the top three destination states for three years running, but it has a high income tax. True, but its overall tax burden is below average, so this only proves that people take into account *all* taxes (business taxes, property taxes, sales taxes, fuel taxes, etc.) when assessing the desirability of a location, not *just* the income tax. We will readily concede, however, that there are some states that don't fit the pattern at all. The most mysterious counterexample to the rule is Vermont. This is a very high-tax state in all regards, but had a big net influx of newcomers in 2006 and 2007. Our explanation is that there are many Americans who are at-

Figure 8-3: State Winners and Losers

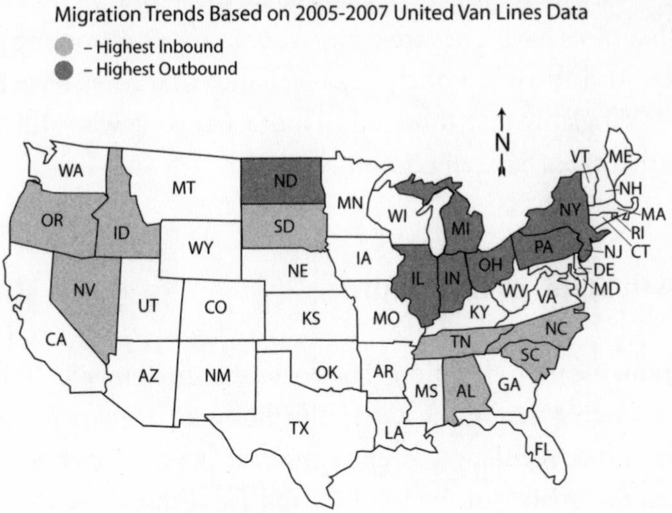

Migration Trends Based on 2005-2007 United Van Lines Data

⬤ – Highest Inbound
⬤ – Highest Outbound

NOTES:

Based on the 2005–2007 United Van Lines Migration Studies using the percentage of inbound versus outbound shipments.

tracted to the liberal culture of Vermont and who are desirous of the Ben & Jerry's lifestyle. We also hope they like the government they're paying for.

Of course, out of fifty states one can always cherry-pick some that do or don't fit the observed pattern. The formal term for these exceptions to the rule is: "statistical outliers." The real issue is whether there is a strong statistical relationship between taxes and a state's interstate migration or whether the observations we've pointed out are just due to chance. The answer to that, according to a new study by John Tatom, former economist at the Federal Reserve Bank of St. Louis, is, yes, taxes do explain a lot. Tatom examined the overall tax burden in a state and studied how that affected migration in and out of the states. He concludes: "The in-migration rate is sensitive to the tax rate . . . A doubling of the state tax rate will cut the in-migration rate by half."[25] That was statistically significant to the 99.9% level of confidence, meaning that the odds are one in one thousand that this result happened by chance. In other words, there is a 999 in 1,000 chance that our premise is right and that taxes have a negative impact on a state's economic performance. And there is a one in 1,000 chance that taxes have no impact. We'll gladly take those odds and bet anyone who still doesn't think that taxes have an economic impact.

Growth States of the Future

Location, location, location. Those are the three magical words in real estate that determine a desirable home or a smart place to invest in. Taxes, regulation, minimum-wage laws, the cost of the tort system, the quality of the schools, and fiscal discipline or the lack thereof, are all factors that affect how fast a state grows and how many people and businesses want to call that state home. America is one massive free trade zone, where businesses, capital, and people can move freely to wherever they wish to settle. States are now openly competing with one another for assets, and they are doing so on the basis of their tax systems, their liability laws, their educational systems, and their quality of life.

We created a state competitiveness index based on tax and regulatory policies in each state. It shows which states are getting it right and which are falling behind, see Table 8-2. If states were like stocks, you'd want to sell places such as New Jersey and Ohio and buy places such as Utah and Tennessee. Think about that before you buy your next house or property.

Hello, Darkness, My Old Friend

As bad as the scene is in many financially troubled states and cities, California is in a distinctive category all its own. California is swimming in a Pacific Ocean of red ink. It has roughly one half trillion dollars of outstanding bonds, making the state far and away the most indebted in the nation. In the early 2000s Moody's downgraded California bond ratings twice. So naturally, this state, the most indebted in the nation, keeps approving ballot initiatives crammed with a slate of populist bond initiatives: $13 billion for schools, $3 billion for water, and $3 billion for low-income-housing construction. That's a lot of new debt even for a state the size of California, and now even the bond traders are starting to flinch.

But that infrastructure and school construction debt is a drop in the Pacific Ocean compared to the real ticking fiscal time bomb in California: public pension costs that have gone berserk. Consider the financial turmoil of the sleepy middle-class town of Vallejo, California. In early 2008 Vallejo came within an eyelash of becoming the first city since Bridgeport, Connecticut, back in 1991, to declare for Chapter 9 bankruptcy. This San Francisco Bay suburb of 120,000 residents declared that it could no longer afford to pay the extravagant salary and retirement benefits it owes to its public employees. Just a few hours before the city council was to file for bankruptcy the unions caved in and granted wage concessions to keep the city operational.[26]

Vallejo's story of financial woe has raised eyebrows because we are not talking here about a desperately poor or dilapidated city, like Newark or Detroit. Vallejo is quintessential middle-class America, with an average family income of about $57,000. The city projects a $20 million budget shortfall this year and next, which is a big bucket of red ink out of an annual budget of $80 million.

Here's how bad it has gotten. Wage contracts are so exorbitant that some of the richest residents of Vallejo are the police and firemen. Ten firemen earned more than $200,000 last year, with overtime. That's a salary nearly four times higher than what the average family in Vallejo earns. Incredibly, 80 percent of the city's budget is consumed by labor and pension costs. "No city or private person

Table 8-2: 2007 ALEC-Laffer Overall State Rankings

Based upon the equal-weighting of 16 policy variables

1	Utah	26	Massachusetts
2	Arizona	27	Iowa
3	South Dakota	28	New Mexico
4	Wyoming	29	Kansas
5	Tennessee	30	Wisconsin
6	Virginia	31	Washington
7	Colorado	32	Maryland
8	Georgia	33	Montana
9	Idaho	34	Nebraska
10	Texas	35	Minnesota
11	Nevada	36	Oregon
12	Indiana	37	Pennsylvania
13	Oklahoma	38	Alaska
14	Florida	39	Connecticut
15	Arkansas	40	West Virginia
16	Michigan	41	California
17	Missouri	42	Illinois
18	Alabama	43	New Jersey
19	North Carolina	44	Maine
20	New Hampshire	45	Hawaii
21	Louisiana	46	Kentucky
22	Delaware	47	Ohio
23	Mississippi	48	Rhode Island
24	North Dakota	49	New York
25	South Carolina	50	Vermont

wants to declare bankruptcy," say Councilwoman Stephanie Gomes, "but if you're facing insolvency, you have no choice but to seek protection."[27]

"Vallejo's fiscal problems aren't unique. They're just the tip of the debt iceberg here in California," warns Keith Richman, a former state legislator and now president of the California Foundation for Fiscal Responsibility. He's right. The California Public Employees' Retirement System (CALPERS) has $26 billion of unfunded liabilities. The teachers' retirement system is another $20 billion in the red, and health benefits add another $48 billion to the shortfall.

These unfunded pensions could be the next great financial bubble in California, coming on the heels of the subprime mortgage meltdown. This fiscal time bomb is creating Enron-level balance sheet problems for cities from end to end in the Golden State and could cause local and state tax bills to double or even triple to cover the shortfalls. California is not the only state facing this fiscal riptide, but it's worst on the Left Coast. Across the state soaring public employee pension costs are crunching municipal budgets, causing service cuts or tax hikes. The Los Angeles County school system health, pension, and workers' compensation liabilities are so mountainous that an estimated one of every three dollars for the L.A. schools will go not for classroom instruction, but for lavish teacher retirement costs. "The three Rs in the L.A. county school system are now reading, writing, and retirement," moans Mr. Richman.[28]

There are other horror stories. The California Foundation for Fiscal Responsibility finds that many cities have a 3 percent rule that allows a worker to accrue a pension benefit of 3 percent of his or her final salary for each year worked. So an employee who started on the job at age twenty-two can retire at age fifty-two with a lifetime pension benefit of 90 percent of the final salary. Oh, and did we mention that these pensions also come with an annual cost-of-living adjustment and lifetime health care benefits? Talk about a gravy train! And thanks to longer life expectancy, most California cities in the twenty-first century are going to be simultaneously paying for three police forces and firefighting services: the active one and two retired ones.[29]

So the luxurious benefits of public employees grow more unaffordable each year while California's cities keep edging closer to the fiscal cliff. We hope we're wrong, but Chapter 9 bankruptcy may be California's last fiscal recourse.

Hasta La Vista, Baby

We warned Arnold in our initial meeting that notwithstanding all of the androids that he had to overcome in his Terminator movies, he had never faced a more tenacious adversary than the Democrats in the state legislature. We should be clear that even though we are critical of policy decisions the governor has made, we *like* Arnold; not only is he impressive for obvious professional reasons, but he's very intelligent and—if you'll forgive the cliché—is genuinely compassionate toward his fellow human beings. But he also has a naïve view that he can gather everyone in a room and, regardless of ideology, they will all come to an agreement on how to make the state a better place to live.

How wrong he is. Politics is mostly about power. We think that November 2005 was a turning point of sorts. Governor Arnold Schwarzenegger called a special election and backed four seminal ballot propositions. One, Proposition 76, would have put a limit on state spending; another, Proposition 77, would have mandated unbiased redistricting of the state's political districts; yet another would have granted state teachers tenure after five years instead of two years; last, Proposition 75 would have required unions to get express written consent from each union member to use his or her dues for political purposes. All four of these propositions are eminently reasonable and should have passed easily. On that fateful day in November, however, all hell broke loose and each of these four propositions went down in flames.

The liberals were empowered and emboldened by their huge victory over Governor Schwarzenegger and are mounting an enormous counteroffensive.

So now spending in California doesn't walk, it runs. Ten years ago the state budget busted at the seams at $65 billion, which rose to $100 billion in five years under Gray Davis and is now approaching $130 billion after four years of Arnold. That's a doubling in spending in just over a decade.

But this story isn't over yet. There's a lot more to come, and none of it is pretty, due to the housing market meltdown in most areas of California. Of course, the mortgage crisis has been a nationwide phenomenon, but California has the farthest to fall, because of by far the most inflated home prices in the nation. The housing bubble sent the median home price in California to $500,000 last year. At the height of this real estate euphoria, fewer than one in twenty residents could afford to buy the average home in San Diego and Los Angeles counties. Only one in ten could afford the average home in San Francisco.[30] This is the very definition of irrational exuberance. There is no way the market could sustain a run-up in prices that rapidly, because there weren't enough people who could buy the homes. Now the state is enduring the inevitable correction, with prices tumbling by double digits in some markets. Homeowners are demanding a revision of their property tax assessments, which is only adding to the revenue drought.

But this brings us back to the California curse of outmigration, which is greatly exacerbating the housing implosion. There's a big pool of sellers and a declining pool of buyers in the Golden State. Prices are going to keep tumbling until someone in Sacramento fixes the antigrowth tax environment. Don't hold your breath.

In his State of the State speech in 2006 Schwarzenegger noted: "Our systems are at the breaking point now. We will need more roads, more hospitals, more schools, more nurses, more teachers, more police and fire, more water, more energy, more ports . . . more, more, more . . ." Yes, he's right, but where in the world will the money come from?

Seemingly oblivious to economic reality, in the summer of 2008 Democrats proposed to raise the California income tax rate to 12%, the highest in the nation. We despair.

• • •

California is more equal than the rest of the nation. But there are limits, even in California. When you treat businesses and entrepreneurs that dare make a profit as if they are enemies of the state and cash machines for government programs, bad things happen. Businesses leave. A state without businesses doesn't have new jobs, and a state without taxpayers doesn't collect revenues to maintain public services. This in a nutshell explains the great reverse gold rush out of California, and why in recent years it has been accelerating. Our prognosis is a dreary one: California is in a death spiral—or should we call it a "debt spiral"—with high taxes driving out wealth producers, which reduces jobs and property values, which depletes revenues for the cities and the state, which causes big deficits, which causes the legislature and towns to raise taxes again, causing more people to flee and the whole unhealthy cycle to repeat itself.

So now the moving vans are headed out of California, not in, driven by the latest wave of exiles, who can't afford all of the state's crazy laws, regulations, and taxes. Perhaps the downward spiral will be arrested when the voters of California finally get so fed up that they rise up in the spirit of Proposition 13.

9

SOCIALISM, NON,
THE LAFFER CURVE, OUI:

SUPPLY-SIDE ECONOMICS TAKES THE
WORLD BY STORM

*A tax cut bidding war is spreading across Europe as leaders of the
continent's biggest economies give up criticizing smaller neighbors
for cutting business tax rates and decide to join them instead.*[1]
— *BLOOMBERG NEWS BULLETIN*, May 28, 2007

FLAT AND HAPPY

Mart Laar is the delightful and charismatic former prime
minister of Estonia. He is also going to have a prominent
spot in the history books for being the first leader to bring the flat
tax to Eastern Europe. This genuine revolutionary is almost singlehandedly responsible for Estonia's widespread adoption of free
market reforms some ten years ago, and for lifting his people out of
poverty.

Mr. Laar told us that when he first started pushing the flat tax
plan, the major opponents were not the Estonian citizens, "who

love the flat tax," but the economists and other wise men of government "both inside and outside of this tiny country." He recalls, "Almost all of the smartest minds told me, 'We cannot have a flat tax. It is untested. It will not work. It will cause budget deficits.'" But Mr. Laar insisted that the plan would work because fortunately, when he was young, he had read about the virtues of the flat tax in Milton Friedman's classic book *Free to Choose*. So in 1994 Mr. Laar heroically and wisely ignored the economic pundits and snapped in place one of the world's first flat taxes at 23 percent. Since then Estonia has had one of the most rapid growth spurts of any nation in the world and the flat tax is widely heralded as a cornerstone of this prosperity story. "We now have so many jobs we now import workers from much of the rest of Europe," he boasts.[2]

Mr. Laar encountered the same academic hostility to his flat tax idea that Reagan, Kemp, and Laffer did when they unleashed supply-side economics. Here again we have a lesson of how wrong conventional-minded intellectuals can be when assessing revolutionary ideas in economics. As we saw in Chapter 5, Ronald Reagan discovered this in 1980 when he was almost universally ridiculed as an affable dunce by the deans of economics for touting supply-side marginal tax rate reductions as a cure for America's high inflation and the economic malaise of the 1970s.

The three of us have spent years debating and defending supply-side economics, and we have heard all the sophisticated arguments, and a lot of the unsophisticated ones, too. There is one question we always pose to our critics for which they have no rational answer, and it is this: If the supply-side tax rate reduction model employed by Ronald Reagan and more recently George W. Bush is truly fool's gold, then why are so many nations around the world adopting these policies at such a frantic pace? Why has Ireland with its bargain basement 12.5 percent corporate tax rate been the economic version of Carl Lewis sprinting past competitors from northern and western Europe for the past decade?[3] Why are Germany, France, and Sweden slashing their tax rates? Why do twenty-four countries now have flat taxes?

We're patiently waiting for an answer. And, sorry, we won't accept the cop-out response that the leaders of about half the nations in the world have been duped or are drinking the same mind-altering Kool-Aid that Arthur Laffer and Steve Forbes have been supposedly serving up to Republicans in Washington.

Here's the stubborn reality: History is moving against the critics of supply-side economics. The Left is losing the policy debate every day, maybe not on the pages of the *New York Times* or the *Washington Post*, but where it really matters: in political capitals all around the world. (In early 2008, newly elected leaders of Poland and Hungary announced they plan to implement a flat tax by 2009. More Kool-Aid drinkers?)

The Globe Tilts to the Supply Side

In the mid-1990s a small group of free market economists were invited to go to Russia and meet with the new Soviet president, Vladimir Putin, to give him advice about reforming the Russian tax system. One of them was our close pal Richard Vedder of Ohio University. Vedder is a top-notch economist, but he doesn't have the Ivy League pedigree from Harvard or Yale. He tells us that before the meeting the group had exchanged notes and decided that they would recommend a 20 percent flat tax for Russia. The high tax rates of more than 50 percent were not raising income tax revenues but were reducing growth. There was massive fraud and evasion. So after eating a luxurious lunch with Mr. Putin in one of the great halls of the Kremlin, "and drinking lots of vodka," the economists made an hour-long presentation about the virtues of a single-rate flat tax with no deductions or loopholes. When they came to the end, they said, "And that is why we recommend for Russia a 20 percent flat tax." There was awkward silence in the room for a few moments, then Putin slammed down his glass of vodka. "Gentlemen," he said. "I like your idea of a flat tax. But a flat tax of 20 percent, *no*. We will have 13 percent." The rest, as they say, is history.

There can be no doubt that over the past twenty-five years and especially in the last five years, global tax rates have fallen at a faster pace than at any time in the last century. We'd argue that this chopping of antigrowth tax rates is the most momentous economic trend around the globe today. Corporate tax rates are declining. Individual income tax rates are being lowered. Wealth taxes are falling or disappearing altogether. While the new Left in America continue to argue on talking-head TV shows and on the floor of the U.S. Congress that tax rates don't matter, the rest of the world has stopped listening to them. Even socialist leaders around the world have been mugged by economic reality in this new age of globalization and quicksilver capital. The socialist government in Bulgaria just instituted a 10 percent flat tax. Keeping tax rates low is a key strategy for a nation that wishes to compete in international markets and achieve rapid growth.

This trend truly started with the Reagan tax cuts in the United States. Other nations started following suit. The average personal income tax rate of industrialized countries in 1980 was 64 percent. That rate fell to 50 percent in 1995 and today stands at 41 percent. See Table 9-1. So personal income tax rates at the top of the income scale have fallen by one-third.

On the corporate income tax side the tax-cutting frenzy is even more pronounced. The average tax rate in industrialized nations has fallen by half, from 48 percent to 25 percent, since the start of the Reagan era. See Table 9-2. We regret to report that the United States today has the second-highest corporate income tax in the world, and in high-tax states like California and Maine, the business tax rate is the highest in the world.[4] And the statutory tax rates are not what many multinational companies face when they locate in a new region. Steve Moore recently met with the lead tax coun-

Table 9-1

Top Personal Income Tax Rates in Developed Countries Are Falling		
	1980	**2007**
Australia	62	49
Austria	62	50
Belgium	76	50
Canada	64	44
Denmark	66	59
Finland	68	51
France	60	48
Germany	65	45
Ireland	60	42
Italy	72	43
Mexico	55	28
Netherlands	72	52
New Zealand	62	39
Norway	75	40
Portugal	84	42
Spain	66	43
Sweden	87	56
Switzerland	38	34
United Kingdom	83	40
United States	73	39
Average	68	45

Source: OECD.

sels from many of the Fortune 500 companies: Intel, Dell Computers, IBM, and Caterpillar. The consensus was that in most countries today large companies can virtually cut their corporate income tax liability to zero. What was more disturbing was that several of the executives, who are in charge of site selection for new plants and factories, said, "The tax rates are way too high in the United States. We don't even consider the U.S. for expansion anymore." We've forfeited our lead.

The tax-cutting trend around the world has been going on for almost three decades now, but in recent years the pace of tax chopping has unquestionably accelerated. "Nowadays," says Scott Hodge, president of the nonpartisan Tax Foundation, "the rates are

Table 9-2

Corporate Tax Rates in Developed Countries Are Falling		
	1980	**2007**
Australia	46.0	30.0
Austria	55.0	25.0
Belgium	48.0	34
Canada	37.8	36.1
Denmark	40.0	25.0
Finland	43.0	26.0
France	50.0	34.40
Germany	56.0	38.90
Ireland	45.0	12.5
Italy	40.0	33.0
Japan	42.0	39.5
Luxembourg	40.0	30.4
Mexico	42.0	28.0
Netherlands	48.0	25.5
New Zealand	45.0	33.0
Norway	29.8	28.0
Portugal	47.2	26.5
Spain	33.0	32.5
Sweden	40.0	28.0
United Kingdom	52.0	30.0
United States	46.0	39.3
Average	**43.5**	**30.3**

Source: OECD.

being cut so quickly around the world, it's hard to keep a good tally of all the latest developments."[5] We believe a primary explanation for this is that nations are sick and tired of losing business to Ireland and the flat tax nations.

There are currently 24 nations with "postcard" flat taxes—and most of these nations are in Eastern Europe (see Table 9-1). What a culture shift. These nations, formerly entrapped behind the Iron Curtain, endured suffocating economic controls and suffered stagnant and even real declines in living standards for half a century. Now they are capitalists par excellence and flat tax fanatics. The average flat tax rate of these twenty-four nations is 20 percent, which

Table 9-3: **Postcards from Around the World**

Albania	10%	Kyrgyzstan	10%
Bulgaria	10	Latvia	25
Czech Republic	15	Lithuania	27
Estonia	22	Macedonia	12
Georgia	12	Mauritius	15
Guernsey	20	Mongolia	10
Hong Kong	16	Montenegro	15
Iceland	35.7	Pridnestrovie	10
Iraq	15	Romania	16
Jamaica	25	Russia	13
Jersey	20	Slovakia	19
Kazakhstan	10	Ukraine	15

Source: The Center for Freedom and Prosperity.

has made the tax rates of Old Europe, of 40 to 60 percent, look as high as the Swiss Alps. The flat tax countries even compete with each other to keep rates low. Russia is at 13 percent. In the wake of the Polish government's announcing a 15 percent flat tax, Bulgaria has said it will do Poland one better and institute a 10 percent flat rate income tax.

For many decades, the only country on the planet with a flat tax was Hong Kong, which adopted the postcard tax system way back in 1947. It was a 15 percent tax rate with no tax on dividends or capital gains or money earned outside the island. Hong Kong also established itself as a free trade zone, which is why this is a capitalist paradise, with skyscraper buildings and merchants buying and selling nearly everything imaginable, from bags of peanuts to Rolex watches, on streets that bustle with activity. The tax code is about 180 pages, compared to tens of thousands for the U.S. code. The result was that Hong Kong over several decades became one of the richest places on earth despite almost no land (which explains the skyscrapers) and no natural resources. The only mystery is why it took nearly half a century for the rest of the world to start copying the Hong Kong flat tax model.

Meanwhile, we need to point out that China's economic revolution has been powered by what Hoover Institution tax scholar Alvin Rabushka has called "The Great Tax Cut of China." It's a fascinating story that hasn't been told enough. In 1978 the late Chinese leader Deng Xiaoping unleashed a whole series of free market–based economic reforms, such as privately owned farms (which caused a near doubling of food output above what the communist state-owned farms produced), coastal economic enterprise zones, more open opportunities for foreign investment, privatization of state-owned enterprises, and tax cuts. But as Rabushka points out, "The application of supply-side tax policies was the main component." Rabushka raked through the data in China and found that in 1978 total government revenues ate up about 31 percent of GDP. With Deng's policies the income tax burden fell to about 11 percent of GDP.[6] Now, this does not include many indirect taxes and the "tax" of government ownership and regulation, but this was more than a halving of the tax burden as a share of GDP over a twenty-year period. It helped generate the double-digit rates of economic growth on the mainland that have become the stuff of economic legend. But if it were not for the chopping of the tax rates, that miraculous and continuing economic boom might never have happened.

Sixty Million Frenchmen Can't All Be Wrong

So now even stodgy old Western Europe, whose tax rates in the past have been hopelessly uncompetitive, is getting into the act. For years Europe has been the economic doormat of the industrialized nations. The economic growth rate of the E.U. nations between 2001 and 2006 was about half the pace of the United States. In the 1990s the unemployment rate in Europe was consistently about 50 percent higher than the jobless rate in the United States. This was no workers' paradise.

The Europeans created a vast constellation of domestic policy interventions that were cloaked in the seductive rhetoric of compassion, fairness, and cultural sophistication. In reality they had obliterated work incentives and entrepreneurial activity. These antigrowth policies include highly generous welfare benefits for the unemployed; state ownership or subsidy of key industries (such as the $15 billion to Airbus); workplace rules that make it difficult for employers to hire and fire workers; prohibitions against closing down plants; heavy protections of labor unions against competitive forces; mandatory worker benefit packages that include health insurance, child care allowances, paid parental leave, and four to six weeks of vacation for employees; super-minimum-wage laws; shortened work weeks; and, alas, high taxes on business and labor to pay for these lavish benefits. In sum, Europe penalizes work and subsidizes nonwork, and no surprise, they have gotten a lot of the latter and far too little of the former.

Germany, France, Spain, and other neighbors on the continent formed the European Union to bring economic integration, pick up the growth rate, and create an economically unified counterforce to the U.S. economic machine. The three of us have supported European integration. But most of the mountainous economic maladies that face France and Germany today are incidental to whether the E.U. gains or loses economic power. The European Union has always been the right answer to the wrong question. It was principally set up to establish a single, stable currency (which has been a good thing) and to reduce trade barriers (another good thing). But for years the European Union purposely ignored the continent's central ailments: high tax rates, bloated welfare benefits, and industrial policies that pick winners and losers—mostly poorly. Indeed, the economic harmonization strategy has been in part motivated by Brussels bureaucrats who wish to inhibit the benign and liberating impact of tax cutting and tax competition among member countries by creating a de facto multistate cartel. The two nations that have refused to comply with "tax harmonization"—Ireland and the United Kingdom—have generally followed much more sensible fiscal policies.

But recently the Europeans looked in the mirror and didn't like what they saw—an unattractive wart on the chin of their socialistic economies. For example, the French economy grew by only 1.3% from 1980–2000 and Germany grew by only 1.5% during the booming 1990s. So now they are undergoing a fairly drastic economic facelift.[7]

The reforms have started with European leaders slowly shedding many of the excesses of cradle-to-grave socialism and the confiscatory tax rates required to pay for the supersized Nordic welfare states. They are turning to the supply-side economics model—though they would never acknowledge that they've adopted the Reagan policies they once disparaged. But two decades of slow growth and double-digit unemployment in Europe have made this U-turn in policy a necessity. In 2007 Germany, under Chancellor Angela Merkel, chopped its corporate income tax rate by 8.9 percentage points. So now, after several rounds of tax cuts Germany, which started this century with a 52 percent top corporate income tax rate, has sliced that to 19.8 percent. Ms. Merkel sounds a lot like Jack Kemp or Ronald Reagan when she says that the purpose of the tax cuts is to boost "Germany's attractiveness as a location for international investment."[8]

Or how about the unlikely transition that is going on in France? When Nicolas Sarkozy, the flagbearer of France's Gaullist right, was elected president in 2007, he promised a "real economic revolution," including offering employees new tax incentives to earn more money by working longer hours. What a concept: rewarding work! He asked the French citizens: "Why have we had an economic growth rate 1 percentage point below that in the better-performing of the free countries over the past 15 years?"[9] Good question, and the French instinctively knew the right answer even if it was hard to swallow. Years of overtaxing work and subsidizing laziness have slowed production and increased the ranks of those who live on the dole. The tax and welfare policy incentives became so perverted that in 2004 a best-selling book in France was entitled *Bonjour, Paresse,* which, translated, means, "Hello, laziness." It outlined how French workers could make a good income by shirking and without working hard.[10]

Sarkozy is so far confronting a predictable wall of political opposition to his reforms, but at least he's pointing the country in the right direction. And let us repeat: we are talking here of *France,* the country that has no word for entrepreneurship, that invented the four-and-and-a-half-day work week, and where past leaders like François Mitterrand have openly disparaged Reaganomics as a prescription for economic chaos and decline.

Meanwhile, France's next-door neighbor, Spain, has a socialist prime minister, José Luis Rodríguez Zapatero, who is also sounding a Reaganite tax-cutting message. He pledged that if he were re-elected, he would cut the corporate income tax by ten percentage points and totally eliminate the nation's wealth tax. Zapatero is a liberal on foreign policy and has taken a staunchly anti-American stand on the war in Iraq. But he recognizes a bad tax when he sees one. An American Enterprise Institute analysis finds that "the Spanish wealth tax is among the highest in the world. It penalizes savings and thrift. Moreover, due to creative accounting, it is one of the easiest taxes to avoid and therefore tends to ensnare middle-class Spaniards rather than the wealthy."[11] Even Zapatero himself seems to understand this economic reality, as he has declared that the tax cut would ensure that "saving is no longer punished."

The surest sign of all that there is a new economic paradigm taking hold in Europe is that just two years ago, Sweden, the social-ist workers' paradise, completely eliminated its estate tax because the political leaders realized that the tax was economically counterproductive. According to the Swedish prime minister, Fredrik Reinfeldt, "We will abolish the wealth tax. We hope to give a boost to the desire to invest in Sweden and to create a condition for new, expansive companies to create more jobs." So now Sweden, and more recently, Russia, have no estate tax, but the land of the free, America, taxes death at 45 percent.[12] What's wrong with this picture?

Some of our favorite supply-side success stories come from the other side of the planet. India cut its top tax rate from 65 percent to 50 percent in 1985 and afterward its stock market jumped 40 percent in one year. South Korea cut its income tax from 87 percent in 1979 down to 40 percent by 1996. Its revenues soared from $1.7 billion in 1980 to $24 billion in 1996. How's that for a Laffer Curve effect? The leaders of the former communist nation of Vietnam announced in the summer of 2007 that they intend to slash the corporate rate from 28 to 25 percent while removing other governmental barriers to growth. All of this is intended to attract foreign investment. So it would seem that a little more than three decades after the end of the Vietnam War, we now know which side won . . . capitalism.

What seems to be motivating this sudden tax-slashing fad in every continent is globalization and free trade. In the information and technology age, borders don't matter much anymore. The world has become one massive shopping market for capital. Nations find themselves in a frenzied contest to try to climb past each other in the race up the economic growth ladder. Singapore, for example, recently approved a corporate tax cut to keep pace with low-tax neighbor Hong Kong. Northern Ireland is making a bid to slash its corporate tax rate to 12.5 percent in order to try to catch up to the economic gazelle of Europe: Ireland. When we recently met with the new prime minister of Scotland, Alex Salmond, he told us the same thing. "Supply side economics works. We've seen that in Ireland." Then he added: "Their low tax rates are attracting all the capital of Europe and if we want to compete our rates need to fall to near theirs." [13]

We call this global phenomenon Reaganomics 2.0. [14] The supply-side economics model that the Gipper installed with such great controversy twenty-eight years ago is now the economic operating system around the globe. Foreigners have witnessed with envy the American prosperity boom of the last quarter century. Where American politicians have decried "tax cuts for the rich," the rest of the world has seen impressive and sustained rates of growth. When Reagan cut tax rates from 70 to 28 percent and cut the inflation rate from 13 to 3 percent, the incentives for production, work, investment, and risk-taking exploded. Those policies proved to be a gravitational pull on foreign investment capital of more than $1 trillion from 1982 to 2002. Now the capital may start to flow back as many of these nations start to treat investors and capital more kindly at home.

The "Irish Miracle"

The greatest supply-side economics success story of recent times (other than the Reagan Revolution) is the Irish Economic Miracle. Ireland turned to the supply-side only when the nation was on its knees and seemingly all other inferior alternatives had been tried.

Ireland is a nation that just over a century and a half ago had some 8 million people. But by 1980 that population had fallen to 5 million (4 million in the Republic), with far more Irish living in America than in Ireland. In the 1960s, 1970s, and 1980s Ireland became a giant welfare state with high taxes, generous benefits for not working, and an industrial base in wreckage. The movie *The Commitments* depicted a rock band with several of the struggling band members collecting welfare benefits from the government. "It beats working," was the famous response of one band member when

Figure 9-1: Ireland Unemployment Rate, 1961–2005

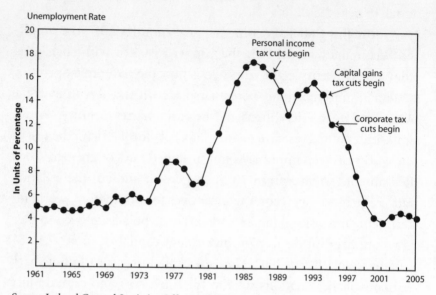

Source: Ireland Central Statistics Office and U.N. International Labour Organization.

asked why he stood in long lines for monthly benefits. Indeed, it did—and Ireland's GDP stagnated.

In the 1990s everything changed. Welfare policy was reformed; government services and enterprises were privatized; and most important, the corporate income tax rate was cut from 48 percent to 12.5 percent—not just the lowest in Euroland, but one-third the average rate on the continent. In the succeeding ten years, the population for the first time in decades grew (to 5.7 million), GDP rose at twice the rate of Europe's, and more than one thousand international companies, such as Intel, Bristol-Myers, Squibb, Microsoft, Dell, and Motorola, moved in. By 2000 Ireland's growth rate hit 8.7 percent a year, its unemployment rate, which had risen to 16.3 percent in 1988 (which we would consider a depression), fell all the way below 5 percent, and perhaps most astonishing of all, with the lowest corporate tax rate in all Europe, it had the biggest budget *surplus* as a share of GDP.[15] Prior to the tax cuts starting in 1980, Ireland collected $1.2 billion in income taxes. By 1997 the nation collected $5.1 billion. Capital gains tax revenues grew by 60 percent from 1993 to 1998 after a series of rate cuts.

Writing in *Commentary*, Carl Schramm, the president of the Kauffman Foundation, beautifully summarized the transformation that took place in Ireland:

> *The leading example of a "hot spot" is Ireland, which only 30 years ago was looked down upon as the poor cousin of Europe, and now boasts one of the highest living standards in the world. Ireland was able to launch its magical economic ride on the strength of a low corporate tax rate, heavy investment in education, and open door policy to foreign investment.*[16]

The biggest winners here were the rank-and-file workers. The average hourly manufacturing wage soared by 126 percent from 1985 to 2004 at a time when many industrial nations were experiencing stagnant wage growth. The Irish on a per capita basis are now twice as rich as they were in 1980, as real GDP has gone from $8,019 per person to $18,772.

In 1991 Germany had a per capita income that was twice that of Ireland. By 2004, Ireland's per capita purchasing power of 25,100 euros exceeded Germany's at 21,700. In less than a decade and a half Ireland climbed from last to first in Europe. That's economic development at warp speed. The Irish brain drain that started way back during the potato famine of 1845 and continued almost unabated for the next 150 years has finally reversed course. Now top minds are coming to Ireland—at a pace of 50,000 newcomers a year. The unemployment rate has fallen from 18 to 5 percent (see Figure 9-1).[17] Ireland created so many new jobs and attracted so many companies that E.U. bureaucrats began to complain of Ireland's "tax poaching." That means cutting tax rates below the level of European rivals to attract capital.[18] These protests are an admission that taxes do matter after all. The Irish are the Celtic Tiger of Europe (just as Hong Kong, Singapore, and Taiwan were the "Asian Tigers" during the 1980s and 1990s) and low tax rates have played a critical role in this amazing economic rehabilitation. In the immortal words of the Irish rock band U2, for Ireland, "It's a beautiful day."

The Laffer Curve Goes Global

As the Irish success story illustrates, one of the taxes that has a large impact on a nation's ability to compete in global markets is the corporate tax rate, which is coming down rapidly just about everywhere. Just in 2006 and 2007 twelve nations have cut their corporate rates, including Germany, Spain, and the Netherlands.

This has put America in a competitive hole. U.S. policymakers may want to take a look at a new study by AEI scholars Kevin Hassett and Aparna Mathur. They find that the burden of the corporate income tax rate is borne in large part by workers in the form of lower wages. They found manufacturing wages were negatively associated with high corporate tax rates in a study of seventy-two nations.[19] In other words, our high corporate tax encourages outsourcing of jobs and hurts American workers most.

One implication of Ireland's success story is that there may be a global Laffer Curve. The lower a nation's tax rates, the higher its growth rate and the more revenue it generates. The Irish, with their 12.5 percent corporate rate, have attracted so much corporate activity that the nation collects 3.6 percent of GDP in corporate revenues, well above the international average. The United States by contrast, with its near 40 percent rate, has been averaging less than 2.5 percent of GDP in corporate receipts. "The United States," warns Kevin Hassett, an economist at the American Enterprise Institute, "appears to be a nation on the wrong side of the Laffer Curve; we might collect more revenues with a lower corporate tax rate." His AEI study concludes that there is "strong statistical evidence of a Laffer Curve effect in the corporate income tax. It is not merely a recent phenomenon."[20] Imagine that.

This Laffer Curve effect of lower international tax rates suggests that nations will increase their economic output and competitive stature in the global race for capital by cutting rates. And our friend Alan Reynolds, an economist at the Cato Institute, has confirmed this relationship: Countries that cut tax rates sharply outperform those that don't. He labeled the tax rate reduction countries "supply-side economies" and the countries that raised tax rates in the 1990s "demand-side economies." His results were shocking. The "supply-side economy" nations—whose tax rates fell from an average of 61.5% to 34%—experienced economic growth rates much faster than the demand-side countries. "Hong Kong, Singapore, and most other economies that have adopted supply-side tax strategies have seen their private consumption and investment, good measures of living standards, increase three times the pace of the demand-side economies," he concludes.[21]

No wonder the Eastern Europeans are getting rich quick.

Healthy, Wealthy, and Wise—Is There a Tradeoff?

Okay, so we've provided some compelling evidence that high tax rates are self-defeating economic strategies because they reduce production within a nation's borders and hurt a nation's economic performance. But critics say: Economic growth is not everything. What about quality of life? What about pollution? What about equality? What about health? We agree these are very important, too.

For years prominent scholars and leaders, from the late great American economist John Kenneth Galbraith, promoted the idea that we should forgo some freedoms to improve economic efficiency and fairness.[22] Galbraith once noted that Americans wouldn't be cheered by news of higher GDP growth if they were choking

Figure 9-2: Supply-Side Countries Are Healthier and Wealthier

Per Capita Income and Life Expectancy

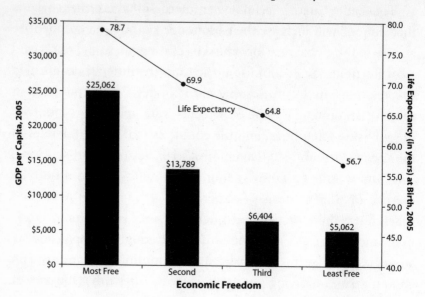

Source: Cato Institute and Fraser Institute, Economic Freedom of the World, 2007.

on the air they were breathing. And we still hear American intellectuals tout the universal health care systems in Canada and even Cuba. It may be that residents of states or nations are willing to sacrifice growth for improvements in other quality-of-life measures—such as a clean environment and equality. Do they have to?

To answer that question, we examined whether economic freedom and growth are correlated with these other measures. We came to a joyous conclusion: The freer a nation is, the richer and healthier its population.

In a Cato Institute study published annually, Professors James Gwartney, Robert Lawson, and Walter Block rank eighty nations on economic freedom and then assign a grade, from A for the most free to F for the least free.[23] The per capita income of the freest nations is $18,000. The average per capita income of the least free nations is about ten times lower, or $1,700. As Adam Smith both understood and predicted two hundred years ago, market-based economic policies, or what he called "the freedom to truck, barter, and exchange," are powerful engines for economic growth.[24] How do those "A" nations fare on other measures of well-being?

The best single measure of health in a society is life expectancy. Life expectancy captures within it all sorts of other trends of health improvement: infant mortality, disease rates, quality of medical care for the population, nutrition, and so on. As Figure 9-2 shows, people living in the free nations have substantially longer life spans (almost thirty years longer) than the citizens of nations that impose restrictions on individual freedom.[25] There is further confirmation of this relationship when we examine what happened in nations that were divided into free and unfree pairs in the second half of the twentieth century. South Korea today has much longer life expectancy than North Korea. Taiwan has longer life expectancy than China (though China is rapidly catching up). By the time the Berlin Wall came down, West Germans had achieved five-years-longer life expectancies than East Germans.[26]

Fortunately, the economically freest people are not just overwhelmingly the richest, they also lead the longest lives and are thus the healthiest. For those, like us, who believe that human freedom is an unequivocal good, and that poverty is bad, it is heartening to know that these forces overpoweringly work together, mutually reinforcing each other and improving the human condition.

It is an extraordinary thing. In all of Europe, the man who was most responsible for ridding the continent of the oppression of communism and told Mr. Gorbachev in Berlin to "tear down this wall" was Ronald Reagan. But there are only two statues of Reagan in all of Euroland: one in Budapest, which was financed by an American, and most recently a second, unveiled on July 4, 2007, in Warsaw, Poland.[27] That's gratitude for you.

Perhaps the residents of Euroland now have another reason to thank Reagan. It has been the application of Reaganomics that is bringing many areas of Europe out of the economic land of the living dead. Not only did the wall of communism come down, but the walls of high tax rates that were ruining Europe are now being jackhammered, too.

And it is here that we come to the sad irony of this story. For twenty-five years the Reagan economics model has created so much wealth and prosperity in the United States that the rest of the world is now emulating it. But now all of the talk in Washington is of higher income taxes, capital gains taxes, dividend taxes, payroll taxes, energy taxes, and hedge fund taxes.

The Left growls that supply-side tax-cutting policies around the world are a mere ploy to enrich the already super-rich and to force a "race to the bottom" where the world's poorest get an even smaller slice of the pie. That is exactly the wrong interpretation of what is happening in these supply-side nations.

Thanks to globalization, trade, and lower income taxes, the global growth rate from 2002 to 2007 rose by 6% annually, the highest rate ever recorded. The 2008 report by the United Nations finds that beginning in 1985 and projected to 2015, the global poverty rate will have fallen in half. That's more than 600 million people (more than were killed during World Wars I and II combined) who will be pushed out of a miserable, destitute existence.[28] If the United Nations is right, this is the greatest human triumph in history. The report reveals that much of the poverty reduction has happened in two nations, China and India, which have moved toward open markets, lower taxes, and capitalism. It's all spectacular news if we want to lift people out of deprivation and poverty.

The worry here is that America's twenty-five-year comparative advantage in the global economy of having nearly the lowest tax rates in the industrialized world is being voluntarily surrendered.[29]

Yikes. This is happening thanks to the tomfoolery of our own politicians, who have deluded themselves into thinking that tax rates can be raised without adverse consequences at the very moment that the Russians, Swedes, Poles, Chinese, Germans, and even the French realize how much they stand to benefit from cutting their tax rates. If that trend continues, this story won't have a happy ending for America.

10

How to Create a
Bull Market:

The Capital Gains Tax

Validates the Laffer Curve

The tax on capital gains directly affects investment decisions, the mobility and flow of risk capital . . . the ease or difficulty experienced by new ventures in obtaining capital, and thereby the strength and potential for growth in the economy.[1]
—President John F. Kennedy, 1963

You're looking at a poor man who thinks the capital gains tax [cut] is the best thing that could happen to this country, because that's when the work will come back. People say capital gains are for the rich, but I've never been hired by a poor man.
—New Jersey painting contractor,
1994, quoted in *Washington Post*

Thirty years ago Congress did something that would seem almost unheard of in these days of partisan hand-to-hand combat: It passed a bipartisan tax reduction bill designed to grow the economy. Many political observers believe that this capital gains tax cut was the first official act of the supply-side revolution in Washington, predating by three years the famous Reagan tax cut of 1981.

A capital gains tax is the levy applied to the appreciated value of an asset when it is sold, such as stock, a family business, a home, a ranch, or a farm. Throughout most of the 1970s the capital gains tax reached 49 percent, and an increasing chorus of economists saw the policy as economically self-defeating, as it reduced capital investment. One of the people convinced of this was the sponsor of that 1978 law, Representative William Steiger, a thirty-nine-year-old Republican from Wisconsin who argued that the capital gains tax in combination with the ratcheting rates of inflation in the 1970s (capital gains have never been indexed for inflation) were dramatically depressing stocks and business activity.

The *Wall Street Journal* editorial page elevated this tax act, which Robert Bartley dubbed "Stupendous Steiger," into a crusade and a rallying cry for the pro-growth counterassault against the policies of stagflation in the 1970s.[2] Jude Wanniski of the *Journal* declared that "the Steiger amendment is not one tax provision among many, but the cutting edge of an important intellectual and financial breakthrough." And indeed he was right. The Steiger amendment passed and the capital gains rate was cut from 35 percent to 28 percent.[3] This was the first major pro-growth tax rate cut to pass Congress since the Kennedy tax cuts of the early 1960s.

It was not to be the last.

Thanks to a series of later reductions in 1981, 1997, and 2003 (the tax was raised in 1986), the capital gains tax has fallen from 49 to 15 percent. These tax cuts stimulated the investment of incubator funding for a generation of new businesses. These dollars are often invested by venture capital funds or so-called "angel investors"—those who put the first at-risk capital into new entrepreneurial business startups. These financing sources provided the indispensable first round of funding for the cascade of what eventually became highly successful American companies in the 1980s and 1990s, ranging from Microsoft to Wal-Mart to Google. But these investors also supply the early stage funds that are the life-givers to thousands of startup businesses and mom and pop stores across the country that are the daily pulse of our economy. These early-stage investors, it turns out, back lots of firms and entrepreneurs, many of whom never earn a penny of profit. Their willingness to put their money at high risk is sensitive to the rate of capital gains tax that must be paid when they successfully back a winner.

As we will show in this chapter, the capital gains tax cut is not just vital for financing the launch and growth of new businesses, but is the one tax in the federal tax code that most consistently validates the Laffer Curve. For the past forty years, every time the capital gains tax rate has been lowered, revenues have increased; every time the capital gains tax rate has been raised, the government has forfeited revenue.[4]

But the politics of the issue have become steeped in controversy over the past decade. In the early 1960s under JFK, and then in 1978 with the passage of the Steiger amendment, lowering the capital gains tax rate was regarded as sound economics and a growth enhancer by members of both parties and most economists. But in recent times the Left has continually denied any benefits of lower capital gains taxes and argued that cutting the tax on the sale of assets only helps the yacht-owner class.

This has brought us to an economics crossroads. Today Senator Barack Obama proposes to enact the largest capital gains tax increase in nearly forty years, with the rate rising from 15 percent to as high as 28 percent in 2009. This would be a double dose of cyanide for the economy, because it would slow economic growth *and* it will likely lose revenue for the Treasury.

Capital Equals Jobs and Higher Wages

It was, of all people, Jesse Jackson who once remarked that inner cities needed more capital because "without capital, capitalism is just another ism." That is one of the most eloquent statements that Jesse Jackson ever uttered on economics.

Capital is the engine of a growing free market economy. A recent study by Dale Jorgenson of Harvard discovered that almost half of the growth of the American economy between 1948 and 1980 was directly attributable to the increase in U.S. capital formation (with most of the rest a result of increases and improvements in the labor force—that is, improvements in human capital).[5]

Most people think of capital as money—the dollars invested in the stock market or in a new business. But it is wrong to think of capital as just financial assets. Capital refers also to physical investment—the plant, the factory, the forklifts, the computers, the fax machines, and other factors of production that make a business operate efficiently. A corner lemonade stand could not exist without capital—the lemons and the stand are the essential capital that make the enterprise run.

The most important source of capital in a productive economy is, of course, the human mind. Knowledge and knowhow are forms of capital. Invention is capital. Technological improvement is capital. The spirit of entrepreneurship is capital.

Capital formation is essential to generating higher incomes for American workers. We often ask students the following puzzler: Why is it that the average U.S. worker earns five to ten times more per hour than a worker in Mexico? (And if they answer, as some invariably do, because we have a higher minimum wage, they instantly get an F for the day.) The answer, of course, is that American workers are five to ten times more productive on the job than the average Mexican worker. U.S. farmers and manufacturing workers, for example, produce more than workers in other nations, which allows employers to pay them more. And what is very clear is that the physical capital Americans have to work with on the job dramatically increases their output. For example, in many areas of the world, people still dig ditches with shovels. In the United States we build ditches with mighty earth-mover machines that move more dirt in an hour than fifty workers can remove in a day.

Our friend the late Milton Friedman once told us a story of being in India in the 1960s and watching thousands of workers build a canal with shovels. Milton asked the lead engineer, Why don't you have tractors to help build this canal? The engineer replied: "You don't understand, Mr. Friedman, this canal is a jobs program to provide work for as many men as possible." Milton responded with his classic wit, "Oh, I see. I thought you were trying to build a canal. If you really want to create jobs, then by all means give these men spoons, not shovels." The point is that with shovels these men would have jobs, but they would never be productive and never be highly paid.

Between 1900 and 1998 real wages in the United States rose about sixfold. In other words, a worker in 1998 earned as much in ten minutes as a worker in 1900 earned in an hour.[6] What explains this surge in the living standards of the American worker? The short answer is capital and productivity.

Punitive taxes on capital are often advocated in the misplaced belief that the returns from capital accrue primarily to the owners of the capital, who tend to be wealthier than the average American worker or family. The capital gains tax cut is often disparaged as a tax cut for "plutocrats." But the productivity of the American labor force depends in large part on how much capital each worker has to work with. This is a point that virtually all economists agree on. For example, here is what Nobel laureate Paul Samuelson, a member of John F. Kennedy's Council of Economic Advisers, has to say about the importance of capital formation to worker well-being:

> *What happens to the wage rate when each person works*
> *with more capital goods? Because each worker has more*

capital to work with, his or her marginal product [or pro-
ductivity] rises. Therefore, the competitive real wage rises as
workers become worth more to capitalists and meet with
spirited bidding up of their market wage rates.[7]

The facts support this economic axiom that capital formation
hugely benefits American workers. Capital formation is the key
ingredient to rising wages. Over the past fifty years, 90 percent of
the fluctuation in wages is explained by the capital-to-labor ratio.
When the ratio rises, wages rise; when the ratio flattens, wages stag-
nate.[8]

Gary Robbins, a former Treasury Department economist, has
found something even more surprising about the impact of capital
accumulation. "The majority of the benefits from an increase in
the capital stock accrues to workers, not to the owners of capital.
This is because wages rise when workers have more capital."[9]

Human capital—training, education, skills, inventiveness, and
knowhow—is also critical to increasing productivity and living
standards. If workers are more skilled, they will produce more, and
thus command higher salaries. Ultimately, this is how U.S. companies and workers will retain their competitive edge against our foreign competitors.

High capital gains taxes don't hurt the rich as much as they hurt
the poor. When capital taxes are high and investment capital grows
scarce, the last areas that will receive funds from the shrinking investment pool will be inner-city neighborhoods with high crime
rates, a poorly educated workforce, and high business bankruptcy
rates.

A report by the members of the U.S. Civil Rights Commission
found that after the 1978 Steiger capital gains cut, when the top
capital gains tax was reduced from 49 percent to 28 percent, "the
number of black-owned businesses increased in a five-year period
by one-third (to 308,000 from 231,200)."[10] After the tax rate was
cut again down to 20 percent, the number then rose by an addi-

tional 38 percent (to 424,000) by 1987. The Commission noted that "expansion has slowed significantly since the capital gains tax rate was raised from 20 to 28 percent in 1986."

So let's walk through the transmission mechanism by which a lower capital gains tax helps the average worker. Consider the chain of events that can be expected when the capital gains tax is lowered:

1. The lower tax raises the expected after-tax return for investors.
2. The higher after-tax rate of return on capital helps give birth to new businesses while increasing the incentive for existing businesses to expand by increasing their long-term investments in capital—equipment, computers, new technologies, and the like. When an airline company purchases a new fleet of planes to expand its flight operations, those planes are the capital for the business.
3. Because capital is now cheaper and the rewards are higher, the cost of production falls and output rises.
4. Because workers have more capital to work with, the average worker's productivity—the amount of goods and services he or she can produce in an hour—rises. Think of how many more boxes a worker can move with a forklift than on his back.
5. Because wages are ultimately a function of productivity, the wage rate (or compensation to workers) will eventually rise.

Since everyone benefits from an increase in capital, the key economic question is: How do we get more of it? One answer is to lighten the tax on capital. That was the motivation for the 1964 and 1978 capital gains cuts, and the subsequent Reagan, Clinton, and Bush cuts.

What History Teaches Us

Over the past forty years a consistent pattern has emerged: Lower capital gains taxes mean more revenue, higher capital gains taxes mean less revenue.

Figure 10-1 summarizes the relationship between the capital gains tax rate and the amount of taxable capital gains. During the most recent periods of capital gains cuts—1981, 1997, and 2003—the capital gains revenues rose after the cut in the rate. So we ask: Why in the world would Barack Obama want to enact a tax increase that will likely yield less money for the government to spend? We can't think of a rational answer.

The government revenue forecasters are always surprised by these Laffer Curve results from capital gains tax changes. One reason is that the government econometric models fail to incorporate even modest economic growth responses from the rate cuts. (In a sense the static models assume in advance that the tax cuts won't work.) They also underestimate the incentive to sell stocks after the

Figure 10-1: **Lower Tax = More Revenues**

Capital Gains Realizations and Tax Rates

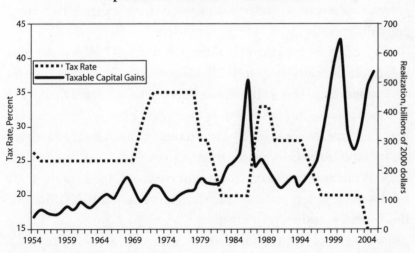

Source: Congressional Budget Office.

capital gains tax is cut, and to hold on to stock after the capital gains tax is raised. (Investors can avoid paying capital gains tax by simply not selling their stock or other asset, so there is no "gain" for government to tax.)

President Bush's Vindication

In early 2003 George Bush won a hard-fought arm-wrestling battle with Congress to lower taxes on investment. The jewel of his tax cut plan was a reduction in the dividend tax, but thanks to some fancy maneuvering by House Ways and Means Committee chairman Bill Thomas, a reduction in the capital gains tax was added to the package. We discuss in Chapter 7 the overall impact of that tax cut, especially the dividend cuts, but here we wish to focus on the latest experiment with the lower capital gains tax, which became law in May 2003.

Five years later we can look back and say that the policy has been an unambiguous success. The rate of business capital investment took a U-turn. In the two years before the tax cut, business investment spending was negative. In the three years after the tax cut average business investment increased by more than 10 percent annually.[11]

Capital gains tax revenues increased from $47 billion the year before the tax cut (2002) to $97 billion in 2006. The latest forecast for receipts in 2007 is $110 billion. This represents more than a 130 percent increase in revenues over four years from a 25 percent cut in the tax rate. As we said, few experiments in fiscal policy have vindicated the Laffer Curve more than this one.[12]

And just like clockwork (or a broken clock), these gains in tax receipts were unexpected by the Congressional Budget Office and the Joint Committee on Taxation. Figure 10-2 compares capital gains revenues with the forecast when the tax cut was proposed.

Figure 10-2: Tax Bonanza

Capital Gains Tax Revenue: Forecast Versus Actual ($BN)

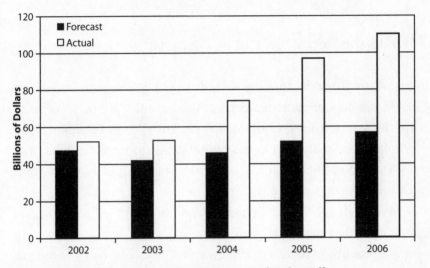

Source: U.S. Department of the Treasury; Congressional Budget Office.

Again, a lot of the increase was due to the sizzling stock market over the past three years. But a lower capital gains cut increased the after-tax return on capital and thus helped create the strong market.

There was a sizable "unlocking effect" from the lower tax rate. The amount of capital liberated for higher-return investment purposes more than doubled, from $300 billion to more than $683 billion from 2002 to 2006. This means that investors voluntarily sold stock and other assets at a much higher volume once the tax rate was reduced. This unlocking effect is highly economically efficient, reallocating capital to higher-return investments for startup ventures and new technologies.

We would add that one reason that billionaire Warren Buffett doesn't pay much income tax is that he has billions of dollars of capital gains on the stocks that he owns. If the capital gains tax were lowered, we would bet that he would sell more of his stocks and thus pay MORE federal taxes. If the tax rate is raised, he will undoubtedly pay less tax.

What's the Fairest Tax Cut of Them All?

For nearly three decades the so-called tax fairness issue has dominated the capital gains tax debate. Who are the winners and who are the losers from a capital gains tax cut? When President Bush proposed the reduction in the capital gains rate in 2003, his critics argued that about 60 percent of the tax break would go to the richest 1 percent of Americans.

Although the wealthy have the vast majority of capital gains, and thus they pay the most in capital gains taxes, millions of middle-income Americans claim capital gains on their tax returns as well. Capital gains are not reported just by wealthy individuals. In fact, 2005 Internal Revenue Service data indicate that 47 percent of all returns reporting capital gains were from households with incomes below $50,000. Seventy-nine percent of all returns were for households with incomes below $100,000 and half had incomes below $50,000.[13] Moreover, these tax return data vastly overstate the income status of those with capital gains, since these sales of assets are often irregular or even a once-in-a-lifetime event. For example, when someone sells a home or ranch, the income from the sale may be $1 million, but the seller may have never earned more than $50,000 in his working life. She appears to be a "rich" and undeserving millionaire in the income statistics because of the cash from the once-in-a-lifetime sale.

One of the most unjust features of the capital gains tax is that it taxes gains that may be attributable only to price changes, not to real gains. This raises the effective tax rate much higher than the statutory rate, since the capital gains tax, unlike most other elements of the U.S. tax code in modern times, is not indexed for inflation. The nonpartisan Tax Foundation reports that that can have major distortion effects on what an individual pays in capital gains taxes and can—indeed, often does—lead to circumstances in which investors "pay effective tax rates that substantially exceed 100 percent of their gain."[14] Princeton economist Alan Blinder, a former member of the Federal Reserve Board, noted in 1980 that, up until that time, "most capital gains were not gains of real purchasing power at all, but simply represented the maintenance of principal in an inflationary world."[15] Inflation is, fortunately, much lower now than in the 1970s, but the longer an asset is held, the more the inflation penalty accumulates. So, ironically, the fact that capital gains taxes are not indexed for inflation rewards the quick turnover of stock, rather than the patient investment Congress has always argued is more desirable.

There is one other large inequity (and inefficiency) of the capital gains tax. It represents a form of double taxation on capital formation. A government can choose to tax either the value of an asset or its yield, but it should not tax both. Take, for example, the capital gains tax paid on a pharmaceutical stock. The value of that stock is based on the discounted present value of all of the future proceeds of the company. If the company is expected to earn $100,000 a year for the next twenty years, the sales price of the stock will reflect those returns. The "gain" that the seller realizes from the sale of the stock will reflect those future returns, and thus the seller will pay capital gains tax on the expected future stream of income. But the company's future $100,000 annual returns will also be taxed when they are earned. So the $100,000 in profits is taxed twice—when the owners sell their shares of stock and when the company actually earns the income. That is why many tax analysts argue that the most equitable and economically optimal rate of tax on capital gains is zero, although Art Laffer takes this a step further and argues that the most economically efficient capital gains tax rate would be negative. We'll gladly settle for zero, though.

Ending Capital Punishment

How does the capital gains cut help U.S. competitiveness in global markets? One answer is that the lower capital gains tax helps infant companies get their initial infusion of capital to get off the ground. Studies from the capital gains cuts in the 1970s, 1980s, and 1990s show that venture capital funding increases in reverse direction to the capital gains tax rate. The lower the rate, the more risk capital to entrepreneurs. This is why the Venture Capital Association says that the low capital gains tax is "one of the top issues for our industry." If we want America to spawn the next generation of Comcasts, Targets, and Dell Computers, we had better keep this tax rate as low as possible.

This argument is all the more salient when we consider what is happening with capital gains taxes in the nations we compete with. The rates are falling like timber. Today, the United States, even if we retain the 2003 rate of 15 percent, still has a higher capital gains tax than many industrial nations. Many of America's principal trading partners have lower rates on capital gains than the United States. In fact, some of our major international competitors—including Germany and Switzerland—impose no tax on long-term capital gains at all. Australia and the United Kingdom have higher capital gains tax rates, but because both those nations allow for indexing of the base, the effective tax rate may still be lower than the U.S. tax rate.

The circumstantial evidence suggests that political uncertainty about where the capital gains tax is headed may now be hurting the stock market and reducing the value of U.S. assets. The fall of the dollar hasn't helped either. After 2010 the capital gains tax is scheduled to go back up to 20 percent. The *Wall Street Journal* reports that investors are already beginning to sell stocks and other assets in anticipation of the higher tax rate in 2011.[16]

In our opinion it is critical not only that Congress extend the life of the tax cuts by making them permanent, but that it do so sooner rather than later, to restore global confidence in U.S. fiscal policy and financial markets. We can't think of anything more directly harmful to the stock market than to raise the capital gains tax, and we only hope that America's 80 million shareholders/voters are paying close attention to what the politicians are promising on this critical issue.

11

THROW MOMMA
FROM THE TRAIN:
THE UNFAIR ESTATE TAX

I think it's so irritating that once I die, 55 percent of my money goes to the United States government . . . You know why it's so irritating? Because you already paid nearly 50 percent when the money was earned.[1]

—OPRAH WINFREY, 1997

You ought to be able to leave your land and the bulk of your fortunes to your children and not the government.[2]

—HILLARY CLINTON, 2000

A DEATH TAX TRAGEDY IS COMING IN 2010

In 2001, Congress concurred with Oprah and Hillary and re-pealed the estate tax. But it was one of the most bizarre tax reduction plans in U.S. history. At that time, the death tax applied to all estates of more than $1 million in net assets. The rate of tax on estates reached as high as 55 percent—meaning the federal government could lay claim to more than half of a person's lifetime savings at the time of his or her death. Since the estate tax was originally enacted in 1916 at rates ranging from 1 to 10 percent, the top death tax rate has increased 500 percent and the lowest rate by more than 1,000 percent.

The case for repeal of the death tax is fairly straightforward: This punitive tax raises very little revenue for the federal government, yet it does significant harm to the economy, imposes very high compliance costs, and fails to achieve its objective of curtailing the transmission of wealth from one generation to the next. It is arguably the most counterproductive tax in the entire internal revenue code. It also causes the misallocation of tens of billions of dollars a year away from the highest wealth-producing investments into entirely unproductive tax shelters.

Because of arcane budget rules in Washington, back in 2001 the estate tax could be cut only for ten years, not permanently repealed. So what passed was a contorted mess. The estate tax falls to 45 percent in 2009 and then in 2010 it is eliminated. And then in 2011 the tax comes back from the dead and is resurrected at the old 55 percent rate. This is going to cause nightmares for those people who have medium to large estates to pass on. If the heir dies on December 31, 2009, a 45 percent estate tax is applied. If the heir dies on January 1, 2010, there is no estate tax whatsoever; but if the death certificate reads January 1, 2011, the 55 percent rate is applied. This is a tax system that only Dr. Kevorkian could love.[3] With millions of dollars at stake, tax advisers are already trying to work out plans to time deaths to coincide with the zero death tax. That's why we call this the "Throw Momma from the Train death tax repeal bill."

Back in 2007 when former first lady Lady Bird Johnson died at the age of ninety-four, her daughter joked at the funeral that "Mom wanted to last until 2010 so she wouldn't have to pay the estate tax."[4] It was a funny moment on a sad occasion, but this is no laughing matter. We could have sons and daughters and grandkids keeping Grandma on life-support systems and living like a vegetable through the end of 2009 to avoid the death tax. We can almost hear them at the nursing home in December 2009: "Come on, Grandma, you can do it. Hold on for just a few more days."

When Steve Moore noted this problem at a speech to a retirement community in Florida, a woman came up to him afterward and said: "What you say about the death tax is absolutely true. My sister and I have decided that if our mother, who is ninety-six years old, dies before 2010, we will put her on ice, so the IRS does not take half her lifetime savings."

But for an even more macabre scene, think of what it will be like at the end of 2010. You could have kids and grandkids disconnecting Grandpa from life-support systems in cases in which there are millions of dollars at stake. You could have elderly people taking the Kevorkian route to elude the grim reaper of the IRS. Retirement planning magazines are already advising the elderly on their options for timing their death.

Studies have documented that when a lot of estate money is at stake, people do exactly that: time their death to minimize their tax bill. In Sweden death rates were down 9% the day before the estate tax was scheduled to fall.[5]

If you think this is madness, we couldn't agree more. The estate tax is the most immoral levy in our tax system. It is immoral because it rewards bad behavior while encouraging licentiousness and recklessness.

Here's an example: Take two people in their late sixties, Mr. Spendthrift and Mr. Frugal. Spendthrift lives a life of ostentatious luxury in retirement. He buys Ferraris and fur coats. Dines on lobster and the most expensive caviar every night. He lights up his $300 Cuban cigars with fifty-dollar bills. He takes baths in tubs full of Dom Perignon champagne. He has a beautiful young woman on each arm accompanying him everywhere he goes and spoils them rotten with his credit card. He takes $250,000 cruises reserved for just himself, a large crew, and his lady friends. He has a penthouse apartment in every major city that he travels to. He feeds his pet

Labrador retriever New York strip steak every night. And he times his death just right so that he kicks the bucket precisely at the time that he has lavishly spent his last dollar. Well done. For all this selfish behavior he is rewarded by Congress. His estate tax bill from the IRS is zero. His gold-plated lifestyle is the greatest tax dodge in history. It's all legal, in fact encouraged.

Now his friend Mr. Frugal lives life differently. He reinvests some of his assets in the family company that his two sons now operate. He works with them to build up the client base, and as the company expands it hires two hundred new workers. He lives in the same home that he bought thirty years ago when his wealth was one-one-hundredth of what it is now. He invests some of his millions in some of his friends' startup businesses to provide needed seed capital. As the family business grows and a few of his venture capital investments pay off, his fortune doubles. He sets some money away for his kids, his most cherished assets of all. Because of his unassuming lifestyle, most people have no idea how much money he has earned through his sweat equity, his savings, and his shrewd investing. So when Mr. Frugal dies he has $40 million to his name, and his reward for helping grow the economy, employing scores of workers, and acting responsibly is a $15 million bill from the IRS handed to his kids at the funeral. But they don't have anywhere near that kind of cash because most of the value is tied up in the family business. So they sell to someone like Warren Buffett, and Mr. Frugal's dream of building a family legacy that could be carried on for several generations is squashed by the tax collectors.

Now you can see why we regard the death tax as immoral and anti-American. Mr. Frugal has clearly lived what most people would view as a more virtuous lifestyle than Mr. Spendthrift, but Frugal is clobbered with a hefty estate tax at death, while Spendthrift pays not a penny of tax. Very few Americans would regard this situation as just or fair.

The Left has concocted a fairy tale that Americans don't have to sell their businesses or farms to pay the death tax, but the reality is it happens all the time. The American Family Business Institute has documented many cases in which family businesses have been destroyed by this tax. At the time of this writing, the longtime owners of the Pittsburgh Steelers, one of the most storied franchises in NFL history, had to sell the team because of the death tax. Some of the death tax victims have testified before Congress with heartbreaking stories of the family legacy sold at auction at death to pay the taxes.[6] At a recent congressional hearing, billionaire Warren Buffett endorsed a higher death tax. But sitting next to him on the panel was a small business owner with a tiny fraction of the wealth that Buffett has. When the small businessman was asked about what would happen if the estate tax were raised back up again, he said his family would have to sell the business and then he pointed to Mr. Buffett and said: "Probably to someone like him." Moreover, a best-selling finance book several years ago, entitled *Die Broke,* described how wealthy people could plan to spend down their assets to zero by the time of their death—in part to cheat the taxman.[7]

The real shame here is that the costs of this oppressive levy are imposed on the economy with virtually no offsetting benefit.

The death tax raises almost no money.

Over the past forty years, the death tax has consistently raised only between 1 and 2 percent of total federal revenues. In 2005 the death tax raised roughly $40 billion in tax revenues out of just under $3 trillion in total federal tax receipts, or less than 1.5 percent of all collections. Because the death tax slows economic growth and thus reduces other tax receipts, the actual net revenue raised by the federal government is well below 1 percent of total receipts. In a 1995 study on the death tax, economist Dick Wagner of George Mason University calculated that the death tax may actually cost the federal government more money than it raises.[8]

Another inequity of the death tax is that the money in estates that is taxed has almost all been taxed already when it was earned. This is Oprah's sensible objection to this tax. She pays nearly 50 percent federal, state, and local income tax on her money when she earns it, but then she has to pay up to 55 percent when she goes to her grave on the 50 percent that was not taxed away already.

For every dollar that she is able to pass to her loved ones, the government keeps up to three dollars. Now some of Mr. Frugal's money may never have been taxed if it was accumulated capital gains. But under the estate tax repeal, capital gains are taxed at 15 percent either at the time of death or at the time of the eventual sale of the stock or business.

The estate tax imposes huge compliance costs that make collection of this tax extremely economically inefficient. One study published in the *Seton Hall Law Review* indicated that in 1992 the compliance costs were more than half the total amount raised by the tax.[9]

More recently, the National Federation of Independent Business estimated that the government and individuals collectively spend sixty-five cents on enforcement, compliance, and legal bills for every dollar the government eventually collects.[10] It is important to note that less than half of the estates that must go through the burdensome process of complying with the paperwork and reporting requirements of the tax actually pay even a nickel of the tax. These small estates sometimes are forced to spend tens of thousands of dollars to comply with regulations for a tax that they don't even owe. No wonder the legions of estate lawyers and tax accountants love this tax.

Many ardent defenders of the death tax in Washington argue that the costs of the death tax are worth absorbing because this tax helps break up huge hoards of wealth in America that are amassed by people whose fortunes were accumulated by birthright, rather than by hard work or individual initiative. But research by Professor Edward McCaffery of USC Law School argues that "if breaking up large concentrations of wealth is the intention of the death tax, then it is a miserable failure."[11] The wealthiest families tend to invest heavily in estate tax planning, which innoculates them against paying this tax at all. Two of America's wealthiest families, the Kennedys and the Rockefellers, for example, have paid very little estate tax over the past several generations, thanks to careful and clever estate planning by lawyers and accountants. Statistics on who pays the death tax bear this out: The billion-dollar-plus mega-estates have for years and years found crafty ways to avoid the tax. The medium-sized estates tend to be the most hobbled by the tax. Almost half of all estates that pay the tax have a net worth of less than $10 million.[12]

Taxes Everlasting

The Left just doesn't understand why a tax that hits mostly the richest 5 percent of families is so loathed by the middle class. The fact that bus drivers and schoolteachers and construction workers and legal secretaries are opposed to imposing a death tax puzzles income redistributors, because this is a tax that will never directly hit most families. They now contemptuously call the estate tax repeal the Paris Hilton tax relief act. We're not here to defend Paris, but what liberals don't get is that most Americans think and hope that someday they will be rich themselves, and they are offended at the idea that the government could take half of what they have built and saved over a lifetime.

Before the Bush tax cut, the United States had the second-highest death tax in the world.[13] In recent years Canada and Australia have repealed their estate taxes. Remarkably, just three years ago Sweden and Russia abolished their death taxes. Now that should give us pause. In both cases, the Swedes, who are among the most socialistic people on the globe, and the Russians, who are among the most authoritarian people in the world, explained that they took this action because they had come to believe that the estate tax is economically counterproductive.

We've been saying that very thing for years, and we're glad that at least the socialists and former communists are listening. When the Swedes and Russians are moving in a more aggressive pro-growth, free market direction than the United States Congress, we've got a big problem in Washington. And people wonder why we've turned bearish.

12

PROTECTIONISM
THEN AND NOW:

THE SMOOT-HAWLEY TARIFF ACT

OF 1930

Today Americans are about as nervous about the economy as a cat straddling the ledge of a swimming pool. In March 2008 a USA Today/Gallup poll captured the extent of voters' fears and anxieties about the direction of the country. It found that three of four voters think we are headed for a recession. But here was the most revealing question:

> How likely do you think it is that the United States will be in an economic depression within the next two years—very likely, somewhat likely, not too likely, or not at all likely?

Figure 12-1 shows how voters answered that question.

When six in ten voters believe we might be headed for a depression, that's about as coyote ugly as it gets. It means Americans are intensely worried about losing their jobs and the indignity of standing in the unemployment lines. But it's safe to say that most Americans today have no idea how bad a depression is—and how

Figure 12-1

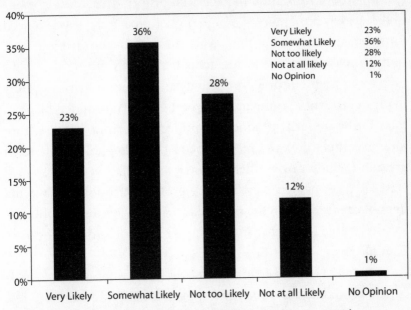

Source: Gallup Poll, as reported in USA Today/Gallup, March 14–16, 2008.[1]

badly an economy can falter. During the decade of the Great Depression, U.S. output and incomes plummeted by half.

So let us review what a depression is really like and the policies that caused the last one—policy mistakes that sent America into a twelve-year spiral of decline. The biggest policy blunder of all was trade protectionism—a failed economic strategy that still has a surprisingly large number of supporters in Congress and on the presidential campaign trail.

Smoot-Hawley: The Killer Tariff

The name of this bill may have a familiar ring but might not immediately register even among well-informed Americans. We know it had something to do with the Great Depression, but we aren't quite sure what that was. Time for a quick refresher.

THE END OF PROSPERITY

The Smoot-Hawley Tariff Act of 1930 is among the most notorious pieces of legislation in American history. The "roaring twenties" is widely remembered as a period of prosperity. It was indeed for most Americans, but this wasn't the case for the farming community. Average farm income actually declined during the 1920s even though agricultural productivity and output were rising. During his presidential campaign, Herbert Hoover promoted plans to raise tariffs on farm products to protect American farmers from foreign competition. In time, this plank of the Republican platform grew to include many other industries as well. Today the Democrats are more associated with trade protectionist policies than the Republicans are, but in the late 1920 and the 1930s the Republicans led the charge for higher import tariffs.[2] Smoot and Hawley were Republicans.

In the 1928 election, Herbert Hoover handily defeated the Democratic candidate, New York governor Al Smith, riding on the crest of prosperity from the Harding and Coolidge years. Upon taking office in March 1929, Hoover called a special session of Congress for the purpose of raising duties on agricultural products. It soon became clear, however, that congressional leaders were considering much more sweeping tariffs than those on agriculture. Northeasterners demanded tariffs on manufactured goods.

The bill was quickly passed in the House but ran into trouble in the Senate. The special session ended in late 1929 without a bill's being passed. That didn't stop other nations from preemptively retaliating against the United States with their own high tariffs. Then the world witnessed the stock market crash of October 1929. See Figure 12-2. When Congress reconvened in spring 1930, the Great Depression was under way. It was the onset of the Great Depression that changed some minds in Congress, which in turn allowed the bill to pass in June 1930. Before the bill was signed, President Hoover received a petition signed by more than one thousand economists warning him of the dire consequences of the bill and urging him not to sign it. The economics profession was then as it

Figure 12-2: Crash of 1929

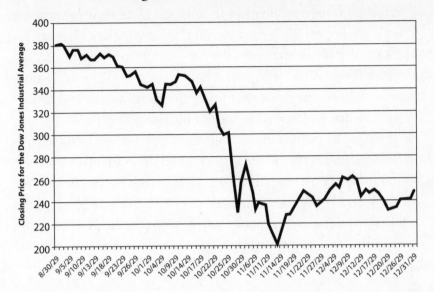

is now virtually unanimous in its support of free trade. Hoover did indeed have some reservations about the bill, worrying that its wide-ranging tariffs might provoke more retaliation from America's trading partners. But he put his reservations aside, signed the bill, and one of the worst pieces of legislation became law on June 17, 1930. The act raised tariffs on more than twenty thousand imported goods and imposed an effective tax rate of 60 percent on more than three thousand products and materials imported into the United States. As expected, many countries retaliated, and American imports and exports plunged.

Did It Cause the Great Depression?

The debate about whether the Smoot-Hawley Act caused the Great Depression of the thirties continues to this day. The majority of economists and historians believe that it not only contributed importantly to the Great Depression, it also triggered the stock market crash of October 1929.[3] Even though the bill was not signed into law until June 1930, investors anticipated its eventual passage. Economist Robert Shiller points out that on Monday, October 28, 1929, the day before the crash, the *New York Times* ran a front-page story on the possible passage of Smoot-Hawley.[4] Many economists believe this was the straw that broke the camel's back and caused Black Tuesday, which was the start of the Great Depression.

Perhaps the most complete and thorough analysis of the effects of Smoot-Hawley on the stock market and the crash of 1929 can be found in our late friend Jude Wanniski's classic book, *The Way the World Works*. Wanniski chronicles the day-by-day progress of the bill that would become Smoot-Hawley as well as the press reaction, foreign reaction, and the stock market gyrations that accompanied the news. It reads like a thriller novel.[5]

> *On Tuesday, October 29 [the day of the Great Crash], all the reports coming out of Washington seemed to be aimed at assuring the stock market that the tariff bill would not be killed, that it would be pushed through somehow, and this new coalition of Republicans and Democrats would see to it.*

Why did trade protectionism unleash a Great Depression? Because protectionism meant that companies lost a huge share of their overseas markets and U.S. workers lost the benefits of low-cost imports, so the effect of the tariffs was to lower their real incomes. Within two years of the bill's passage, twenty-five countries had retaliated with protective measures of their own. In 1929, the United States GDP was $104 billion (nominal—not inflation adjusted), and the country exported $5.2 billion in goods. By 1932, GDP had tumbled to $68 billion, and exports had tumbled to $1.6 billion.

Whether one believes that Smoot-Hawley caused the Great Depression or not, what is inarguable is that it did not create jobs or raise incomes in America by keeping out imports. Those who today support tariffs against China and Japan and other nations that sell us goods and services, as a way to save America's manufacturing jobs, should take a close look at what happened after the Smoot-Hawley bill was passed. The United States didn't preserve jobs, it shed millions of them. The unemployment rate by 1933 soared to 25.1 percent—four to five times higher than it is today.[6] Trade protectionism clearly was not a blessing for workers or American industry. Recently, Smoot and Hawley[7] were declared "the most depressing couple in U.S. history." They would have our vote for that ignominious distinction.

The Poverty of Closed Borders

Now let's fast-forward back to 2008. Trade protectionism has many proponents among voters and the politicians. Protectionism comes in many forms: saving American jobs, immigration control, equal treatment for workers, "fair trade" practices, reducing the "trade deficit," and a bunch of other populist catchphrases.

We find this a remarkably wrong-headed mentality. America must "compete, not retreat,"[8] as President Bill Clinton once put it. And America has been competing, and winning. Over the past twenty-five to thirty years the United States and the world have been on a bipartisan free trade binge that has helped us drive our unemployment rate down and has helped create some 40 million new jobs on these shores. The more closed economies in Europe have seen only a fraction the number of new jobs the United States, has. Import duties per dollar of imports are at a fifty-year low, and the flow of goods and services across borders has soared.[9] The U.S. Trade Representative Office tells us that about one of four new jobs in America is a result of international trade.

How then is it possible that free trade has come to be seen as a force of evil, not good?

A Tale of Two States

In early 2008, Democratic primaries occurred on the same day in two very different states, Ohio and Texas. During that campaign, Barack Obama and Hillary Clinton raced around Ohio spreading economic doom and gloom, American declinism, and worst of all, phony prescriptions like trade protectionism and higher taxes on the rich to bring back jobs. At a General Motors plant in Lordstown, Ohio, Senator Clinton told workers they are living through a financial "perfect storm" with declining paychecks and higher prices for everything from gas, to milk, to college tuition.[10] A few days later, Mr. Obama told a crowd at a Youngstown factory that Ohioans have "watched job after job after job disappear because of bad trade deals like NAFTA" that "don't put food on the table."[11]

Yes, times are tough in the rust-belt state of Ohio. Two hundred thousand manufacturing jobs have been lost there, plants are closing, home foreclosures are at record levels, and family incomes are $4,000 lower now than at the start of the decade. But that slide is anything but indicative of the economies of most other states. No state's economic conditions are more polar opposite to Ohio's than those of another big state, Texas. The Texas economy has boomed since 2004, with nearly twice the job creation and industrial production growth rates of the rest of the nation.[12] The explanation for the Lone Star State's success and Ohio's misfortunes reveals why it is so critical that the U.S. embrace trade and globalization.

Texas's growth spurt gives the lie to the claim that free trade deals cost America jobs. The anti-NAFTA rhetoric by Senators Obama and Clinton doesn't play well in places like El Paso, Austin, and Houston, which have become gateway cities for trade and commerce with Central America and have flourished since NAFTA was signed into law in 1993.

Mr. Obama's claim that 1 million jobs have been lost due to trade deals is laughable in Texas, the state most heavily affected by NAFTA. Texas has *gained* thirty-six thousand manufacturing jobs since 2004, and it has ranked as the nation's top exporting state for six years in a row, with $168 billion of exports in 2007, which translates into hundreds of thousands of jobs.[13] Ohio and Michigan are bleeding auto jobs—but many of these "runaway plants" are not fleeing to China or Mexico, but rather to more business-friendly Texas. GM, for example, just recently announced it is opening a new plant to build hybrids. Guess where? Arlington, Texas.

Ohio governor Ted Strickland whined that Ohio's miseries are a result of Bush's failed national economic policies.[14] Think again. It's true that the U.S. economy has slowed to a crawl in recent months, but Ohio's decade-long economic wounds are mostly self-inflicted.

This is a state that decries plant closings even as it imposes the third-highest corporate income tax rate in the country (10.5 percent). The joke is that Ohio lays out the red carpet for companies—but when they leave, not when they come.

Meanwhile, Texas is one of the world's largest insourcers of jobs. In 2006 the state *exported* $5.5 billion worth of cars and trucks to Mexico and $2.4 billion worth to Canada. Nearly one thousand new plants have been built in Texas since 2005, including facilities owned by such industry giants as Microsoft, Samsung, and Fujitsu. Foreign-owned companies supplied the state with 345,000 jobs. No wonder Texans don't fear globalism.

The economic populist chorus of class warfare and trade protectionism may play to voters in depressed Ohio, but it falls flat in Texas. After one of Hillary Clinton's diatribes against trade deals, a Clinton spokesman was forced to concede, "I think people in Texas . . . would have a different view of NAFTA than folks (*who got fired*) in Ohio would."[15] Yeah, no kidding.

So we have here two different economic models: one that works, another that is putting people by the thousands in the unemployment lines. The challenge for our national economy to remain prosperous over the next decade is to make America more like Texas and less like Ohio.

The South Carolina Resurgence

During the presidential campaign Barack Obama ran a radio ad that said: "NAFTA . . . has cost South Carolina thousands of jobs. It's what's wrong with politics today." [16]

Oh, really? South Carolina happens to be an excellent example of how dynamic economies more than replace "outsourced" jobs with "insourced" ones. Many people view South Carolina as a state in economic decline due to imports. Textiles, which a hundred years ago were a growing staple of the state's economy ("outsourced" from New England in the late nineteenth century), are under severe pressure from developing countries using "cheap labor" and "sub–Western civilization labor standards." American textile workers, liberal politicians say, are losing their good-paying jobs and have few alternatives. Going from a false premise to an inappropriate conclusion, they conclude that the only way to stem this unreasonable loss of jobs is to keep out the cheap textiles from Central America, India, China, and other suspect countries.

The reality is that South Carolina has come a long way from textiles. The lower-wage textile positions are being replaced by higher-paying, higher-tech production jobs. South Carolina is home to the domestic plants of foreign companies that offer opportunities in expanding industries.[17] For example, China's largest appliance and electronics manufacturer (Haier) opened a plant in Camden, South Carolina, that makes refrigerators and other appliances for the U.S. market. BMW has invested $3.5 billion in its South Carolina operations and employs more than 5,400 workers. In April 2008, BMW announced it will spend $750 million to expand its South Carolina production plant during the next three years and create 500 new jobs. And if you happen to see a BMW X5 SUV or a Z4 sports coupe, you don't have to guess if it was made in Germany or somewhere else—they are all manufactured in South Carolina. Michelin produces tires, several companies produce auto parts, one produces fire trucks, and another produces electronic and mechanical guiding devices.[18] Those who believe manufacturing is disappearing in America should travel down to the heart of Dixie, South Carolina.

The Dreaded Trade Deficit

Politicians from Democrat Barack Obama to independent Ross Perot (remember, he was the one who talked about "that giant sucking sound" of jobs leaving the U.S.) to Republicans Pat Buchanan and Mike Huckabee have argued that the trade deficit is the biggest problem with our international trade situation today. One economist, Peter Morice of the University of Maryland, has calculated that "were the U.S. trade deficit cut in half, GDP would increase by nearly $300 billion, or about $2,000 for every worker in America." The word "deficit" sounds troublesome, but the reality is that the United States has run a trade "deficit" for most of the past twenty years because we have also run a capital surplus. We also ran a trade deficit throughout much of the nineteenth century. As the United States became an attractive place to invest, foreigners sold us more goods than we sold them, and then they used those extra dollars to invest in plants and equipment and factories in the United States. (Remember all those foreign-owned plants in South Carolina and Texas.)

But still the politicians say: We must eliminate our trade deficit. Well, the best way to do that is to slow the economy and slide into the ditch of a recession. Because there is an amazing relationship between jobs and the trade deficit that may shock the reader. When the trade deficit goes *up*, the unemployment rate goes *down*. And when the trade deficit goes *down*, the unemployment rate goes *up* (see Figure 12-3).

So again we find that trade protectionism tends not to create jobs, but to destroy them. It is no accident that as the U.S. economy is now slowing down in 2008, the trade deficit has fallen.

Figure 12-3: **When the Trade Deficit Falls, Unemployment Rises**

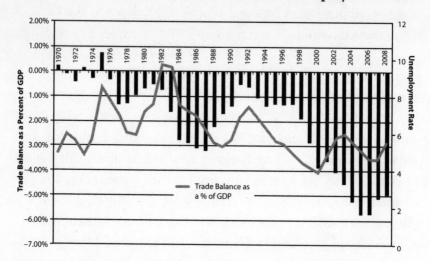

Source: Unemployment rate from the Bureau of Labor Statistics; Trade Balance Data from the Bureau of Economic Analysis, Table 1, International Transactions.

The Outsourcing Boogeyman

A new word has entered our vocabulary: "outsourcing." It has come to mean companies closing plants in the U.S. and moving their operations abroad. One prominent example of outsourcing is call centers moving from America to India or some other developing country. These changes have given the media new sources for human interest stories about the sad plight of displaced workers. Media personalities such as Lou Dobbs have assumed the mantle of "Defender of American Jobs," exploiting these continuing images to oppose free trade and immigration and to create loyal viewers who share that perspective. Television images of people suffering, of course, become red meat for politicians. Opposition to "outsourcing" and "harmful trade" becomes a major plank in politicians' platforms, as it provides an excellent opportunity to play on the vulnerabilities and fears of the American public. No one wants to see his job outsourced to another nation, but international trade has not cost American jobs on balance.

A favorite story illustrates some of the complexity and irony. A young woman who worked for one of us a few years ago as the "outsourcing" issue was developing described how her mother was becoming more and more worked up over the issue. The mother would religiously watch Lou Dobbs and attend worker meetings to discuss what to do about this looming threat. When asked one day what company her mother worked for, the young woman replied "Honda." The woman had not even considered that without free trade her job would not even exist.

Just as the disappearance of older jobs is called "outsourcing," many have taken to calling the other side of the equation "insourcing," the creation of jobs from foreign-owned businesses opening in the United States, and domestic businesses expanding to foreign markets. Prominent examples of insourcing abound. Honda, Toyota, Nissan, and Hyundai have established sizable production facilities in the United States. Mercedes-Benz produces its M-Class, R-Class, and GL-Class SUVs in Alabama. Citizens Bank, once a sleepy little Rhode Island bank, but now the eighth-largest bank in the United States, is owned by the Royal Bank of Scotland.

Insourcing is significant and growing rapidly. The Organization for International Investment estimates that the U.S. subsidiaries of foreign firms employ 5.4 million Americans, and 34 percent of the jobs are in manufacturing.[19] The payrolls of these subsidiaries total $307 billion, and the companies pay on average 31 percent more than all U.S. companies. In fact, based on new jobs created, the United States has been on net a massive insourcer, not outsourcer of jobs since 1980. It is Europe, with its absurd labor protections, high tax rates, generous welfare policies, and restrictive tariffs that has been outsourcing millions of jobs. We should not want to be more like Europe.

It is undeniable that some people are harmed by trade just as some are hurt by technological innovation. But people are also harmed by businesses in California that move to Texas. Protectionist solutions are counterproductive. Sound state economic policies that are pro-growth and pro-jobs combined with transitional support, through retraining, relocation aid, temporary financial relief, and similar measures, are the answer.

The simple response to the protectionists' preoccupation with outsourcing is that total jobs in the United States are *rising*, not falling, at a time when our trade deficit is huge. The protectionists might counter that manufacturing jobs are declining. That is true, but manufacturing jobs have been in steady decline since 1979, over a period of tremendous expansion in the U.S. economy. The number of manufacturing employees has fallen by almost 5.5 million since 1979, but simultaneously the real (dollar) value of manufacturing has risen, a tribute to the rising productivity of American workers.[20] Even if there were no trade, the tremendous rise in productivity would have meant that fewer manufacturing jobs would be needed, so the decline cannot be blamed on trade. The U.S. has "lost" more jobs in agriculture than manufacturing over the last fifty years, even though we are net exporters of food and net importers of manufactured items. If we wanted to create more jobs we could do so by abolishing farm tractors, but it is self-evident that this would make us poorer, not richer.

Even as manufacturing and agricultural jobs decline, total jobs grow. Over the last ten years, the number of people receiving wages and salaries in nonagricultural, private industries grew by 12.2 million.[21] Since 2000, private sector job growth has been over a million per year.

The protectionists simply overlook all the new jobs that were created while manufacturing jobs declined. Since 1979 there has been the revolution in personal computers. Besides production and sales, new opportunities appeared for programmers, system analysts, and other technicians. Myriad software companies (think Microsoft) have sprung up, employing programmers and software designers who are creating everything from sophisticated business inventory systems to improved weapons technology. Electronics are miniaturized more and more, permitting new applications from computers to medical instruments. The internet has entered most homes, requiring content companies like eBay, Google, and Yahoo. The high-definition television revolution is continuing. Cable television has permitted the rise of ESPN, HBO, CNN, and hundreds of other channels employing millions of people. New financial market instruments based on advances in financial theory continue to appear, such as futures, structured notes, options, and ETFs. More complex financial accounting creates opportunities for more sophisticated financial experts.

Yes, we have a large trade deficit. But that trade deficit translates into a *capital surplus* for the United States as foreign investors flock to investments here in America, creating jobs and prosperity and all that the additional capital implies. As we showed in Figure 12-3, when the U.S. economy is booming and creating jobs, our trade deficit goes up. When the U.S. economy goes into recession, the trade deficit goes down, and even disappears. That's because Americans buy fewer goods and services when the economy is lousy. So if Lou Dobbs really wants to end the trade deficit he should be cheering for a recession that will put Americans out of work.

Closed Minds and Closed Borders

We are concerned that Congress at some point may pass trade legislation as devastating as the Smoot-Hawley Tariff Act of 1930. We have to assume and hope that along the way some lessons have been learned and that wisdom will prevail. But the siren song of protectionist trade policies is wafting through the halls of Congress and out on the presidential campaign trail. The seductive arguments are the same false promises of saving jobs that Messrs. Smoot and Hawley made more than seventy years ago. Make no mistake about it: Those politicians on the left and on the right who are advocating protectionism and American isolationism threaten to launch a spike in the very heart of America's unique source of economic strength. Great nations with world-class workers thrive on free trade. Seemingly well-meaning attempts to raise trade barriers for worthy social and economic ends may be politically tempting, but woe to those who neither heed nor learn from the lessons of the past.

13

MANY HAPPY RETURNS:

THE FLAT TAX SOLUTION

Dear IRS: Please take me off your mailing list.
　　—SNOOPY, typing a letter, from a 1960s *Peanuts* cartoon

In this chapter we argue that the fairest (and most pro-growth) tax system is one that imposes a low flat rate tax on everyone. We can already hear our critics protesting: a flat tax hurts the poor and gives the rich a big tax break. A progressive rate tax structure, they say, will take money from the well-to-do, who can afford to pay more, and redistribute those dollars to the poor, who need the money. They want a Robin Hood–style tax system to promote justice and equity. So we thought we would begin this chapter by telling the real-world version of the Robin Hood legend as a way to explain why "stealing from the rich to give to the poor" may not be such a smart long-term economic strategy after all.

The Supply-Side Version of Robin Hood

The story begins with Robin and his band of merry men in the English town of Nottingham. They would wake up in the morning and don their light green leisure suits and go zipping off into Sherwood Forest, where they would hide among the trees, waiting for hapless travelers on the trans-forest thruway.

If a rich merchant came by—and by rich we mean a super richie (this guy didn't have a silver spoon in his mouth, he had a golden goblet down his throat)—Robin would stop him, chat with him for a few minutes, and then take everything the guy had. He'd make the guy run naked back into the forest.

But don't forget, the guy who got robbed is so rich that when he gets back to his castle he will have many other golden goblets, and lots of other jewels and wealth.

If a prosperous merchant came through the forest, one who was just rich but not super rich, Robin would take almost everything the guy had, but not quite everything. If a normal, everyday average businessman came through the forest, Robin would take just a moderate chunk of what the man had. And if a poor merchant came through the forest, one who could barely make ends meet, Robin would just take a little token from that guy.

In the vernacular of our modern-day society, Robin had a progressive stealing structure for the merchants who came through the forest.

At the end of the day, Robin and his men would take their contraband and go back into Nottingham, where they'd wander the streets. If they found someone who was down-and-out and had absolutely nothing, Robin would stop him and say, "Hi, my name's Robin Hood. I'm your local redistributionist agent and I'd just like to tell you how much I love you." And then Robin would give the destitute man a whole pile of goodies.

When Robin and his men found another person whom we'd call "working poor," with an income around $10,000 a year at about minimum wage, they would give him a smaller bundle of goodies than they gave to the guy who had nothing. And if Robin Hood found some normal, everyday average citizen walking around the streets of Nottingham, Robin would give the man a small token equivalent to our modern-day tax rebate. Robin would add, "You and your wife go out to dinner and the wine's on me."

The more a person makes, the less Robin gives him, and the less a person makes, the more he gives him. You follow the model: he stole from the rich and gave to the poor. The richer you were the more he'd steal from you, the poorer you were the more he'd give you. This is the legend of Robin Hood.

But wait. Think about what happens *next*. Imagine for a moment that you are a merchant back in the ancient days of Nottingham: *If you were rich, how long would it take you to learn not to go through the forest? If* you're smart, not long for sure.

Those merchants who couldn't afford armed guards would have to go all the way around the forest in order to trade with the neighboring villages. The route around the forest is a lot longer and full of rocks, bumps, logs, holes, etc.—it is far more costly doing commerce when you're traveling around the forest rather than going through the forest.

Those merchants who could afford armed guards (and by the way, today we call these armed guards lawyers, tax accountants, and lobbyists) would go through the forest and Robin couldn't rip them off. And those armed guards were as expensive then as they are today. So at the end of the second day, Robin Hood had no contraband whatsoever to give to the poor. All he had succeeded in doing was driving up the cost of doing business, which meant the poor had to pay higher prices and were made worse off.

So you see the tale of Robin Hood has a less happy ending. By stealing from the rich and by giving to the poor, Robin Hood made everyone, but especially the poor, worse off.

How to Fix the Tax System Once and for All

We don't believe that anyone would argue that America has a twenty-first-century, pro-growth tax system. At least we have never met such a person. In fact, the U.S. tax code fails on every count. It is not simple (a truth we all rediscover every April 15); it is not fair, according to most voters; and it does not promote a strong economy that creates jobs and wealth.

We think that one of the most important steps that our politicians could take to re-energize the U.S. economy would be to scrap the income tax and put in place a simple, pro-growth flat tax. We noted in Chapter 9 that some two dozen nations have a flat tax, and it works brilliantly in these countries, many of which are balancing their budgets and getting rich because of it.

Our favorite example is Hong Kong, which adopted a 15 percent flat tax fifty years ago and has been a glittering model of tax efficiency and sanity ever since. Hong Kong is now one of the wealthiest places on the globe, thanks in part to low tax rates and tax simplicity. There was worry when Hong Kong was given back to China that the flat tax would be swallowed up by the Chinese tax system. Just the opposite has occurred. The capitalistic impulse of the Chinese has led the mainland to move incrementally toward the Hong Kong system through tax rate reductions. Even Russia, the home of communism, now has converted to a 13 percent flat tax. Why not the United States?

Why Do Governments Impose Taxes on Citizens?

The flip answer to that question is because they can. A more thoughtful answer is that the government imposes taxes on us for three reasons.

1. Raise Revenue

The first reason we need to pay taxes is pretty obvious. The government (local, state, and federal) has the responsibility of running the country. That means paying most vitally for our national defense, but also for police and firefighters, building roads, parks, and other public facilities, funding services like the FBI and the CIA, and paying the millions of people who work for the government, from diplomats to social workers. The government also spends enormous amounts of money to provide services to the elderly, the retired, the poor, our veterans, and others. Few would argue with the need to pay taxes to fund these activities, which are designed for the collective good.

2. Redistribute Income

While most of us will agree that taxes need to be imposed to pay for public services, the Left also wants to use the tax code as a way to rob Peter and pay Paul. They want to redistribute income from the rich to the poor by taxing the rich at a higher rate than all other income earners. Why do that? To confiscate some of their wealth and perhaps use the additional revenue to help the less fortunate or the less successful. Proponents of the graduated income tax believe not only that the wealthy should be taxed at a higher rate, but that they won't really mind it, since at certain levels of income, paying more taxes won't hurt much. We even have people like Warren Buffett who say they *want* to pay more taxes.[1] (There is nothing stopping them from voluntarily paying more taxes, by the way.) Many of the current crop of presidential candidates want the rich to pay more for this very reason. Perhaps readers remember this exchange between Senator Hillary Clinton and Senator Barack Obama during the Democratic debate in Los Angeles on January 30, 2008:[2]

> **Question:** If either one of you become president, and let
> the Bush tax cuts lapse, there will be effectively tax
> increases on millions of Americans.
> **Obama:** On wealthy Americans.
> **Clinton:** That's right.

Obama: I'm not bashful about it.

Clinton: Absolutely.

Obama: I suspect a lot of this crowd—it looks like a
pretty well-dressed crowd—potentially will pay a little bit
more. I will pay a little bit more. But that investment will
pay huge dividends over the long term, and the place
where it will pay the biggest dividends is in Medicare and
Medicaid. Because if we can get a healthier population,
that is the only way over the long term that we can
actually control that spending that is going to break the
federal budget.

Clinton: It's just really important to underscore here that
we will go back to the tax rates we had before George
Bush became president. And my memory is, people did
really well during that time period. And they will keep
doing really well.

Could they be any clearer about their governing philosophy
or their intention to raise taxes on "the Wealthy?" A Democratic
president will most assuredly raise taxes and potentially lead the
nation off an economic cliff—and we're not convinced Republicans might not feel compelled to do the same.

3. Social Engineering

The tax code is also used to regulate behavior, to reward certain activities and to punish others. This is social engineering via the tax system. So we cattle-prod people with tax breaks for everything from giving money to the Boy Scouts, to buying a home, to paying for college tuition, to buying energy-efficient refrigerators and washers and dryers. And then we punish for activities we don't approve of like drinking and smoking.[3] But frequently we perversely penalize activities that we view as virtuous, through dividend taxes, estate taxes, capital gains taxes, and yes, even the income tax. We double- and triple-tax people on savings—then Congress complains Americans aren't saving enough.

We believe these multiple taxes on savings deny ownership opportunities to those with the lowest incomes. Thomas Kelly, president of the Savers and Investors League, calculates that if Americans could save just $1,000 a year tax free from the time they started working to the time they retire forty-five years later, most workers would have about $1.75 million in their nest eggs.[4] But he finds that because of multiple taxes on savings in our economy, about 60 percent of that nest egg would be wiped out. America has one of the lowest rates of savings in the world, in part because we have a perverse tax code that penalizes Americans for saving.

Why don't we just use the tax code to raise the money necessary to pay for government at the lowest possible rate, and then let individuals decide how to spend and invest their own money?

The Income Tax Monstrosity

There is a wonderful old story about W. C. Fields, who was once discovered by a young boy reading the Holy Bible. "Mr. Fields," asks the surprised kid, "what are you of all people doing reading the Bible." W. C. Fields responds: "Looking for loopholes, my boy."[5] This practice of looking for loopholes in the tax code is now a massive industry in America.

In 1980 Jimmy Carter called the income tax "a disgrace to the human race," and he was right—but as with so much in Washington, he didn't fix it.

So now we have undoubtedly the most complex and incomprehensible tax code in the world.[6] The Internal Revenue Service employs 115,000 people, has an annual budget of $11 billion, and is the largest federal bureaucracy. The IRS sends out 8 billion pages of forms and instructions each year. Laid end to end, they would stretch twenty-eight times around the earth. This can't be good for the economy or the environment.[7]

All of this complexity means lots of work for tax lobbyists and accountants who make money puncturing holes in the tax code and helping their clients find clever and mostly legal ways to minimize their tax payments. Firms like H & R Block and the big accounting companies do billions of dollars of business a year, thanks to tax complexity—and, by the way, these companies are some of the biggest opponents of the flat tax.

The higher the tax rate, the greater the value of special-interest loopholes and carve-outs and the more coveted insider lobbyists become. Think about it: At a 40 percent tax rate a tax deduction is worth twice what a tax deduction is at a 20 percent tax rate. This is something that Barack Obama does not seem to understand. He says he wants to rid Washington of the lobbyists who get favors from Congress for their clients, but by raising tax rates to 50 percent or more, he makes lobbyists a prized commodity. If Mr. Obama succeeds in raising tax rates, he will create beehives of K Street influence peddlers in Washington. If Mr. Obama really wants to put a muzzle on the undue influence of lobbyists, he should embrace a low flat rate tax with *no* deductions and loopholes that can be bought and sold inside congressional committee rooms.

Flat Means Fair

There is one bedrock principle of the flat tax and only one—a single rate tax. Everyone pays the same rate of tax on the income they earn. Some people say this isn't fair.

We take the opposite view. What is patently unfair is that two people can live right across the street from each other, have the same income, the same four-bedroom home, the same number of children, and the same lifestyle, but one pays three or four times more tax than the other. One takes clever advantage of every deduction and loophole he and his accountant can find; the other doesn't do any tax planning or sheltering of income. The current tax code violates the constitutional principle of treating all people equally under the law. The tax system fosters inequality.

Now assume we have a flat tax of, say, 15 percent. That would be the tax rate on all of your income regardless of its source. There would be no deductions except for mortgage interest, charitable donations, and pre-existing municipal bond interest. In this scenario, the fellow who makes $100,000 a year would pay $15,000 in taxes and everyone else who makes $100,000 would pay the same tax. We call this tax justice.

Now what about the person who earns $1 million a year? She pays $150,000 in taxes, or ten times more than the guy who made $100,000. Ten times more income; ten times more tax. We think this is a fair principle, and we hope voters will agree with us on that proposition.

But we know there are plenty of people who believe that the earner who makes $1 million a year should pay *more* than ten times what the fellow who makes ten times less pays. These folks, mostly Democrats, but a lot of Republicans, too, think that the richer fellow should be taxed at a higher rate. Why? Because we are told that he can afford to pay more. But throughout this book we have shown that higher tax rates merely discourage rich people from working, investing, saving, and taking risks to start businesses, which winds up hurting everyone by damaging the productive capacity of the U.S. economy. Remember Robin Hood.

But then people say, Why not just tax the rich people at a slightly higher tax rate? This won't hurt the economy. But this is a booby trap. Remember, the first income tax was just 7 percent. Everyone could afford that. Within less than ten years it was at 77 percent. And liberals have raised it to as high as 93 percent. But here is an amazing statistic. The percentage of taxes paid as a share of GDP has stayed remarkably consistent between 18 and 20 percent of national GDP and the effective tax rate on the rich has remained essentially flat over the past fifty years whether tax rates were 90 percent or 28 percent. High tax rates don't mean more revenue, they mean more loopholes.

Washington politicians and special interests get together when tax rates are high to provide tax breaks for this friend, and that political contributor. When we move away from the principle of a flat tax, the system degenerates quickly, like a sand castle when the tide rolls in. That is the lesson of history. That is why we favor a tax code that is flat and simple and doesn't play favorites, and *stays* flat forever. No more soak the rich, but rather a tax system that tries to make more and more Americans rich. Isn't that the fairest tax code of all?

All Aboard the Flat Tax Express

In 1992, the year Bill Clinton was elected president, California's former governor Jerry Brown almost upset Clinton's quest for the Democratic nomination, running on the platform of a 13 percent flat tax, which would have replaced all federal taxes save sin taxes. It was designed by Arthur Laffer.[8]

Our friend Steve Forbes ran for president in 1996 on the idea of the flat tax.[9] At first people laughed that this magazine publisher would think that he could run for president with crazy ideas like the flat tax. But then something strange happened. His ideas started to catch on. The flat tax was surprisingly popular with voters for its simplicity and its capacity to grow the economy. The special interest groups, such as the housing lobby, spent millions of dollars to defeat Forbes. And their attack ads cleary worked. Forbes's lead in New Hampshire sank and Bob Dole went on to win the Republican nomination. But Forbes helped penetrate the culture with the flat tax idea. We contend he was not wrong but ahead of his time.

Then another amazing thing happened. America did not adopt Steve Forbes's flat tax, but Eastern Europe did. More than twenty countries got flat tax fever and more are added to the list every year. These nations are real-life laboratories that show the flat tax can and does work.

So when people say it cannot be done, they are wrong. Yes, there have been many flat tax proposals over the years, and none have been enacted. The biggest problem, as Steve Forbes discovered, was not persuading the American people of the wisdom of the flat tax, but overcoming the special interests that want to protect their tax loopholes.

The Laffer Flat Tax

Under a flat tax plan that Arthur Laffer first presented in 1984, all but a small number of federal taxes would be eliminated, including existing income taxes, Social Security payroll taxes, corporate profit taxes, capital gains taxes, and estate and gift taxes.[10] These taxes would be replaced by two single-rate taxes, one on business and another on personal income. With a minimum amount of deductions, a flat tax of 12.1 percent would produce higher revenues than the taxes they replace, even without the benefit of the Laffer Curve effect on revenues. Once the Laffer Curve effect takes hold, revenues would increase further.[11]

Remember an important principle from Chapter 2: A good tax system has a low tax rate and a broad tax base. One advantage of the low flat tax rate is it would minimize incentives for taxpayers to seek inventive ways to either pay less tax or avoid paying more taxes. People will always seek positive incentives and avoid negative incentives.

Flat and Happy

While no specific flat tax proposal has been enacted in the United States, the many attempts to institute a flat tax have succeeded to some extent, because tax rates have fallen dramatically and the tax base has grown. One reason for the lack of success is that many of the earlier attempts at a flat tax were piecemeal approaches that tended to address a specific tax and leave others in place. To succeed, true tax reform has to take into account the entire tax code, not bits and pieces of it.

Three federal taxes account for the bulk of tax revenues: the personal income tax, corporate profit taxes, and federal payroll taxes. These three account for over 85 percent of total federal revenues. Therefore, any flat tax proposal should incorporate all three forms of taxation.

Critics, including Warren Buffett, complain that the rich don't pay their fair share of taxes. In many respects, that is true. But the reason they don't lies in the excruciating complexity of the existing tax code with its endless array of exclusions, deductions, exemptions, and tax shelters that expensive advisers and accountants can use to the advantage of their wealthy clients. The alternative minimum tax was another attempt at leveling the playing field by applying a separate way to figure taxes that would capture more revenue from those who pay very little. As we all know, over time that tax had the most deleterious effect on the middle class.

Corporate taxes are similarly flawed. We have one of the highest corporate tax rates in the world and one of the lowest collection rates as a share of our GDP.[12] What's wrong with this picture? An army of rich lobbyists on Capitol Hill continue to represent their corporate clients' interests by insuring that many of them pay little or no tax and therefore contribute little or nothing to the government they use.

Social Security taxes are also flawed. They are a second layer of income tax on worker income. They also create a wedge between

248

the cost of hiring a worker and the wage paid to the worker. So they reduce new job creation and the number of Americans willing to work. The payroll tax also is capped; in 2008, for example, wages and incomes over $100,000 were not subject to payroll taxes, so the tax has a regressive feature to it. The more income you make, the lower the share of your income that goes to payroll tax.

How Will It Work?

The Laffer flat tax would replace most federal taxes: the personal tax, the corporate income tax, Social Security payroll taxes, the estate and gift taxes, and a large number of lesser taxes. Many of these taxes raise little revenue relative to their economic cost in terms of incentives, recordkeeping, and collection. This flat rate tax would eliminate much of the inefficiency from the U.S. federal tax system by both broadening the tax base and significantly lowering the highest marginal tax rates. By having the largest possible tax base combined with the lowest possible tax rate, we would provide people the least opportunity to avoid paying taxes and the lowest incentive to do so. Reduced incentives to avoid or evade taxes result in a reduction in the associated costs of monitoring these activities. In addition, lower tax rates go hand in hand with greater incentives to work and produce.

What Is the Flat Tax Rate?

Now we come to the critical issue. What rate of tax can we apply to all income and all business value added to replace all the tax revenues generated from the current tax system? The rate is surprisingly low and affordable. We find that by stretching the tax base, and allowing the deduction of rent, the tax rate for our flat tax for 2008 is 12.1 percent on personal income and 12.1 percent on business value added. Yes, this will raise as much money as the entire current federal tax code. And this does not assume any economic growth kickback from the tax policy. This tax works because lower tax rates generate more income and growth and thus more tax revenue. The flat tax will have a positive impact in helping to balance the budget, and we would hope that as more revenue comes into the Treasury, Congress will do what other flat tax nations have done: lower the tax rate even more. Russia, for example, found that it got more revenue from its 13 percent flat tax than from its 50 percent plus tax rates before the flat tax.[13]

Because this rate is so surprisingly low and some readers may want to challenge our math, we present a series of tables at the end of this chapter that lay out the calculations.

In addition to being fair and simple and pro-growth, it is also a transparent tax system. With only one source of revenue and a single tax rate, everyone will know exactly what taxes are in effect. There will be no hidden taxes whatsoever.

Another big advantage of this tax system is that it provides a much more stable and predictable revenue stream from year to year because the tax rates do not vary with income gains and losses. That means that we shouldn't see the wild swings in the budget deficit that we've witnessed over the last three decades.

Flat Tax Versus Fair Tax

Many readers will have heard about an alternative tax overhaul plan called the fair tax. Laffer and Moore have worked closely with the founders of the fair tax movement. We have done studies on the distortions of the current tax code for Americans for Fair Taxation, so we are not opposed to this idea. In fact, we like it and see many similarities between the fair tax and the Laffer flat tax.[14]

The fair tax is a plan that would eliminate all federal taxes: the personal income tax, the corporate income tax, the estate tax, the payroll tax, and excise taxes. The fair tax rate would be roughly 23 percent on all goods and services purchased in the United States. Low-income households would be protected by exempting their first $15,000 of income from the tax. Our friend Representative Jon Linder of Georgia is spearheading the crusade for this repeal of the income tax. Linder says that abolition of the income tax and implementation of a national sales tax would create thunderous rates of growth for the economy, which would be liberated from the shackles of high tax rates on work and income. The fair tax plan would also get the IRS out of our lives and out of our pocketbooks. How much money you make would no longer be the government's business.

Americans would pay all their taxes at the cash register when they buy goods and services. This means that if you buy a Grape Slurpee from 7-Eleven or a Mustang from a Ford dealer, you would pay a 23 percent sales tax. But costs would not rise because the income and payroll tax under the current tax code make everything more expensive. So the cost of making a car would be lower and the final price tag might not be higher at all.

Exports would not be taxed and capital investment would not be taxed, so the fair tax would dramatically increase the competitiveness of American firms.

The idea of getting the IRS out of people's financial records is attractive, too. This is an agency that has gone after Girl Scouts who sell too many cookies and don't declare the income.

The tax bases of the fair tax and the Laffer flat tax are nearly identical. Both systems have almost no loopholes and tax everything at a uniform rate. The Laffer flat tax divides the tax into two components: a business tax on value added and a tax on wages and salaries. But adding the two tax rates of 12.1 percent together yields a 24.2 percent tax rate, almost identical to the fair tax rate.

One reason we believe the flat tax is more achievable is that imposing all tax on the retail level of the economic system may cause some problems with evasion and noncompliance (though the incentive to cheat is highest under our current system, with its high income tax rates). We believe that a system that spreads the tax burden to all producers may lead to less leakage and tax evasion.

Moreover, the fact that so many other nations have a flat tax today and that it is a popular success suggests that this may be the most politically appealing option to the politicians and the electorate. We would be thrilled if the United States would adopt either plan.

Why a Flat Tax Works

Excessive taxation is detrimental to labor and capital, poor and rich, men and women, and old and young. Excessive taxation is an equal opportunity tormentor. While the world is dynamic and many of its ups and downs are beyond the control of government, there are a number of criteria for judging the efficacy of a tax system. These were summarized well by nineteenth-century American economist Henry George:

1. That it bear as lightly as possible upon production.
2. That it be easily and cheaply collected.
3. That it be certain—so as to give the least opportunity for tyranny or corruption on the part of officials, and the least temptation to lawbreaking and evasion on the part of the taxpayers.
4. That it bear equally—so as to give no citizen an advantage or put any at a disadvantage, as compared with others.

Changes to marginal tax rates are critical for growth because they change incentives to demand, and to supply, work effort, and capital. Firms base their decisions to employ workers, in part, on the workers' total cost to the firm. Holding all else equal, the greater the cost to the firm of employing each additional worker, the fewer workers the firm will employ. Conversely, the lower the cost of hiring a worker, the more workers the firm will hire. For the firm, the decision to employ is based upon gross wages paid, a concept that encompasses all costs borne by the firm.

Workers, on the other hand, care little about the cost to the firm of employing them. Of concern from a worker's standpoint is how much the worker receives for providing work effort, net of all deductions and taxes. Workers concentrate on net wages received. The greater net wages received, the more willing a worker is to work. If wages received fall, workers find work effort less attractive and they will do less of it. The difference between what it costs a firm to employ a worker and what that worker receives net is the tax wedge.

A marginal tax rate cut—ideally to a flat rate—has two types of effects. Because the decrease in marginal tax rates lowers the cost to the employer in the form of lower wages paid, firms will employ more workers. On the supply-side, a reduction in marginal tax rates raises net wages received. Again, more work effort will be supplied. Eliminating the payroll tax will therefore increase the number of jobs, perhaps dramatically.

Under a flat rate tax, average tax rates will remain approximately constant for a given level of income or output. However, the rewards for incremental work by labor, the employment of additional capital, and the more efficient combination of the two will all be higher with the flat tax. As a result, more employment, output, and production is expected. Economic growth rates will accelerate until these effects are fully incorporated into the workings of the economy.

History proves that high tax rates do not generate big increases in revenues. In Figure 13-1 we show federal tax rates and federal tax revenues over the past several decades. Tax revenues have gone up when high tax rates were lowered. This provides powerful evidence that lowering tax rates can generate the receipts we need to balance the budget while maximizing economic growth, wages, and jobs.

A flat single rate tax system without deductions will reduce the wild annual fluctuations in tax revenues. Thus, politicians will not be so tempted to build up expensive spending programs during boom times that will be unaffordable during tough times. It is the

Figure 13-1: Real Federal Revenues and the Top Marginal Income Tax Rate

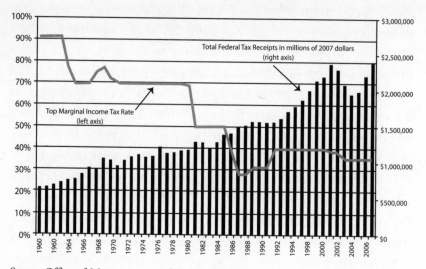

Source: Office of Management and Budget, Budget of the United States Government, *Fiscal Year 2008.*

volatility of spending, whereby spending actually is cut during bad times, that causes so much hardship among those most vulnerable. A flat tax may well be the most moral tax structure as well as the most productive tax structure.

The flat tax proposal is not regressive, as its critics may charge— it is a proportional tax system. Everyone pays the same rate of tax on all of their income.

And don't for a moment think that progressive tax structures help the poor, the minorities, or the disenfranchised. In spite of the statutory progressivity of the tax codes, deductions, exemptions, and exclusions of all sorts have rendered the actual income tax neither fair nor efficient. Those people struggling to become wealthy who cannot afford fancy lawyers to help them take advantage of tax avoidance schemes pay much more in taxes, rarely getting the rewards they rightly deserve.

But the personal income tax is not alone in its failure to serve its appointed task. The corporate income tax has also become a farce. Businesses that make highly desirable products and conserve our precious natural resources without adhering to the dictates of sophisticated tax counsel are taxed at incredibly onerous rates. If, on the other hand, a business squanders resources, makes a lousy product, retains the gilded lobbyists and tax lawyers, and thereby reports horrendous losses, it stands a good chance of qualifying for government subsidies and most assuredly doesn't pay for the government it uses. Perhaps the single most serious problem with the current tax system is the immense distortions introduced by the existing business tax code. Not only has the business tax code caused higher unemployment and lower productivity growth than otherwise would have occurred, but, even as this has occurred, government revenue from business taxes has dwindled.

One final point. To us the best form of welfare is still a good, high-paying job. There is no alternative to economic growth. And a tax system that destroys jobs and wealth is the most regressive tax of all. That is why we believe the best way to spur economic growth is to enact a flat rate tax now.

Appendix: The Flat Tax Math

In the tables that follow we verify how we raised the same amount of revenue as the current system with a flat tax of 12.1 percent. In fiscal year 2006, federal government revenues were $2.4 trillion (Table 13-1). This included all tax and budget receipts. In the Laffer complete flat tax plan, certain taxes and fees (Table 13-2) will be maintained, including the "sin" taxes we discussed earlier, for a total of $139 billion in retained revenues. The plan calls for the repeal of all personal and corporate income taxes, payroll taxes, estate and gift taxes, and some other taxes (Table 13-3) totaling $2.267 trillion in repealed taxes.

Mortgage interest deduction and charitable contribution deductions will be retained and some Social Security income will become deductible, as will a credit for rental expense benefiting mostly lower-income taxpayers who rent rather than own their homes (Table 13-4). This is how the personal income tax base of $8.2 trillion is calculated.

Our flat rate business tax takes total business sales and deducts from that all business investment, which yields a business value-added tax base of $10,489 billion (Table 13-5). To arrive at the amount of flat tax income needed to fund the government, again based on FY 2006 data, divide the total tax base of $18.7 trillion ($8.2 trillion in individual income plus $10.5 trillion in business value added) by the required revenue of $2,267 billion that must be provided by the flat tax. That computes to a flat tax of 12.13 percent (Table 13-6). It's as simple as that.

Here are the updated flat rate tax calculations.

Table 13-1: Total Tax Collections—Current System (FY2006, in $billions)

	Revenue	Percent of Total Revenue
Individual Income Taxes	$1,043.9	43.4%
Corporate Income Taxes	$353.9	14.7%
Old Age Survivors, Disability and Health Insurance (OASDHI)	$790.0	32.8%
Total Income and Federal Payroll Taxes	$2,187.9	90.9%
Estate and Gift Taxes	$27.9	1.2%
Other Taxes and Budget Receipts	$190.9	7.9%
Total Budget Receipts	$2,406.7	100.0%

Source: U.S. Treasury Combined Statement of Receipts, Outlays and Balances, 2006.

Table 13-2: Taxes to Be Retained (FY2006, in $billions)

Classification	Revenue
Railroad Retirement Accounts	$4.2
Unemployment Insurance	$43.4
Federal Employees' Retirement Contribution	$4.3
Civil Service Retirement and Disability Fund	$0.1
Excise Taxes:	
Federal Alcohol Tax	$8.5
Federal Tobacco Tax	$7.7
Other (Firearms, Motorboat Fuels, Misc. Funds, etc.)	$1.9
Custom Duties	$24.8
Misc. Receipts and Taxes, Including:	$44.4
- Deposit of Earnings, Federal Reserve System	
- Fees for Permits, Regulatory and Judicial Services	
- Fines, Penalties, and Forfeitures	
- Gifts and Contributions	
- Other	
Total Budget Revenues Maintained	$139.3

Source: U.S. Treasury Combined Statement of Receipts, Outlays and Balances, 2006.

Table 13-3: Taxes to Be Repealed (FY2006, in $billions)

	Revenue	Totals
Individual Income Taxes	$1,043.9	
Corporate Income Taxes	$353.9	
Old Age Survivors, Disability and Health Insurance (OASDHI)	$790.0	
Total Income and Payroll Taxes Repealed		$2,187.9
Estate and Gift Taxes	$27.9	
Selected Excise and Other Taxes	$51.7	
Total Other Taxes Repealed		$79.6
Total Taxes Repealed		$2,267.5

Source: U.S. Treasury Combined Statement of Receipts, Outlays and Balances, 2006.

Table 13-4: Flat Tax Personal Income Tax Base
(2006, in $billions)

Personal Income	$10,983.4
plus capital gains*	$668.0
less charitable contributions*	−$183.4
less mortgage interest payments*	−$383.7
less transfer payments (tax exempt)	−$1,585.3
less monetary rent	−$277.0
less imputed rent	−$1,014.5
Equals Tax Base for Personal Income	$8,207.5

* Based on 2005 data.
Source: NIPA Tables, Bureau of Economic Analysis; Statistics of Income, IRS.

Table 13-5: Flat Tax Business Value-Added Tax Base
(2006, in $billions)

Final Sales	$13,194.7
less business investment	
Fixed nonresidential	−$1,397.7
Business-fixed residential*	−$153.0
Depreciation**	−$1,081.4
Business Transfers***	−$27.2
Increase (+ if decrease) in business inventories	−$46.7
Equals Tax Base for Business Value-Added	$10,488.70

* Estimate based on all farm structures and 20 percent of nonfarm structures.
** Capital consumption allowance without capital consumption adjustment.
*** Charitable contributions plus bad debts.
Source: NIPA Tables, Bureau of Economic Analysis.

Table 13-6: Calculation of Flat Tax Rate (2006, in $billions)

Tax Base, Personal Income	$8,207.5
plus Tax Base, Business Value-Added	$10,488.7
Total Tax Base	$18,696.2
FY2006 Targeted Budget Revenue	$2,406.7
less Budget Revenue elsewhere obtained	–$139.3
Requisite Flat Tax Revenues	$2,267.4

Flat Tax Rate = Revenues / Tax Base = $2,267.4 / $18,696.2 =12.13%

14

THE DEATH OF
ECONOMIC SANITY

The problem is not that we don't know what works, or that we don't know what the answers are. The problem is that there are so many self-proclaimed economic experts who know what is not so.[1]

—MILTON FRIEDMAN, 1980

THE AMERICA SELL-OFF

Wayne Gretzky was once asked what made him one of the greatest hockey players of all time. His answer was advice to live by: Most players, he said, skate to the puck. I always skated to where the puck was going next. Similarly, world champion chess players will tell you that the key to beating your opponent is to visualize the board as it will look three, four, or five moves ahead.

There's a whole lot of wisdom in this strategic advice about how to succeed in sports and board games that carries over to economics and investment.

In assessing the health of the American economy, we're worried about where the puck is going. So, evidently, are the shrewd and successful investors who make their money anticipating seismic economic and political changes—the tipping points—and reacting before the herd. All over the globe, capitalists are looking ahead at where the United States is headed, and for the first time in more than a generation, they aren't liking what they're seeing. What they are anticipating is the torrent of bearish policy mistakes that we wrote this book to warn about. It pains us to say this, but wise money managers are protecting their own assets, and their clients' assets, by selling America. They're getting out of Dodge the same way people scatter out of town after the emergency weather reports, but before the hurling winds of a tornado actually crash down and bring destruction. It's amazing to us that foreigners see the storm coming before we Americans do ourselves.

Here are some of the cyclones that have already arrived or are coming:

- Tax rates on investment are headed up, not down.
- America has nearly the highest corporate tax in the world.
- The alternative minimum tax will hit 25 million annually.
- The dollar is falling relative to other currencies and relative to such commodities as oil and food.
- America is turning its back on trade and globalization.
- An economically masochistic "cap and trade" global warming regulatory and tax monster threatens to send our jobs and factories and capital to China, India, Malaysia, the Philippines, and other developing nations.
- The federal budget is spiraling out of control, and neither party is even half serious about halting the multi-trillion-dollar liabilities that could cause an ocean of future debt and taxes.
- Unions are gaining more power in the workplace.
- The health care system, which is one-sixth of our economy, may be nationalized.
- National energy policies raise prices, limit access to domestic oil and gas resources, and make America more dependent on foreign oil.

Whew. That's a lot of economically dimwitted ideas for any country to absorb all at once. Each individually might be enough to shift the economy into a lower growth gear or to stall the engine completely, but the combination of these antistimulants could do severe and lasting damage. The reason we told the story of the 1970s in so much gory detail was to warn about how bad things can get when the policies work against growth, not for it.

This list of economic body blows explains why, for the first time in years, hot capital is escaping over the borders out of the United States and flowing into China, India, Europe, and even Japan. International investors can see the very storm brewing in Washington, D.C.—the onslaught from the Left—that frightens us so much. We have noted in previous chapters that the $5.2 trillion net flow of funds into the United States since 1980 has been one of the lubricants of the surging U.S. economy over the past quarter century. Following the 2003 Bush reduction in capital taxes, in 2003 foreigners invested $64 billion[2] in the United States. That number tripled to $204 billion in 2007.

But starting in late 2007 foreigners started pulling their money out of the United States, and Americans started investing more abroad. Global investors are losing confidence in the U.S. The result is a falling stock market and a collapse of the dollar. Right now the outmigration of capital is still a trickle, but we fear it could turn into the river wild. The last time the United States was an exporter of capital was . . . the 1970s.

November 4, 2008: Fright Night

There is a palpable wave of fear and loathing in financial markets in anticipation of what will happen policywise if liberals score a knockout punch in the 2008 elections and seize control of the White House and win big majorities in Congress. A recent issue of *The Economist* says on its cover that politically America is lurching to the left. We're not too thrilled with either party's performance of late, so this book is anything but an endorsement of the Republican Party. To steal a line from late-night comedian Joan Rivers, choosing between the Republicans and Democrats these days is like being asked which is your favorite Menendez brother. But a clean sweep for the Democrats is assuredly not a happy outcome for the U.S. economy and the financial markets.

Over the last forty years, the markets have not been at all bullish about a Democratic monopoly on power. And for good reason. The last three times Democrats controlled all the levers of power in Washington, 1965–68, 1977–80, and 1993–95, they were pushed by the unions, environmental groups, the poverty lobby, and trial lawyers to pass sweeping antigrowth changes in tax, regulatory, and spending policies that torpedoed the economy. Experience shows that the U.S. job market and financial markets perform best with divided government to provide checks and balances on the excesses of each party. The worst outcome politically is when Democrats control every branch of government (and the second worst is when Republicans have complete control).

What is different—actually, worse—now from the Carter and early Clinton years is that Barack Obama is not even pretending to be a moderate or a Clinton "New Democrat." In fact virtually none of the eight Democrats who ran for president tried to occupy the political center. The field all squeezed to the left and debated issues between the end zone and the twenty yard line on the liberal side of the football field. The Democratic debates were a horrifying contest to see who would raise taxes, spending, and regulations the most and who would pander the most to unions, trial lawyers, and radical anti-growth environmental groups. Mr. Obama has told the American people unabashedly what he intends to do on the economy. He says, "We have to disaggregate tax policy between the wealthy and the working class or middle class. We have to be able to say that we are going to at once raise taxes on some people and lower taxes on others."[3] Here's the translation of this economic gobbledygook. He will raise the highest marginal tax rates through the roof to try to get more money out of the rich. He also wants to expand liberal entitlement programs, not shave their costs. He wants trade protectionism, not trade expansionism.

Question: Who will be the countervailing force to Barack Obama's liberal instincts?

Answer: We don't have a clue.

If Obama wins the White House in 2008, there will be little or no veto power over how far his administration might go to redistribute income and grow the government both in spending and in harassment of business through regulatory expansion and oversight. The Democrats even have a shot at getting to sixty seats in the Senate, which would mean Republicans would lose the power to block through the filibuster the most dangerous ideas. This would liberate House Speaker Nancy Pelosi and Senate majority leader Harry Reid to do pretty much whatever they wish. The Democrats in Congress are already prowling impatiently back and forth like tigers waiting to lurch when they're freed from their cages.

Even if John McCain is able to pull out a victory, he and a Democratic Congress could easily cook up a dangerous potion of tax increase and regulatory populism that could severely wound the U.S. economy. We know John McCain and we like him, and we hope for the best if he wins, but he could unleash a firestorm of bad laws in the name of "getting things done" and in the spirit of "bipartisanship" and in wracking up what the media will praise as "accomplishments."

Are we being irrational and paranoid here? There's an old saying that it's not paranoia if someone really is out there trying to get you. The markets are already expressing fear that the political class in Washington will launch an assault on growth economics. We believe this is one reason why the stock market plunged in the first half of 2008. An analysis by Professor William Perry at the University of Michigan has found that whenever Barack Obama has moved up in the polls, the stock market has slid farther south. The risk factor of bad policies in 2009 has escalated dramatically, so we don't believe that investor fears or ours are misplaced or exaggerated.

Onslaught from the Left

We've been keeping close track of the economic agenda items endorsed by Mr. Obama, Mr. McCain, and members of Congress, and we haven't seen such an array of prosperity killers for many years. We need to lay out these threats, but we will issue a warning: What you are about to read contains scenes of graphic violence to the economy and reader discretion is advised.

Tax the Rich

"The project of the next president is to figure out how do you create bottom-up economic growth as opposed to trickle down economic growth that George Bush has been so enamored with," proclaims Barack Obama about his economic governing philosophy.[4]

Step one is to soak the rich, and Figure 14-1 shows what is likely to happen to tax rates under a Barack Obama presidency based on the promises he's already made. (We will give Senator Obama credit: Most Democrats wait until *after* they are elected to roll out their tax hike surprise; Senator Obama has been quite forthcoming about what he intends to do.) Nearly every tax rate rises, in some cases significantly. For the first time since the Jimmy Carter years the highest tax rate on income would rise to above 50 percent. That means the government gets *more than half* of each additional dollar earned or invested.

In Table 14-1 we show what happens to the combined federal and state income tax plus payroll tax in the five highest-income-tax states. Our condolences to people who live in these tax hells.

Figure 14-1: The Obama Tax Plan

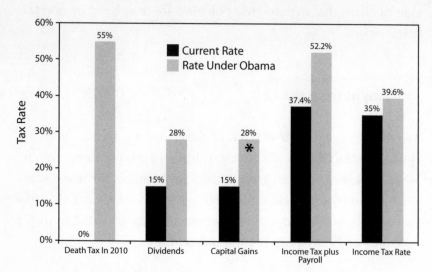

* Obama campaign says it would raise these rates to "as high as 28 percent."
Source: The Wall Street Journal.

These would be some of the highest income tax rates in the world. While liberals may regard this as some kind of triumph for tax fairness, we have a grimmer assessment. Not long ago America was one of the world's tax havens, with the lowest tax rates. In a couple of years America could have nearly the highest tax rates on the planet and will be categorized as a "tax hell" country. What a depressing turn to the dark side.

Liberals will, of course, pooh-pooh our concerns and for the umpteenth time they will fall back on the defense that raising tax rates did not hurt the economy in the 1990s, so it won't inflict damage now. But even if one believed that this was true of the 1990 and 1993 tax hikes, two things need to be remembered. First, the Democrats today are talking about raising taxes a lot higher than they were even under Clinton. And second, the potential damage from 50 to 60 percent tax rates is exacerbated by the trend in the rest of the world over the last decade to lower and flatten rates. Does anyone really believe that American companies can compete effectively

Table 14-1: **Combined Federal and State Tax Rates Under the Obama Plan**

New York	58.2%
California	58.1%
New Jersey	57.8%
Iowa	57.6%
Ohio	57.5%

Source: The Wall Street Journal.

in global markets when we have a 52 percent marginal tax rate, and the rest of the world is on a mission to get to the 15 to 30 percent range? Can America compete with Eastern Europe when those nations have flat tax rates that are only about one-third as onerous as ours?

What makes this threat all the greater is that Congress and the next president will not have to enact a legislated tax increase to trigger most of these higher rates. The Bush tax cuts are scheduled to expire at the end of 2010. So if Congress simply does *nothing*, tax rates on capital gains, dividends, inheritance, and personal income taxes will rise automatically. This will raise average and marginal tax rates sharply. Figure 14-2 shows that under this automatic pilot scenario, the tax share of GDP rises from 18 percent of GDP to about 25 percent of GDP in the next thirty years.

This mother of all tax hikes also means that the capital gains would go automatically from 15 to 20 percent. (Mr. Obama has endorsed raising the rate to as high as 24 to 28 percent—higher than under Bill Clinton.) The dividend tax would rise from 15 percent all the way up to near 40 percent. Since the tax on stocks directly affects the after-tax return on investment, a higher dividend and capital gains tax will necessarily mean lower stock values.

Here's why these investment tax hikes will sock it to America's 100 million worker/investors. If investors are only permitted to keep sixty cents on the dollar of all dividends earned on a share of stock because of a 40 percent tax, the share value by definition has

Figure 14-2: Tax Time Bomb

Federal Taxes as % of GDP

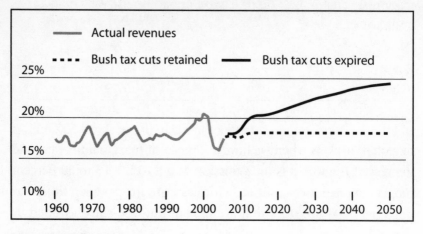

Source: The Wall Street Journal.

to be lower than if investors can keep eighty-five cents on the dollar from the dividend payments with the 15 percent tax. Since share prices are based on the stream of future earnings of the company *after taxes are paid*, the higher the tax imposed on the earnings, the lower the value of the stock. When George W. Bush cut the taxes on dividends and capital gains the share values of U.S. stocks rose by 10 to 15 percent within weeks of the new law's enactment, as the market capitalized the higher after-tax earnings per share just as stock value rose after the 1997 capital gains cut under Bill Clinton.[5] But if you play the record in reverse and raise those taxes back to where they were (or higher), the market reacts in reverse fashion.

This isn't some untested ideological theory. It is a financial fact of life, and the question isn't *whether* share prices will fall, but how much they will fall. A 2008 study by Wall Street economist Michael Darda found that the price of stocks is inversely related to the capital gains tax and the inflation rate, both of which are rising now.[6] Even Senator Obama himself acknowledged on CNBC TV in March that his tax plan might have negative consequences for the economy and therefore he might delay the higher tax rates until financial conditions improve. But if these tax hikes would hurt the economy, Senator, why do it in good or bad times? Why do it all?

Tax the Middle Class

Oops. There is a hole in the Left's soak the rich strategy. Even liberal think tanks agree that taxing the rich will get about $32 billion a year in 2010 in new revenues, and even all of the upper-bound estimates are about $60 billion a year. But the budget deficit is $400 billion. Hmm, that leaves a $340 billion budget hole.[7] Where oh where will the rest of the money come from to a) balance the budget, and b) expand social programs and c) give tax cuts to some groups? We have a hunch where the money will come from: the wallets of the middle class.

Democrats swear that they will give the middle class a big tax cut in 2009, but the middle class isn't likely to get away unplucked in 2009—thanks to the sinister alternative minimum tax. If you haven't heard of it, you will in the months and years ahead. The AMT is a ticking time bomb that is set to detonate in the laps of some 25 to 30 million tax filers by 2010. This would be, according to the *Wall Street Journal*, the largest one-year tax increase on middle-class America in the nation's history.[8]

Ironically, this AMT was a tax that was originally designed back in 1969 to load higher taxes onto the backs of a few hundred of the wealthiest Americans who weren't paying income taxes. But one of the lessons that we learn over and over in Washington is that when politicians talk about soaking only the rich with higher taxes, you'd better get your umbrella out, because everyone's going to get wet. The AMT was conveniently never indexed for inflation, so if you make between $75,000 and $100,000 a year and you have two or more kids, Congress thinks you're rich and there's a high probability that you will be sucked into this fiendish tax system in the next five years. For those who reside in such high-tax states as California, New Jersey, and New York, the pain in the pocketbook will be more severe, because under the AMT you lose your federal tax deduction for state and local taxes paid.[9]

Democrats say they would like to wipe out this tax for many reasons, not the least of which is that this is a "Blue State tax," with eight of the ten states with the most tax filers hit by the AMT living in Democratic country. But Congress craves the $50 billion to $60 billion of revenues each year to sustain their spending programs even more. What this means is that for an ever-increasing share of American families, the first page of the IRS 1040 instruction code might as well read: Don't even bother wasting your time filling out all these forms and booklet. Go directly to the AMT and pay even more, or about $2,000 extra tax on average each year. Isn't it nice to know the politicians in Washington consider you rich?

Red Tape Rising

Rules, rules, rules. Politicians love to pass them, and officious bureaucrats love to enforce them—it's in their nature. Thou shalt do this. Thou shalt not do that.

God was able to instruct us in the Bible how to live a good and holy life by consolidating the rules down to Ten Commandments. These are pretty simple rules to live by. Don't kill, don't steal, don't lie, don't covet your neighbor's wife. But the Cato Institute now says that there are not ten, but ten thousand commandments established by Washington regulating everything from toothpaste to the temperature at which restaurants can serve coffee. The cost of the hyper-regulatory system is now estimated at just over $1 trillion. This is a stealth tax on Americans that costs about $8,000 in lost output for every U.S. household. This is the equivalent to imposing a second income tax on every U.S. family.

Here's what makes us nervous. More rules are coming. The atti-

tude of the Left is that free markets have been allowed to run unin-
hibited for much too long. Government needs to build an electric
fence around industry to keep them from roaming too far afield.
This is the view of Senator Hillary Clinton, who wants a new rule
book for business and more powers for government. Earlier this year
she declared, "I want to get back to the appropriate balance of power
between government and the market." She even said that she longed
for a return to the 1960s and 1970s when "labor unions grew" and
tax rates were "confiscatory" by today's standard.[10] She longs for an
era when tax rates were "*confiscatory*"? This is one of the more
frightening things we've heard a politician say in a long, long time.

When Hillary Clinton says she wants to get back to an "appropriate balance" of power between government and industry, what
she is really saying is she wants more regulation.[11] But deregulation
has been, for the most part, an enormous benefit to consumers and
workers, as we demonstrated in Chapter 5. The gains have been in
the magnitude of $50 billion to $100 billion a year, mostly through
lower customer prices.

Stricter mortgage rules are especially problematic. There's no
doubt that banks and borrowers got greedy and share a big responsibility for the sub-prime mortgage mess. But it's also true that for
years Congress commanded banks through the Community Re-
investment Act to lower credit standards and make more loans to
low-income and minority borrowers, thus contributing to the subprime lending debacle. Government forced banks to make these
loans or face losing their bank charter. So with this congressional
gun to their heads, the banks and mortgage companies made more
and more loans to people with poor credit ratings, low down payments, and low incomes. But when borrowers defaulted on many
of these subprime loans, Congress shouted: Where did all these
subprime loans come from? What happened to underwriting standards? Then an indignant Congress moved to pass "anti-predatory-
lending" laws that punish banks for pushing these same aspiring
homeowners into loans they can't afford.

This rush to regulate the financial industry could not come at a worse time. All of the evidence points to America's already slowly surrendering its status as the financial center of the global economy. This has become such a problem in recent years that New York City mayor Michael Bloomberg, then–New York governor Elliot Spitzer, and New York senator Chuck Schumer chaired a commission for the State of New York on the future of Wall Street. The commission found that Wall Street is losing its dominance as the world's financial capital.[12] More and more transactions are taking place on foreign exchanges in London, Hong Kong, and Zurich. Already Europe is advertising itself as a "Sarbanes-Oxley Free Zone," meaning it doesn't have the onerous regulations that the United States has on publicly traded companies. This can hardly be good news for Wall Street, New York City, or the nation. It would be like the movie studios' migrating out of Hollywood to Europe.

Unfree Trade

Economist William Niskanen of the Cato Institute once neatly summarized the folly of protectionism: Trade barriers to keep out foreign goods are the policies that nations impose on themselves during peacetime that our enemies impose on us during times of war. He's right. Consider Britain in World Wars I and II. Germany tried to put a naval blockade around Britain and even torpedoed ships trying to enter to keep out vessels that were trying to stock the British people with low-priced products and supplies. But in peacetime, high tariffs accomplish what the German torpedoes did during war: They prevent foreign ships from bringing low-priced foreign products that we want and need.

The modern U.S. economy is highly dependent on open international markets and benefits from the reduction in trade barriers. One benefit of imports is that the international competition holds down prices. Industries that are most influenced by trade—

computer software, electronic equipment, cars and trucks, and apparel—are the sectors of the economy where prices tend to fall the fastest. Prices have been rising fastest in areas like health care and education that are generally sheltered from the pressures of imports.

Trade is not just associated with less inflation, but also with more growth. According to Moises Naim, the editor-in-chief of *Foreign Policy* magazine, "Despite all the misgivings about international trade, countries where the share of economic activity related to exports is rising grow 1.5 times faster than those with stagnant exports."[13]

The union bosses and the Democrats they help elect to office dispute this economic reality. In Ohio and Michigan Democratic presidential candidates Hillary Clinton and Barack Obama promised a new "time out" on trade deals. They both have said they wish to renegotiate the free trade agreement with Canada and Mexico (NAFTA) to include labor and environmental protections. We know they know better. This is simply a roundabout way of saying they want to keep foreign goods out of the U.S. markets.

What the Democrats and some Republicans are really supporting is a highly regressive tax on the very poor Americans they say they intend to help. Go to a Wal-Mart and you will see that thousands of products now sell for less than ten dollars. Many items sell for ninety-nine cents, and many of these are made in China. A recent study on the impact of Wal-Mart and foreign trade finds that in combination the two have done more to raise the living standard of the poor than all of the antipoverty programs since the Great Society was instituted.[14] We wonder if the Democrats would cry foul if the Chinese agreed to give our poor all these products for free.

The last trade protectionist president was Herbert Hoover, and as we explained in an earlier chapter, Hoover-style trade protectionism in the late 1920s through the Smoot-Hawley Tariff Act essentially shut down world trade and was one of the contributing factors to the Great Depression—which went global. The flow of trade among countries slowed to a trickle and the United States cut its imports by more than 80 percent. The U.S. unemployment rate surged to an all-time high of 25 percent, and the motto of the era was: "Brother, can you spare a dime." All those high-paying jobs that were supposed to emerge once we locked out all those terrible low-priced products, well, they never materialized.

Hoover was by our reckoning one of the worst presidents of the twentieth century. We shudder to think what will happen if American voters elect another Herbert Hoover on trade.

The Incredible Sinking Dollar

Ronald Reagan declared in the early 1980s, when inflation raged out of control, that his goal was to make the dollar as good as gold again. But in this decade the dollar has continuously lost value relative to gold. In 2000 gold sold at $300 an ounce; by early 2008 its price briefly topped $1,000.[15] When the price of gold rises as it has during this decade, it is a sign that something is desperately wrong with the economy. The dollar has also fallen relative to virtually every major currency—by about one-third since 2002—and in late 2007 the U.S. dollar reached a new symbolic and ignominious low: It fell below the Canadian dollar in value for the first time in over thirty years. It is a rarity indeed when a strong country has a weak currency. And the U.S. today is no exception.

The main reason the dollar has collapsed is lower demand for dollars. Other countries are cutting tax rates, and international traders are seeing higher tax rates out of Washington, D.C., as an irresistible political force in 2009. So they have been dumping dollars and buying Euros, other currencies, and gold. Antigrowth fiscal policy and the promise to raise taxes are contributing to the dollar meltdown. If Congress would simply declare that it will leave the investment tax rates where they are today, we believe the dollar

Figure 14-3: The Dollar's Decline

U.S. Dollar Against Major World Currencies

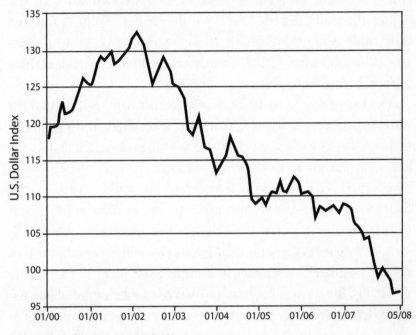

Source: Federal Reserve Bank of Atlanta.

would rally strongly. But we don't see the light bulbs going on in the halls of Congress any time soon.

For these reasons global investors want out of the U.S. to invest abroad and this mandates a decline in the trade deficit or perhaps even a trade surplus. Many economists cheer the fall of the dollar as a way to reduce the U.S. trade deficit. But the main reason the U.S. has run high trade deficits over the past twenty-five years is the phenomenon we described above: as a result of our bullish supply-side policies, foreigners wanted to invest more here on net than Americans wanted to invest abroad. And to get dollars to invest here, foreigners have to sell Americans more goods than we sell them. The U.S. has led the industrialized world in growth and jobs while we ran enormous trade deficits and now we are seeing paltry and even negative job gains as our trade deficit falls.

If anything, over the past thirty years the trade deficit is a symptom of prosperity: The stronger the growth of the U.S. economy and the greater the gains in income of American workers, the higher the trade deficit. The trade deficit has fallen in modern times only when the economy has gone into recession or near-recession—as in early 2008. The United States ran a trade surplus during the Great Depression. Hooray.

Devaluing the dollar to increase exports works only by making Americans accept a paycheck that buys fewer goods and services so that companies can sell more products abroad. So a falling dollar is like a pay cut for all workers. By the logic of the economists who have supported this devaluation policy, we could depreciate the dollar to the value of a dime to make our goods cheaper to sell and to increase our exports, but the value of everything Americans own, and their savings and their paychecks, which are all priced in dollars, would fall closer and closer to zero.

Finally, the dollar's fall has not succeeded much in reducing the trade deficit. It is true that our exports have risen, but so has the cost of our imports. There is no better example of this than the upward trend in oil prices over the past several years. The price of oil has risen to as high as $140 a barrel in 2008, up from about $20 a barrel only a few years ago. This happened mostly because of the dollar's slide.[16] The oil price has risen almost in perfect tandem with other commodities, especially gold.[17]

In the 1970s the twin killers of growth were the combination of high tax rates and inflationary increases in the money supply. The weak-dollar, high-tax-rate combination gave America the worst of all worlds: high unemployment and high inflation. We fear that policymakers may fall right back into that Keynesian stagflation trap. Perhaps you've seen the program on TV: it's called *That '70s Show*.

Big Labor's Big Comeback

The Democratic Party today in America is highly reminiscent of the dominant and self-destructive Labor parties of Europe in the 1960s and 1970s. Those parties were essentially fully owned subsidiaries of big labor bosses, and they continued to press socialized economic policies, lifetime job protection, absurdly generous benefit programs for workers, cradle-to-grave welfare policies, and other economic losers that bankrupted many of the European states and created massive unemployment in these nations as factories and capital left. By the late 1980s and through the 1990s, no company in its right mind would invest tens of millions of dollars to build a plant or factory in France or Germany or Italy.

In Britain it took the election of Margaret Thatcher to break the chokehold of the labor unions on the political system that was gradually converting the proud British empire into a third world state. Thatcher liberated the United Kingdom from the militant unions, privatized assets, got salary demands under control, and cut tax rates. These policies helped restore Britain to first world power status.

In 1981 Ronald Reagan tamed union militancy by firing the illegally striking air traffic controllers. But now unions are flexing their muscles again, and the latest scam from Big Labor is called union card check, which would allow union organizers to dispense with secret elections to organize workplaces. It's an outrageous infringement on workers' right to choose, and by some estimates this scheme could nearly double the unions' membership, political dollars, and lobbying clout. It would institute sham elections and in effect *force* workers to join unions and pay union dues. This new law could also tip the political balance for a generation in favor of the union agenda, which is to make America more like old Europe. One of the first bills that a Democratic Congress and president would pass if they sweep the elections in 2008 would be the union card check bill. If they succeed, be afraid. Be very afraid.

Let's Spend Again

There was a wonderful TV ad a number of years ago for an insurance company that showed King Kong ravaging the city of New York—toppling buildings, destroying Madison Square Garden, trampling cars and buses, and then grabbing the beautiful blond Fay Wray lookalike, who shouts up at him from the palm of his gigantic paws: "Hey, you big ape, who's gonna pay for all this?" Yes, well, we wish we knew who's going to pay for the drunken-sailor spending binge in Washington after $50 billion for housing giants Fannie Mae and Freddie Mac, the $50 to $100 billion in sub-prime housing bailouts and the $150 billion giveaway in tax rebates. This does not even include the gigantic budget increases that are planned for the next four years.

The federal budget spiraled out of control under George W. Bush. Bush was the biggest spender to sit in the White House since LBJ.[18] The budget grew from $2.2 trillion to $3.1 trillion in eight years. Republicans became addicted to earmark spending projects, such as indoor rainforests, and teapot museums, and shark research.[19]

These spendthrift policies were one (good) reason Republicans lost control of Congress in 2006. At first Democrats under Speaker Nancy Pelosi promised to govern as fiscal conservatives, to live by "pay-as-you-go" spending rules to keep the budget deficit under control, and to bring down overall spending. This hasn't happened. We didn't think Democrats could outspend the profligate Republicans, but they are doing so. The federal budget was up 8 percent last year. In 2008 the Democrats with the help of Republican big spenders passed a $300 billion farm bill for corporate special agriculture interests even though farmers are having their best year on the farm *ever*. Meanwhile, on the presidential campaign trail, Democratic nominee Barack Obama has promised $344 billion dollars of annual new wasteful social programs, according to the National Taxpayers Union.

In a moment of rare candor, Hillary Clinton declared in 2007 that "America cannot afford all of my ideas."[20] Barack Obama could have said the same thing. Our fear is that 2009 could see the largest federal spending bonanza since the 1960s, financed through a combination of taxes and the already $5 trillion overdrawn federal credit card. Democrats in 2006 promised a new era of fiscal responsibility and "pay-as-you-go" financing. But today in Washington what we have is "pay-as-you-gorge" financing.

Here Comes Hillary Care

America has arrived at a crossroads of sorts with our medical care system. Either the medical system is going to be driven by the competitive forces of the free market to give health care consumers more options, and to drive down costs while improving efficiency and quality of care, or we will adopt a government-run "universal health care system" modeled after what so many other industrialized nations have. That decision is likely to rest in the hands of the next president.

We hope that everyone remembers the folly of Hillary care in 1993, with its flow chart of bureaucracies that looked as if it had been designed by the Soviet Politburo. Fortunately, that blew up, but the Left has not at all given up on its grand design for a "universal health care system"—by which they mean a government-operated system. And they are getting perilously close to achieving their dream. For the last two decades health care has moved incrementally toward socialized care: first veterans, then seniors, then the poor, then children, then the uninsured. The idea is to suck more and more of the population into the "free" government-run system, and once the tipping point is reached, the private sector system collapses. It's near collapse now. It's bankrupting businesses that pay for their employees' health care. The massive government encroachment into the health care market already constrains the ability of private sector health plans to control costs because programs like Medicare and Medicaid have become the tail that wags the dog of the health care system.

The idea that additional government management and control of the health care market can reduce costs of the system without drastically harming the quality of medical care is a fantasy disproved by the experience of the last forty years. The introduction of Medicare and Medicaid in the mid-1960s corresponded to the ramp up of inflation in health care costs that Hillary and the business community complain of so much these days. Medicare and Medicaid, along with the expansion of private insurance programs subsidized through the tax code, have made patients less and less sensitive to the cost of their doctor and hospital bills—since they don't pay them. This is called the third-party-payer problem. If we move toward a universal insurance system with a single payer, patients will be even less cost-conscious in making medical care decisions.

In recent years, the divergence in prices for health care and everything else has been depressingly widened. Yes, some of this explosion in health care costs is attributable to huge technological advances in health care that are expensive but life saving. But much of the cost inflation is a result of a third-party-payer system that is entirely dysfunctional.

Medicare and Medicaid's costs are growing at about twice the pace of Social Security, so these programs are the real debt drivers. Medicare's costs skyrocketed with the passage last year of the Medicare prescription drug bill for seniors. That drug benefit financial burden was just readjusted, and its ten-year price tag is now over $700 billion.

Health care gobbles up almost 15 percent of the U.S. economy. To put this entire industry under the direction of government—right now health care is almost 50 percent government controlled—would be the largest power grab by government in a generation. We've seen the disastrous financing deficits of Medicare. The Medicare program now has larger unfunded liabilities than even Social Security. To pay Medicare and Medicaid's unfunded costs by 2050 would require a near doubling of the 15 percent payroll tax. What happens when the government runs health care? Costs spiral out of control.

What is far more troubling is the impact of a federal health care system on quality of care. First, consider drug treatments. Of the twenty-five latest wonder drugs introduced on the market over the last decade, more than 80 percent were developed on the shores of the United States by our for-profit pharmaceutical industry. If the U.S. tilts toward socialized medicine, medical progress could be halted dramatically. Where will the wonder drugs of the future come from? The rest of the world for a quarter century has been piggy-backing off U.S. medical breakthroughs, and if we join the ranks of price controls and government management, all the citizens of the world will be the poorer and less healthy for it.

We've seen the decline in health care access and quality in Canada and Britain. Quality deteriorated so much in Canada that now for the first time they are allowing private health plans and alternatives to the national system. The U.S. has higher survival rates from many forms of cancer because we do a much better job diagnosing and treating the disease.[21]

Other nations, it is true, hold down inflation better than we do. But at what cost to quality? Medical costs are restrained in these countries through waiting lines, denial of care, and a virtual triage system in treating the chronically ill. When people get seriously ill in Canada, they come to the United States for treatment. Under a government-run system, if a loved one gets diagnosed with a life-threatening form of cancer, it is increasingly not the patient and the doctor who decide on the best treatment, but a government official who plays God and decides who gets treated and who doesn't. That, in our opinion, to steal a line from Michael Moore, really is "sicko."

Running on Empty

In the 1970s the United States imposed price controls on oil and natural gas, installed a windfall profits tax on oil companies, and poured massive subsidies into "alternative" and renewable fuels and conservation programs. The program was one of the most ill-conceived public policy blunders in our nation's history. The result was runaway energy prices, a huge increase in America's dependence on foreign oil, gasoline lines and even rationing, and stampeding inflation. One prominent study by the Congressional Research Service found that the windfall profits tax on domestic oil companies caused a 6 percent increase in imported oil and a decline in domestic energy investment.[22]

Now for the sequel, twenty-five years later we are back with the politicians in both parties, but mostly Democrats, proposing an entire replica of the 1970s policies that didn't work: windfall profits taxes on oil companies, price controls, and billions of federal tax dollars directed to conservation and alternative fuels. (Liberal groups even want to bring back the universally despised and disobeyed 55 MPH federal speed limit law.) The only difference between now and the 1970s is that at least in that earlier decade we didn't have irrefutable evidence of how disastrous those policies would turn out to be. The likely result will be even higher fuel prices, massive wastes of taxpayer money in wind and solar power, and more oil imported from the Middle East and all of OPEC.

Meanwhile, the one policy that *would* help reduce dependence on foreign oil and help drive down costs is one that Congress won't tolerate, and that is drilling for more oil here at home in Alaska, and offshore in California and the Gulf of Mexico, where there is more gas and oil than in all of Saudi Arabia. At a time when American leaders are jawboning the Saudis and other OPEC nations to increase their oil production, we won't increase our own. Go figure. Meanwhile, Congress has continued to place restrictions on other sources of energy that are cost-efficient and abundant, such as nuclear power, coal, shale, and natural gas. Even with oil as high as $140 a barrel, the U.S. government blocks nuclear power, one of the few fuel sources that emits no greenhouse gases, while China is building more than thirty such plants. Which country ten years from now will have lower energy prices?

Our prediction is that one result of these dimwitted energy policies is that in the next few years it's going to cost a lot more to fill your tank and heat your home, but we voters have only ourselves to blame. We elected these people.

Cap and Kill—The Economy

One of the few policies that the two presidential candidates of 2008, John McCain and Barack Obama, agree on is the need for a so-called cap and trade system to reduce CO_2 greenhouse gases. This is one of the most economically debilitating ideas that has come down the pike in many years, and it is important that Americans know what the politicians and some environmental groups have in mind and how it will put millions of jobs in jeopardy.

Our purpose here is not to debate the science of global warming. It's hard to know who or what to believe, given that some of the scientific findings point to a major warming crisis and other studies question whether recent trends in warming are a result of man's footprint on the earth or of normal climate changes that have been happening for tens of thousands of years on the earth. Just thirty years ago many of the top climatologists were warning of a cooling earth and the return of a global ice age.[23]

But let us suppose that we decide as a nation that we must reduce greenhouse gases. What we can say with certainty as economists is that the *most* economically costly way to respond is through an international treaty like Kyoto, or through a cap and trade system that regulates energy use. What is particularly outrageous is that environmental groups argue with a straight face that cap and trade will actually be good for the economy, because it will help re-tool firms and households for twenty-first-century energy consumption. This is a pipe dream. It's like saying that the destruction of Hurricane Katrina was good for New Orleans because it has led to new buildings and houses.

The cap and trade system regulates energy use of industries and requires industries that use more energy to purchase credits from the government or from industries that use less energy. Since energy is the essential component of everything that we create in our modern economy, bureaucrats will be regulating all sectors of the industrial economy and all activities of every business in America. Almost every activity that we as human beings engage in in our daily lives—including breathing—involves the release of greenhouse gases. In California there is talk of allowing the government to control the thermostats in people's homes and forcing Americans to buy fluorescent light bulbs. The bottom line: If you think the IRS is heavy-handed and intrusive, wait till companies have to comply with the new Green Police.

The overall macroeconomic effect of cap and trade will be to impose a massive though hidden tax on energy. By some estimates this tax will raise as much as $1 trillion for the federal government—which liberals are very eager to spend. A study by the economic consulting firm Arduin, Laffer & Moore Econometrics predicted that the impact of cap and trade will be as follows:

- The U.S. economy could be 5.2 percent smaller in 2020 compared to what would otherwise be expected.
- A potential income loss of about $10,800 for a family of four. That's far more than the average family pays today in income taxes.[24]

And a study by the American Council for Capital Formation predicted:

- Electricity prices could be 129 percent higher by 2030.[25]

Americans might be willing to absorb these giant sacrifices if it would stop global warming. It won't. According to climatologist Pat Michaels of the University of Virginia, cap and trade would reduce global temperatures by just 0.013 C. by 2050.[26] But what cap and trade *will* do is immediately put U.S. companies at a competitive disadvantage in world markets for two reasons. First, the global bureaucrats want the United States to reduce its emissions to a much greater extent than other countries would have to. Second, other nations, especially the Europeans, have already shown a penchant for cheating on Kyoto. In fact, in 2007, the United States reduced its carbon emissions, as a result of high energy prices, more than most industrial nations, and we *aren't* a signatory to Kyoto, while dozens of noncomplying nations in Europe *are*.

It is highly doubtful that China, India, and other fast-developing nations are going to go along with a system that would stunt their own development. Nor should they. These are countries that are pulling hundreds of millions of their citizens out of abject poverty through free market development and energy use. Why should these nations feel compelled to keep their citizens poor, hungry, malnourished, and deprived of modern living standards? In the long run economic growth for poor countries will do much more to improve living standards in the world—now and for future generations—than reducing CO_2 emissions.

If China and India, in particular, don't comply with greenhouse gas emission requirements, then businesses and capital and jobs will leave nations like the United States and migrate to Asia, where costs are already lower, but now with cap and trade will be lower still. We would suspect that hard-hat union jobs will be the first casualties, as steel, textile, chemical, electric power, computer parts, auto, engineering, and other industrial-sector firms say adios to America.

And where does it stop? The economic havoc is trivial to some of the more militant leaders of the global warming alarmism coalition. Back in 1992, U.N. climate chief Maurice Strong was remarkably candid about the green movement's real purpose: "Isn't the only hope for the planet that the industrialized civilizations collapse? Isn't our responsibility to bring that about?"[27] If that is the goal, then cap and trade schemes are the ideal solution.

The tragedy here is that there is a much better way to reduce greenhouse gases, one that is highly consistent with pro-growth policies of supply-side economics. If we were to shift our taxing system away from investment and savings and toward consumption and energy use, we could grow the economy and increase the cost of CO_2 emissions while reducing the cost of financing new technologies that will eventually solve the greenhouse gases problem. It turns out that both the Laffer flat tax and the fair tax would do exactly that. Who knew that the flat tax and the fair tax are the greenest tax systems of all?

Return of the Nativists

The Left in America doesn't have a monopoly on bad ideas. The right's infatuation with restrictionist immigration policies would also slow economic growth substantially. Immigration is one of America's greatest comparative advantages in the global economy.

The restrictionists have it all wrong.[28] Immigrants are economically vital for many reasons. First, they have a high labor force participation rate and fill vital niches in the workforce that help make our economy operate efficiently. There is very little evidence from the past twenty-five years that immigrants displace native workers from jobs or depress wages on average. States with high levels of immigration have lower overall rates of unemployment than states with few immigrants.

Second, most immigrants climb the economic ladder of success fairly rapidly and become productive and valued citizens. An analysis of the most recent 2005 data from the U.S. Census Bureau's Current Population Survey shows that foreign-born, naturalized citizen householders actually have a *higher* average income, ($65,309) than U.S.-born householders ($61,264). The federal taxes paid by naturalized citizen householders average slightly higher—$6,293 per year, compared with $6,202 for U.S.-born families.[29]

Third, immigrants have been vital to the high-tech explosion in places like Silicon Valley. An estimated one-third of all scientists and engineers in Silicon Valley are immigrants. One of us (Moore) conducted a study for the Cato Institute that identified ten high-tech firms, such as Intel, founded by immigrants whose total revenues topped $88 billion in 2005 and whose total employment totaled over 230,000 Americans.[30]

Most important, immigrants are free human capital from the rest of the world—a gift of brains, talent, and ambition. Most immigrants arrive in the United States in the prime of their working years. For example, more than 70 percent of immigrants are over the age of eighteen when they arrive in the United States. That means there are roughly 26 million immigrants in the United States today whose education and upbringing were paid for mostly by the citizens of the country of origin, not American taxpayers. The windfall to the United States of obtaining this human capital at no expense to American taxpayers is roughly $2.8 trillion. So, immigration can be thought of as a multitrillion-dollar transfer of wealth from the rest of the world to the United States.[31]

Slamming shut the golden gates and making it more difficult for immigrants to come to the United States would slow the rate of growth of the economy. The best solution to our immigration "problem," which is really better described as our immigration "advantage," is not to build fences and harass employers and create national ID cards, but to find ways for more immigrants who want to work here to get into the country with green cards legally.

But if policymakers really want to keep immigrants out, by far the best way to dissuade hard-working people from coming is to ruin the economy through higher taxes and the catalog of other cockeyed policies that we have listed above. More immigrants left the U.S. than came to these shores during the Great Depression.

A Hard Rain's a Gonna Fall

The unofficial definition of insanity is to try the same thing over and over again and expect a different result from the first one hundred times. We've summarized here the blizzard of policy ideas that are coming down the pike. Both in the United States and abroad, these ideas have been tested again and again, always with negative consequences.

When we have given speeches and informal talks to people around the country on this coming assault on economic common sense, the audiences are invariably flabbergasted. Why would the politicians do these things that are so obviously economically masochistic? Don't they get the basic economics here? Don't they see this is going against the grain of what most other nations are doing to bolster their competitiveness?

Some politicians, and we would put Barack Obama in this camp, will vote for these economy killers because they are first and foremost obsessed with creating a "fair society," with equality of income. They are willing to sacrifice growth for equity.

Dick Morris, a Bill Clinton political consultant, recently told us a story about being in the Clinton White House and getting a complaint from then First Lady Hillary Clinton about the bipartisan tax plan that her husband was about to sign into law even though it included a capital gains tax cut. Mrs. Clinton thought that this would be a giveaway to the rich and she opposed the policy. After Morris explained to her patiently that "all of the evidence indicates that this tax cut will *raise* revenue for the government and will help the economy, she responded by saying, 'Dick, that may be so, but I still think it is unfair.' "[32] Her ideology has trumped common sense. One gets the feeling that for some politicians the main purpose of tax increase plans is to punish the rich, not to help the poor—or the economy.

We would have hoped that policymakers learned from the 1970s and 1980s what works and what doesn't. But they haven't and are intent on giving the policy failures of the 1930s and 1970s one more chance.

Many liberal economists who we respect contend that the U.S. economy has the resilience to take these punches. Yes, the U.S. economy is remarkably sturdy. And we are living in an exciting period of technological change that is raising living standards at a breakneck pace. These technological trends may hopefully in the end outweigh the negative effects of policy mistakes. That happened, fortunately, in the mid-1990s. Barack Obama justifies his tax increase proposals by saying time and again that the Clinton era demonstrated that high taxes and growth are compatible. Maybe. But to us, this is as much folly as playing a game of Russian roulette with five chambers and one bullet and concluding, this game is entirely safe. The logic seems to be: The last time I stuck the gun to my temple and pulled the trigger nothing happened. By raising taxes, trade barriers, and regulatory hurdles, dear reader, America is tempting fate. We fervently hope that the economy can continue to speed forward even as the politicians fasten ever-heavier ankle weights around our legs. But even if the economy can continue to trudge forward with these growth inhibitors, why not allow the economy to grow much faster, without such restraints?

We call this chapter The Death of Economic Sanity. Perhaps a modicum of common sense will prevail and the Left will go slow instead of launching its entire arsenal of economy killers all at once. But either way prosperity is in great peril. The young people who are the loudest and most energetic supporters of Barack Obama take an expanding economy for granted, since this has been the norm for the past generation. They haven't a clue what a painful recession or double-digit unemployment or a bear market feel like. We fear they are soon going to find out.

15

PROTECTING YOUR
INVESTMENTS IN THE
TROUBLED TIMES AHEAD

W hat happens if, despite the advice in this book, taxes are raised, trade barriers are imposed, and the economy begins to decline? As the investment consultant among the authors of this book, Peter Tanous will guide us through the turbulence that may come our way. In addition to sharing some basics of constructing a good, long-term portfolio, we will point to some specific asset classes that you should consider to protect your investments during periods of stock market turbulence and decline, rising inflation, and greater volatility and risk in the financial arena.

A well-designed, intelligent portfolio should be built to endure the market's ups and downs through the years. You will likely own some real estate, starting with your home, which may well be one of your more valuable personal assets, but for most of us, the investment portfolio you will build on your own, including IRAs and 401(k) plans, will become your most important savings vehicle. Of course you will have to make changes as you go along, but as most investors know, it is the asset allocation decision, that is, what areas of the market to put your money in and in what proportion, that drives your ultimate returns more than any other decision you might make.

How Do We Build a Portfolio for the Ages?

The first thing we think about is risk. We measure risk in investment by looking at how a stock, or group of stocks, or an asset class, such as large-cap stocks, international stocks, or growth stocks, have performed in the past. We measure risk by standard deviation, which is a statistical measure of volatility. For example, in observing how large-cap stocks have fluctuated in the past, we can get an idea of how much they might fluctuate in the future. An asset class that has a high frequency of ups and downs, like emerging market stocks, is likely to continue to behave that way in the future. Wide fluctuations make those stocks riskier than the stocks that fluctuate less. The less dramatic the fluctuations, the more predictable the future returns, or so the theory goes.

The idea in constructing a sound portfolio is to have a variety of asset classes that behave differently from one another, or to put it in technical terms, asset classes with low correlation to one another. That way, if one type of stock, such as value stocks, is going down, your growth stocks may be behaving better and therefore might offset the declines in the value stocks.

A Typical Well-Balanced Portfolio

Let's make some assumptions. You are investing for a period of about twenty years—in other words, for the long term—which might include your retirement, your kids' college educations, a country house, and an estate to leave to your loved ones. Here is a typical portfolio that will likely do the job for you:

Domestic Stocks	30%
International Stocks	20%
Fixed Income	30%
Other	20%
Total:	100%

Understand that while this may be a typical portfolio, yours may be slightly different depending on a variety of factors, including your age, risk tolerance, and investment time objective so be sure to consult your personal financial adviser for more specific advice.

Domestic Stocks

This portion of your allocation should include growth stocks, value stocks, large-cap stocks, and small-cap stocks. Some quick definitions:

> *Growth stocks* are companies that have consistent growth over time, such as Coca Cola, Microsoft, Intel, General Electric, and more recently Google. Investors tend to pay a premium for companies with strong, predictable growth.
>
> *Value stocks* are stocks for bargain hunters. You shop at Neiman Marcus; they shop at Filene's Basement. Value stock buyers look for a way to buy a dollar bill for sixty or seventy cents. The companies in this group are often cyclical, or down on their luck, and often hold valuable assets that are not recognized in the current price of the stock. An example might be a company with large real estate holdings where the real estate is valued on the books of the company at a price that is far less than the current market price of the property. The

real value of the holdings might not be reflected in the company's stock price.

Large-cap stocks are simply companies whose capitalization, or the total worth of the company, is large, say $10 billion or more.

Small-cap stocks are companies that are small and are worth less than large-cap stocks, say $1 billion to $3 billion total value. There are also mid-cap stocks, those between large and small caps.

International Stocks

There was a time when the United States was by far the largest and most liquid market for stocks in the world. Most investors worldwide wanted to have most of their assets invested in the United States. The world has changed. Today, the U.S. market accounts for about half the market capitalization of the world stock markets, so investors will be wise to diversify their investment portfolio by owning some foreign stocks as well. Foreign stocks range from blue-chip names like Phillips, Nestle, Carrefour, BP, Shell, and others to small, emerging markets in such faraway places as Egypt, Turkey, and Indonesia. A smart way to invest in large international stocks is to buy a fund that mimics the EAFE (which stands for Europe, Australasia, Far East). The EAFE index offers comprehensive participation in major overseas developed markets around the world. IShares offers an ETF that tracks the EAFE index. Its symbol is EFA.

A small allocation to emerging markets is a good thing to have, but it should be small since this will likely be the most volatile asset class in any portfolio. Indeed, emerging markets have been on a tear, with gains over the past few years exceeding 30 percent per annum. We believe that in many cases these gains are directly attributable to the low-tax policies many of these countries have adopted, which allowed their economies, and their stock markets, to soar. The key to investing in emerging markets is to diversify as much as possible given the huge volatility in these markets and the fact that they are generally not as well regulated and mature as the equity markets in developed countries such as the United States and European countries. An emerging market fund worth looking at is T. Rowe Price Emerging Markets Stock fund (symbol PRMSX). Another choice is an emerging markets ETF. (ETFs are funds that trade like stocks.) A choice here would include BLDRS Emerging Markets 50 ADR. This fund invests in the stocks of the fifty most actively traded stocks from emerging markets.

Fixed Income

This will be the bond allocation of your portfolio. It is designed to provide some ballast to the fluctuations of your equities, or stocks. To insure that it does provide a safe harbor, you will want to invest in U.S. government securities or highly rated corporate or agency bonds, preferably with shorter maturities. The longer the maturity, the more the price of the bond is likely to fluctuate. It is true that the shorter-maturity bonds will pay less income, since their interest rates will be lower, but this part of your portfolio is primarily for safety, so take the shorter maturity even if it means a bit lower income. You may also want to consider municipal bonds since these are exempt from federal taxes, and in some cases state and city taxes as well, if you happen to live in a state or city that taxes your income. Municipal bonds will be especially important if a new administration raises taxes on "the wealthy" (which is bound to include you!). We suggest that you not try to pick municipal bonds yourself. This is a tricky field. Unlike Treasury bonds, municipal bonds vary in risk. Some have defaulted in the past. This is a risk you should not assume. Instead, consider hiring a professional bond manager if your portfolio is large enough, or select one or more mutual funds to do the job. Two good fund choices for short-term municipal bonds are T. Rowe Price Tax-Free Short-Intermediate (PRFSX) and Fidelity Short-Intermediate Muni Income (FSTFX). Both have good records and both funds performed well during the subprime crisis meltdown that wreaked havoc on some other bond funds. And once again, if you live in New York, California, or another state with high taxes, seek out a fund that specializes in municipal bonds from your state to get relief from both federal and state taxes.

These asset classes, different types of stocks and bonds, will provide an intelligent balance of investment vehicles that generally behave differently from one another. For your diverse equity allocations, each of these types of stocks will grow, but history shows that they will not all grow at the same time, thus providing some balance to your portfolio's long-term growth.

How Many Stocks and Bonds Should You Choose?

This answer may surprise you: How about . . . none! Let us explain. If you decide to spend the time picking stocks and bonds for your portfolio, the first question that arises is how much time will you spend on this activity? A couple of hours a week? An hour a day? Perhaps some other amount of time? Whatever length of time you choose, you ought to consider whether you are likely to do better than a professional who spends *all day* researching stocks and bonds while assembling a portfolio. If you don't have a good answer to that challenging question, the solution is to buy mutual funds and leave the stock and bond selection to professionals.

How to Invest in These Different Asset Classes

So for most of us, the easiest and most practical way to invest in the asset classes above is to buy mutual funds. By doing that, you will let the professionals pick the stocks for your investments in each of the aforementioned categories. The biggest question is whether to go "active" or passive." Active investing involves picking a mutual fund where a fund manager will pick stocks and try to beat an index, such as the S&P 500. Passive investing is simply buying the index, which you can do by buying an index fund. That way, you don't take a chance on the manager's not meeting his goal of beating the index. You are pretty much guaranteed to get the index's return. You won't underperform. Of course, you won't outperform the index either—that's the tradeoff.

So what should you do? Well, consider this: Over time, most mutual funds that use the S&P 500 as their benchmark do not beat it. One reason is that the mutual funds charge a fee, usually about 1 percent a year, and they have to make up the fee through performance just to stay even with their index benchmark. History shows that this has been very hard to do. Morningstar tracks about 350 large-cap funds that have been operating for fifteen years or longer and that use the S&P 500 as their benchmark. Fewer than half beat the S&P 500 over fifteen years and, more significantly, only a handful of them beat the index by a large enough margin that it would have been really worthwhile to have invested in them. So our advice is that you use index funds for all or part of the large-cap, international, and emerging markets portions of your portfolio. In so doing, you will pay a fraction of the fees an actively managed mutual fund will charge you. And you will never have to worry about underperforming the market. Two good choices for index funds are the Vanguard 500 Index Fund (VFINX) and the ETF with the nickname "Spiders," whose initials are SPDR and whose stock symbol is SPY.

In the other areas of mutual funds, specifically small caps and specialized investment strategies, you might try to seek out talented mutual fund managers who have a record of outperforming their segment of the market. Fund groups like Morningstar can help you find these managers.

One last bit of advice on the subject of mutual funds: There are two types of mutual funds, load funds, and no-load funds. The load funds charge a front-end or back-end fee and sometimes both, often as high as 5 percent. Most of that goes to the salesman who sells the fund to you. In our opinion, unless you have a lifelong penchant for supporting the livelihood of mutual fund salesmen, stick to no-load funds that charge no sales commission at all. There are plenty of very good no-load funds.

Other Investments

The "Other" category we have included in your portfolio recommendations is something that most portfolios would not have had a decade or so ago. So why is it there today? Suppose you had good reasons to believe that the economy was going to suffer as a result of misguided tax and trade policies, which would in turn hurt business prospects for an extended period? If that were to happen, a savvy investor should adjust his or her asset allocation to reflect the changed outlook. That is our challenge here.

We know that your investment portfolio will consist of the fairly traditional investments we discussed, such as large-cap stocks, small-cap stocks, some international stocks, and Treasury, corporate, and municipal bonds. Depending on the size of your portfolio, you might also have some exposure to hedge funds, either individually or through funds of funds. Now let's think about what happens during times of market turbulence and economic stress.

Earlier, we described in some detail what will happen to the economy if our leaders make unwise decisions about taxes, trade,

297

and protectionism. The most obvious possibility is that the stock market will go down as the economy deteriorates and earnings falter. The single most important factor contributing to stock price movements is earnings. Earnings support stock prices more than anything else. In times of ebullience, stocks may get a bit ahead of themselves as investor enthusiasm causes buyers to bid up the price for anticipated earnings. The classic example of this was the dot-com boom in the late 1990s. Companies with no earnings at all were bid up to stratospheric prices based on the expectation that high earnings would eventually materialize. When they didn't, the stock prices crashed. Similarly, when earnings increase at a fast clip, this trend is reflected in the rising price of the stock. So it is normal that when investors anticipate that earnings will go down, not up, stocks tend to decline.

Some of the negative factors that we want to hedge are these:

- Declining corporate earnings.
- Rising commodity prices.
- Inflation.

To address these issues, we will make three recommendations that will allow you to bulletproof your portfolio through the bad times, or at least until politicians come to their senses and adopt the timely and proven economic measures we have discussed in this book. In essence, we recommend that you allocate approximately 20 percent of your portfolio to some new asset classes designed to protect you in the event of economic downturns due to various causes.

Beating Inflation—Tips

Here's a good tip: TIPS. TIPS stands for Treasury Inflation Protected Securities. These are the safest bonds you can buy, U.S. government bonds, with the wrinkle that these bonds adjust for inflation. They were first issued in 1997. Here's how they work.

A regular U.S. Treasury security pays you the same interest rate for the life of the loan. So if you buy a Treasury note with a coupon of 4 percent, twice a year you will get a check that pays you the equivalent of 4 percent each year. TIPS are different. With TIPS, the U.S. Treasury adjusts the *principal amount* of the bond each month (after a two-month lag) to keep pace with inflation. The calculation is based on the Consumer Price Index. Because of this important inflation-hedging feature, TIPS have a lower interest rate than regular Treasury securities. This creates a judgment issue: When is it a good time to buy TIPS?

To answer that question, you must become familiar with "the spread." The TIPS spread is the difference between the yield on the regular Treasury securities and the TIPS securities of the same maturity. So if the regular ten-year Treasuries are yielding 4 percent and the TIPS yield 1.8 percent, the spread is 2.2 percent. That 2.2 percent is the magic number that reflects what investors believe the inflation rate to be. Since the principal amount of TIPS adjusts for inflation, the way to look at this is that if you think inflation will be *above* 2.2 percent you are better off buying TIPS, and if you believe inflation will be *below* 2.2 percent you will do better with the regular Treasury bonds. In general, however, it is a good idea to allocate some portion of your portfolio to TIPS to protect against inflation in the long run, whether the result of misguided government policies or a spate of rising prices.

TIPS can be bought directly from the U.S. Treasury (www .Treasurydirect.gov). There are also several TIPS bond funds, including the PIMCO-managed Harbor Real Return Institutional Fund and the Vanguard Inflation Protected Securities fund, which has a low expense ratio of 0.20 percent. Consider splitting the fixed-income allocation of your portfolio evenly between regular bonds and TIPS.

Gold

Gold is an investment that covers a broad swath of conflicting characteristics and is unlike any other investment choice you might make. When the United States went off the gold standard in 1971 and stopped backing the dollar with gold at the rate of $35 per ounce of gold, as stipulated in the Bretton Woods Agreement of 1944, gold became an investment commodity available to millions of Americans.

One thing everyone knew for sure: Gold was a hedge against both inflation and political turmoil. Indeed, Europeans grew up hoarding gold against emergencies when no paper currency would have any value. The French saved gold Napoleon coins religiously—and still do.

But the history of gold as an investment commodity for Americans is a turbulent one. Take a look at Figure 15-1.

This chart shows the history of gold prices since 1970. Note that gold reached a price of around $850 in 1980 and didn't see that price again until 2008, when gold topped $1,000 an ounce for

Figure 15-1: **Gold price (US$/oz.)**

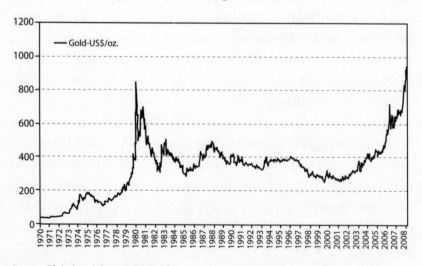

Source: Global Insight, World Gold.

300

the first time in history. An investment in gold was a very poor investment through most of the eighties and nineties.

Why Is Gold Going Up Now?

Remember, gold is not used only as a store of value, it is always a prominent item in jewelry (as if you didn't know!). Growing demand from developing countries, and especially from India, is fueling heightened demand for the precious metal. Indeed, India alone accounts for more than 30 percent of demand for the precious metal, and as the Indian economy grows and prospers, so will its demand for gold. Add to that the traditional reason to buy gold as a store of value and protection against inflation, and with millions of new buyers in the market every year it isn't hard to understand why the demand, and the price, for gold is rising.

Another point: In recent years China has maintained a tight peg between its currency and the U.S. dollar. It does so by investing its reserves in U.S. dollars through Treasury and other U.S. agency bonds. There is increasing demand by the United States for China to float its currency to bring its prices more in line with those of other countries. If China does so (and it seems the process has started), it may limit its future U.S. bond purchases and increase its investments in other real assets. China might no longer find U.S. dollar denominated bonds as attractive as in the past if the dollar is going down in value compared to its own currency. In that case, China might increase its investment in other real assets, such as gold.

Gold as an inflation hedge: Gold has traditionally been considered one of the best inflation hedges. In fact, throughout history, its correlation with inflation is among the best compared to the other commodities.

Should You Own Gold?

In the old days, when you visited your portfolio manager at your bank or your investment firm, the fellow in the three-piece suit sat behind his mahogany desk and developed a portfolio for you that was likely the traditional 60/40 model, that is, 60 percent in stocks, mostly blue chips, and 40 percent in bonds, mostly U.S. government and triple-A-rated corporates. Indeed, some still do just that.

You, however, would be well advised to add some different asset classes to your modern portfolio in view of the uncertainties that lurk ahead. Political and economic uncertainty are with us and are likely to be around for longer than we want. Inflation is also a risk. A good way to hedge all of these bets is to own some gold assets. You don't have to go out and buy bullion, unless you have a place to store it safely and you enjoy looking at it from time to time. You can buy a gold ETF, a security that trades like a stock and is the paper equivalent of buying gold. It will go up and down in the same proportion as the price of gold. The symbol for one of the most liquid gold ETFs is GLD. Or you can buy a gold fund, one that invests both in the commodity and in gold-producing companies' stocks. A good choice of gold funds is the Tocqueville Gold Fund, which has an excellent record.

How much of your assets should you put in gold? It will depend to some extent on your personal level of anxiety. If you are concerned that economic policies will wreak havoc with the economy for a spell, you will likely have a larger allocation to gold than someone who is not quite as concerned as you are. In any event, don't put more than 10 percent of the portfolio in gold under any circumstance. There have been periods when gold was a poor investment for a long time.

Should You Invest in Oil?

The oil price is highly unstable over time. The oil market has gone through wild price gyrations, as in the 1970s and now, when the price has skyrocketed and oil investors got rich, and in the 1980s and the 1990s, when it plummeted and oil investors went bust. The oil price is highly correlated with inflation, the price of gold, geopolitical unrest, especially in the Middle East, and domestic politics (think of all the witless congressional restrictions on drilling for oil in the U.S.—in Alaska, the outer continental shelf, and on public lands in the continental states).

Oil will continue to be a volatile commodity. And the problem of producing enough of it to satisfy global demand may not go away for decades to come. So investors should consider an allocation to oil/energy for some part of their *long-term* portfolio. Like gold, oil does not correlate well with stocks, so if the stock market goes into a tailspin as a result of higher taxes and other misguided economic policies, oil may well be a refuge from the decline. Similarly, if an unforeseen adverse political development takes place in any of the major oil-producing countries, the bad news will be reflected in a higher oil price.

There are a number of ways to invest in oil and energy. One of the best is the Vanguard Energy Fund, which invests in oil and energy companies and has daily liquidity and very low expenses. Another is the oil ETF, symbol XLE, which offers a pure participation in the price of oil and trades daily like a stock. For most portfolios, an allocation of no more than 10 percent may be appropriate, given the volatility of this particular asset class.

Over the long term, history shows that an intelligently allocated portfolio of stocks and bonds will provide a good return through the economy's ups and downs. But if you foresee a period ahead in which the economy may be headed for trouble as a result of poor economic policy decisions, higher taxes, and harmful protectionist initiatives, then you will be well advised to adjust your investments accordingly. Over time, the economy will continue to grow. Political leaders who promote harmful economic policies will eventually be replaced, and better policies will follow. But in the meantime it makes sense to protect one's assets.

NOTES

Chapter 1. The Gathering Economic Storm

1. Ronald Reagan, acceptance speech at the 1980 Republican convention, Detroit, MI, July 17, 1980, http://www.nationalcenter.org/ReaganConvention1980.html
2. The Beatles, *The Beatles Anthology* (San Francisco: Chronicle Books, 2000).
3. Chalmers Johnson, *MITI and the Japanese Miracle* (Stanford, CA: Stanford University Press, 1982).
4. Nikkei Net Interactive, www.nni.nikkei.co.jp
5. Federal Reserve Board, *Flow of Funds Report*, B.100 Balance Sheet of Households and Nonprofit Organizations, Line 41, June 2008, http://www.federalreserve.gov/Releases/Z1/Current/z1r-5.pdf
6. Census Bureau, *2008 Statistical Abstract of the United States*, Tables 670 and 671, http://www.census.gov/compendia/statab/cats/income_expenditures_poverty_wealth/household_income.html; Internal Revenue Service, Statistics of Income, *SOI Bulletin* article—Individual Income Tax Rates and Tax Shares, Table 5, http://www.irs.gov/taxstats/indtaxstats/article/0,,id=133521,00.html
7. Bruce Bartlett and Peter Orzsag, *Rich Man, Poor Man: Income Inequality*, Hoover Institution, July 18, 2001, http://www.hoover.org/multimedia/uk/3003921.html
8. Drew Carey, "Living Large: America's Middle Class," Reason.tv, http://reason.tv/video/show/61.html
9. Paul Skeldon, *Musical Mobile*. Juniper Research, http://techpolicy.typepad.com/tpp/juniper_ringtone.pdf
10. Giving USA Foundation, "U.S. charitable giving estimated to be $306.39 billion in 2007," press release, June 23, 2008, www.givingusa.org/press_releases/releases/20080622.html

11. Barbara Ehrenreich, "Is the Middle Class Doomed?" *New York Times Magazine*, September 7, 1986.
12. Census Bureau, *2008 Statistical Abstract of the United States*, Table 673, http://www.census.gov/compendia/statab/tables/08s0673.pdf
13. Robert Fogel, *The Fourth Great Awakening & the Future of Egalitarianism* (Chicago: University of Chicago Press, 2000).
14. The Congressional Budget Office, "Changes in the Economic Resources of Low-Income Households with Children," May 2007, http://www.cbo .gov/doc.cfm?index=8113
15. Department of the Treasury, *Income Mobility in the U.S. from 1996 to 2005*, November 13, 2007.
16. P. J. O'Rourke, *Parliament of Whores* (Grove/Atlantic, Inc., 2003).
17. ABC Democratic candidates presidential debate, Philadelphia, PA, April 16, 2008.
18. Amity Schlaes, *The Forgotten Man: A New History of the Great Depression* (HarperCollins, 2007).
19. Arthur Laffer, "The Condition of Our Nation," 2008. Thinking Economically, http://www.texaspolicy.com/pdf/TE-Lesson4-Laffer-final.pdf
20. Calculations based on Bureau of Economic Analysis, Table 1: International Transactions Account Data.
21. Calculations based on net change in number of employed persons, Bureau of Labor Statistics data, series LNS12000000, http://www.bls.gov/ data/home.htm
22. Bureau of Economic Analysis, National Income Product Accounts Tables.
23. Peter Goodman, "The Free Market: A False Idol After All?" *New York Times Magazine*, December 30, 2007.
24. 2007 Democratic primary debate at Howard University, June 28, 2007.
25. Robert Reich, "An Introduction to Economic Populism," Robert Reich's blog, http://robertreich.blogspot.com/2006/12/introduction-to-economic-populism.html
26. 2007 AFL-CIO Democratic primary forum, August 8, 2007.

Chapter 2. How a Cocktail Napkin Changed the World: The Laffer Curve

1. Henry George, *Progress and Poverty* (New York: Cosimo Inc., 2006) 307. Originally published in 1879.
2. Jude Wanniski, "Taxes, Revenues, and the 'Laffer Curve,'" *The Public Interest*, Winter 1978.
3. Cheney, Richard. Interview of the vice president by Nina Easton, *Fortune* magazine, November 9, 2007, Office of the Vice President, press release, http://www.whitehouse.gov/news/releases/2007/11/20071109-11.html

4. Stephen Moore, "The Supply-Side Solution," *The Wall Street Journal*, November 9, 2007, http://www.opinionjournal.com/extra/?id=110010844

5. Adam Smith, *An Inquiry into the Nature and Causes of the Wealth of Nations*, 1776, Book Five, Chapter II, Article IV, http://www.adamsmith.org/smith/won-b5-c2-article-4-ss5.htm

6. Keynes, John Maynard Keynes, *The Collected Writings of John Maynard Keynes* (London: Macmillan Cambridge University Press, 1972).

7. Thomas Jefferson, first inaugural address, Washington, DC, March 4, 1801.

8. Bruce Bartlett, "Rock and Taxes," *National Review*, December 5, 2001, http://www.nationalreview.com/nrof_bartlett/bartlett120501.shtml

9. "Bono Avoids Taxes, Joins Forbes," NewsMax.com Wires, August 8, 2006, http://archive.newsmax.com/archives/articles/2006/8/7/145346.shtml?s=lh

10. John Maynard Keynes, "The General Theory on Employment, Interest, and Money," 1936.

11. Edward Prescott, "Why Do Americans Work So Much More than Europeans?" NBER Working Paper w10316, February 2004. This and subsequent NBER working papers are viewable at www.nber.org.

12. Raj Chetty and Emmanuel Saez, "Do Dividend Payments Respond to Taxes? Preliminary Evidence from the 2003 Dividend Tax Cut," NBER Working Paper w10572, June 2004.

13. Christina Romer and David Romer, *The Macroeconomic Effects of Tax Changes: Estimates Based on a New Measure of Fiscal Shocks* (Berkeley, CA: University of California, November 2006), http://www.economics.ucr.edu/seminars/fall06/ets/Romer11-27-06.pdf

14. Tax Foundation Staff, "Cross-Border Shopping by Beer and Cigarette Buyers Highlights Tax Competition Among States," Tax Foundation, December 15, 2002, http://www.taxfoundation.org/news/show/239.html

15. Daniel J. Mitchell, *The Impact of Higher Taxes: More Spending, Economic Stagnation, Fewer Jobs, and Higher Deficits*, Heritage Foundation *Backgrounder #925*, February 10, 1993, http://www.heritage.org/Research/Taxes/bg925.cfm

16. Oyez Project, *McCulloch v. Maryland*, 17 U.S. 316 (1819), viewable at http://www.oyez.org/cases/1792-1850/1819/1819_0/

17. Jonathan Chait, "Feast of the Wingnuts," *New Republic*, September 10, 2007, http://www.tnr.com/columnists/story.html?id=880f4273-e2d6-4914-b15b-ffcce401155a

18. Jonathan Chait, "Less Is Moore," *New Republic*, June 30, 1997.

19. Paul Krugman, "Reckonings; Being Bob Forehead," *New York Times*, January 26, 2000, http://query.nytimes.com/gst/fullpage.html?res=9501E7DA143CF935A15752C0A9669C8B63

20. Department of the Treasury, "Income Mobility in the U.S. from 1996 to 2005," November 2007.

21. Robert Frank, "Reshaping the Debate on Raising Taxes," *New York Times*, December 9, 2007.

22. Arthur B. Laffer, "The Virtues of the Invisible Hand," Laffer Associates, June 5, 2008.

Chapter 3. "We Can Do Bettah": Tax-Cutting Lessons from the Twentieth Century

1. William Ahern, "Comparing the Kennedy, Reagan and Bush Tax Cuts," Tax Foundation, *Fiscal Fact No. 15*, August 24, 2004, http://www.taxfoun dation.org/news/show/323.html

2. Stephen Moore, "Remembering the real economic legacy of JFK," *Human Events*, May 19, 2003.

3. "The Great Consensus," *Time*, December 21, 1962, http://www.time.com/time/magazine/article/0,9171,940125,00.html (From a speech John F. Kennedy gave to the Economic Club of New York in December, 1962).

4. Ibid.

5. Cited in: Stephen Moore. "Our Income-Tax Monstrosity." *National Review*, April 15, 2003, http://www.nationalreview.com/moore/moore041503.asp

6. Cited in: Walter Williams, J. Kenneth Blackwell, John Fund, and Steve Forbes, "The Flat Tax: Revitalizing the American Dream," Heritage Lecture #569, Heritage Foundation, April 8, 1996.

7. Cited in: Lawrence Reed, "The Power to Tax," *The Freeman: Ideas on Liberty*, Vol. 45, No. 10, Foundation for Economic Education, October 1995, http://www.fee.org/Publications/the-Freeman/article.asp?aid=4640&print _view=true.

8. "Warren G. Harding: The Return to Normalcy," Encyclopedia Britannica, 2008, http://www.britannica.com/eb/article-9116882/Document-Warren -G-Harding-The-Return-to-Normalcy

9. "Expression." *Time*, February 18, 1924, http://www.time.com/time/printout/0,8816,717719,00.html

10. Joint Economic Committee, "The Mellon and Kennedy Tax Cuts: A Review and Analysis," staff study, June 18, 1982.

11. Quoted in: Jude Wanniski, Supply Side U *Lesson #6*, Spring 1998.

12. Quoted in: Robert E. Keleher and William P. Orzechowski, "Supply-Side Fiscal Policy: An Historical Analysis of a Rejuvenated Idea," in *Supply-Side Economics: a Critical Appraisal*, ed. Richard H. Fink (Frederick, MD: University Publications of America, 1982), 146–147.

13. Ibid.

14. Office of Management and Budget, *Historical Tables of the United States Government*, Table 1.1—Summary of Receipts, Outlays, and Surpluses or Deficits (-): 1789–2009, http://www.whitehouse.gov/omb/budget/fy2005/hist.html

15. Murray N. Rothbard, *America's Great Depression* (Auburn, AL: Mises Institute, 2005), 5th Edition, 285–321.

16. Bureau of Economic Analysis, NIPA Tables. Table 1.71-1.7.4; Bureau of Labor Statistics, number of employed persons, Bureau of Labor Statistics, detailed employment statistical tables, http://www.bls.gov/data/home.htm

17. Mark Shields, "Bush's Growing Credibility Gap," CNN, October 17, 2005, http://www.cnn.com/2005/POLITICS/10/17/bush.credibility/index.html

18. Opening statement, first presidential candidate debate, delivered September 26, 1960, Chicago, IL, http://www.americanrhetoric.com/speeches/jfkopeningstatementnixondebate1.htm

19. John T. Woolley and Gerhard Peters, The American Presidency Project [online]. Santa Barbara, CA: University of California (hosted), Gerhard Peters (database), http://www.presidency.ucsb.edu/ws/?pid=29602

20. Tax Foundation, "U.S. Federal Individual Income Tax Rates History, 1913–2008," January 7, 2008, http://www.taxfoundation.org/taxdata/show/151.html. Based on IRS data.

21. David Halberstam, *The Best and the Brightest* (New York: Ballantine Books, 1993), 20th anniversary edition.

22. Quoted in: Bruce Bartlett, "The Kennedy Tax Cuts," in *Supply-Side Economics: a Critical Appraisal*, ed. Richard H. Fink (Frederick, MD: University Publications of America, 1982), 276–277.

23. 1963 Economic Report of the President, U.S. Government Printing Office, Washington, DC, 1963, available through the St. Louis Federal Reserve Bank at http://fraser.stlouisfed.org/publications/ERP/issue/1080

24. Bartlett, "The Kennedy Tax Cuts," in *Supply-Side Economics: a Critical Appraisal*, 278.

25. Ibid.

26. Walter W. Heller, "Kennedy Economics Revisited," in *Supply-Side Economics: a Critical Appraisal*, ed. Richard H. Fink (Frederick, MD: University Publications of America, 1982), 290–292.

27. *U.S. News & World Report*, June 13, 1966.

28. Arthur Okun, "The 1964 Tax Cut," in *Perspectives on Economic Growth*, ed. Walter W. Heller (New York: Random House, 1968).

29. Joint Economic Committee, "The Mellon and Kennedy Tax Cuts: A Review and Analysis," staff study, June 18, 1982.

30. Quoted in: Robert L. Bartley, *The Seven Fat Years* (New York: Free Press, 1992), 74.

Chapter 4. Honey, We Shrunk the Economy: The Awful 1970s

1. William Simon, "30 years ago in Reason," *Reason* magazine, February 2008.

2. Andy Behrens, "Disco Demolition: Bell Bottoms be gone!" ESPN, August 11, 2004, http://sports.espn.go.com/espn/page3/story?page=behrens/040809

3. Tony Kornheiser and Tom Zito, "John Lennon: Kevto a Cultural Phenomenon," *Washington Post*, December 10, 1980, A1.

4. John Kenneth Galbraith, *The Affluent Society* (Mariner Books edition, 1998).

5. "The Cities: The Price of Optimism," *Time*, August 1, 1969.

6. Dow Jones Indexes, data available at http://www.djindexes.com/mdsidx/index.cfm?event=showAverages

7. Office of Management and Budget, *Historical Tables of the United States Government*, Table 1.1—Summary of Receipts, Outlays, and Surpluses or Deficits: 1789–2009, http://www.whitehouse.gov/omb/budget/fy2005/hist.html

8. George Herring, *LBJ and Vietnam: A Different Kind of War* (Austin, TX: University of Texas Press, 1996).

9. Lee Edwards, "Lyndon Johnson's Watergate," Heritage Foundation, June 7, 2005, http://www.heritage.org/press/commentary/ed060705b.cfm

10. Census Bureau, *1981 Current Population Survey*.

11. Martin Feldstein, "The Conceptual Foundations of Supply-Side Economics," in *Supply-Side Economics in the 1980s*, ed. Donald L. Koch (Westport, CT: Quoram Books, 1982), 145.

12. Patrick Fleenor and Andrew Chamberlain, "Backgrounder on the Individual Alternative Minimum Tax (AMT)," The Tax Foundation, *Fiscal Fact No. 26*, May 24, 2005, http://www.taxfoundation.org/publications/show/498.html

13. Ibid.

14. Daniel Yergin and Joseph Stanislaw, *The Commanding Heights* (New York: Simon & Schuster, 1998), 60–64.

15. Ibid.

16. Arthur Laffer, "The Bitter Fruits of Devaluation," *Wall Street Journal*, January 10, 1974.

17. Ayn Rand, *Atlas Shrugged* (New York: Random House, 1957).

18. "A Bolt of Blue Lightning," *Time*, August 23, 1971, http://www.time.com/time/magazine/article/0,9171,877278-1,00.html

19. See Note 7.

20. Paul Craig Roberts, "The Breakdown of the Keynesian Model," in *Supply-Side Economics: a Critical Appraisal*, ed. Richard H. Fink (Frederick, MD: University Publications of America, 1982), 146–147.

21. Stephen Moore, "Government: America's #1 Growth Industry," Institute for Policy Innovation 1995, 41–43.

22. Gerald R. Ford, presidential address to a joint session of Congress on the economy, October 8, 1974, http://www.ford.utexas.edu/LIBRARY/speeches/740121.htm

23. Office of Management and Budget, *Historical Tables of the United States Government*, Table 1.1—Summary of Receipts, Outlays, and Surpluses

or Deficits: 1789–2009, http://www.whitehouse.gov/omb/budget/fy2005/hist.html

24. Stephen Hayward, *The Real Jimmy Carter: How Our Worst Ex-President Undermines American Foreign Policy, Coddles Dictators and Created the Party of Clinton and Kerry* (Washington, DC: Regnery, 2004).

25. Ibid.

26. Robert L. Bartley, *The Seven Fat Years* (New York: Free Press, 1992), 67–70.

27. James Gwartney and Richard Stroup, "Marginal Tax Rates, Tax Avoidance, and the Reagan Tax Cut," in *Supply-Side Economics in the 1980s*, ed. Donald L. Koch (Westport, CT: Quoram Books, 1982).

28. Bartley, 74.

29. Based on data from the Department of Energy Information Administration's history of crude prices, available at http://tonto.eia.doe.gov/oog/info/twip/twip_crude.html

30. "The President's Proposed Energy Policy." *Jimmy Carter*. American Experience, PBS, http://www.pbs.org/wgbh/amex/carter/filmmore/ps_energy.html

31. Hayward, 100.

32. Ibid., 101.

33. Stephen Moore, "The Coming Age of Abundance," *Progress and the Planet*, Competitive Enterprise Institute, February 1995, http://www.heartland.org/pdf/23734a.pdf

34. Federal Reserve Board, *Flow of Funds Report*, B.100. Balance Sheet of Households and Nonprofit Organizations, Line 41, June 2008, http://www.federalreserve.gov/Releases/Z1/Current/z1r-5.pdf

35. Federal Reserve Bank of Minneapolis, Consumer Price Index, http://www.minneapolisfed.org/research/data/us/calc/hist1913.cfm

36. Treasury Department, Data on the Federal Funds Rate and Treasury Bills,http://www.ustreas.gov/offices/domestic-finance/debt-management/interest-rate/

37. Jimmy Carter, *Anti-Inflation Policy Remarks to Members of the American Society of Newspaper Editors Announcing the Administration's Policy*, April 11, 1978, http://www.presidency.ucsb.edu/ws/index.php?pid=30652

38. Stephen Moore, "Half-Truths and Consequences: The Legacy of the Global 2000," Heritage Foundation, http://www.heritage.org/Research/EnergyandEnvironment/IA34.cfm

39. Kurt Anderson, "America's Upbeat Mood," *Time*, September 24, 1984, http://www.time.com/time/magazine/article/0,9171,923635,00.html

40. Census Bureau, *Historical Income Tables*, Table H-1, http://www.census.gov/hhes/www/income/histinc/h01ar.html

41. Bureau of Labor Statistics, *Employment and Earnings, 2008*, Table 1, http://www.bls.gov/cps/cpsa2007.pdf and Federal Reserve Bank of Min-

neapolis, Consumer Price Index. http://www.minneapolisfed.org/
research/data/us/calc/hist1913.cfm

Chapter 5. The Twenty-Five-Year Boom:
The Reagan Economic Revolution

1. "Afternoon with Barack Obama," interview with the *Reno Gazette-Journal*, video available at http://news.rgj.com/apps/pbcs.dll/article?
AID=/20080115/VIDEO/80115026
2. Based on data from the National Association of Realtors.
3. Alan Blinder, "The Republican Riverboat Gamble," *New York Times*, August 20, 1996, http://query.nytimes.com/gst/fullpage.html?res=9F0DE5D
71430F933A1575BC0A960958260
4. Yahoo! Finance, http://finance.yahoo.com/q/hp?s=%5EDJI
5. Bureau of Labor Statistics, http://www.bls.gov/data/#unemployment
6. National Association of Realtors, "Real Estate Sales Statistics: Existing
Home Sales and Pending Home Sales." http://www.realtor.org/research/
research/ehspage
7. William Greider, "The Education of David Stockman," *The Atlantic*, December 1981.
8. Michael Wachter and Susan Wachter, *Towards a New U.S. Industrial Policy?* (Philadelphia: University of Pennsylvania Press, 1981), 371.
9. James Pethokoukis, "The Return of Big Government," *U.S. News & World Report*, April 11, 2008, http://www.usnews.com/articles/business/economy/
2008/04/11/the-return-of-big-government.html
10. Richard McKenzie. *Public or Private Choices*, Cato Institute, 1984.
11. Daniel Mitchell, "The Results are in on the 1990 Budget Agreement," Heritage Foundation, *Backgrounder #842*, July 18, 1991, http://www.heritage
.org/research/budget/bg842.cfm
12. Jack Kemp, "Supply-Side Economics: An American Renaissance," *Supply-Side Economics in the 1980s*, ed. Donald L. Koch (Westport, CT: Quoram
Books, 1982), 50.
13. "At Last a Tax Cut," *Wall Street Journal*, Review and Outlook. January 3,
1983.
14. Stephen Moore, "Clinton's Dismal Scientists—Bill Clinton's Economic
Advisers," *National Review*, March 19, 1993.
15. Chalmers Johnson, *MITI and the Japanese Miracle*. (Stanford, CA: Stanford University Press, 1982).
16. Moore, *National Review*, March 19, 1993.
17. Bureau of Economic Analysis, NIPA Tables 1.1.5 and 1.1.6, http://www
.bea.gov/national/nipaweb/SelectTable.asp
18. Charles Alexander, "Cheers for a Banner Year," *Time*, January 2, 1984.

19. Jeffrey Birnbaum, *The Showdown at Gucci Gulch* (New York: Vintage, 1988).
20. NBER, Working Papers, 1999.
21. Robert L. Bartley, *The Seven Fat Years*. (New York: Free Press, 1992), 74.
22. Ibid.
23. Martin Anderson, *Revolution*, Harcourt, first edition, May 1988.
24. Bartley, *The Seven Fat Years*, 43–60.
25. Ibid.
26. Paul Craig Roberts, "Theoretical Foundations of Supply-Side Economics," in *Supply-Side Economics in the 1980s*, ed. Donald L. Koch (Westport, CT: Quoram Books, 1982), 50.
27. Author calculations based on Bureau of Economic Analysis, Table 1: International Transactions.
28. Testimony in front of the Joint Economic Committee, 1982.
29. Dale W. Jorgenson and Kun-Young Yun, *Lifting the Burden: Tax Reform, the Cost of Capital, and U.S. Economic Growth* (Cambridge, MA: The MIT Press, 2001).
30. Warren Brookes, "The Tax Capitalization Hypothesis," *Policy Review*, Winter 1987.
31. Lawrence B. Lindsey, "Individual Taxpayer Response to Tax Cuts: 1982–1984: With implications for the revenue maximizing tax rate," *Journal of Public Economics*, 1987, Vol. 33, issue 2, 173–206.
32. Moore, *National Review*, March 19, 1993.
33. See Note 14.
34. Jude Wanniski, "It's Time to Cut Taxes," *Wall Street Journal*, December 11, 1974.
35. *The New Republic*, editorial, September 9, 1985, 7.
36. Authors' calculations based on data from the Federal Reserve and U.S. Treasury.
37. Robert Heilbroner, "How I Learned to Love the Deficit," *New York Times*, September 4, 1988, http://query.nytimes.com/gst/fullpage.html?res=940DEFDB1F3BF937A3575AC0A96E948260
38. Congressional Budget Office, *Historical Budget Tables*, 2008, http://www.cbo.gov/budget/historical.shtml
39. Ibid. Also Bureau of Economic Analysis, NIPA Tables 1.1.5 and 1.1.6.
40. U.S. Small Business Administration, Office of the Chief Counsel for Advocacy, The Changing Burden of Regulation, Paperwork, and Tax Compliance on Small Business: A Report to Congress, Washington, D.C., October 1995.
41. James Bianco, "A Bull Market-in Regulation," *National Review*, September 16, 2002.
42. Robert Crandall and Jerry Elig, *Economic Deregulation and Customer Choice: Lessons for the Electric Industry*, Center for Market Processes, 1997.

313

43. Census Bureau, *Statistical Abstract of the United States*, 2008, Table 641. http://www.census.gov/compendia/statab/tables/08s0641.pdf
44. Ibid.
45. Bureau of Economic Analysis, International Transactions, Table One, June 2008.
46. Ibid.
47. Thomas M. Humbert, *The Case for Tax Cuts Now*, Backgrounder #161, January 14, 1982. http://www.heritage.org/Research/Taxes/bg161.cfm
48. Ibid.
49. *Survey of Consumer Finances, 2004.*
50. Nina Shapiro, "Can the Rich Be Good?" *The Seattle Weekly*, April 16, 2003, http://www.seattleweekly.com/2003-04-16/news/can-the-rich-be-good.php
51. Michael Cox and Richard Alm, *The Myth of Rich and Poor* (New York: Basic Books, 2000).
52. Census Bureau, *2008 Statistical Abstract of the United States*, Tables 670 and 671, http://www.census.gov/compendia/statab/cats/income_expenditures_poverty_wealth/household_income.html
53. Census Bureau. *Historical Income Tables*. Table H-1. http://www.census.gov/hhes/www/income/histinc/h01ar.html
54. Montgomery County, MD, Department of Finance.
55. William Niskanen and Stephen Moore, "Supply-Side Tax Cuts and the Truth about the Reagan Economic Record," Octo-ber 22, 1996, Policy Analysis no. 261. http://www.cato.org/pub_display.php?pub_id=1120
56. Ibid.
57. David Rosenbaum, "The Push and Pull Over Taxes," *New York Times*, December 8, 1992.
58. See Note 55.
59. Sylvia Nasar, "The Rich Get Richer, But the Question Is by How Much." *New York Times*, July 20, 1992.
60. Internal Revenue Service, *Statistics of Income, SOI Bulletin* article-Individual Income Tax Rates and Tax Shares, Table 5.
61. Ronald Reagan, presidential farewell address to the nation, January 11, 1989.

Chapter 6. What Bill Clinton Could Teach Barack Obama

1. Joe Holley, "Richard Darman; Influenced Policy of 4 GOP Presidents," *Washington Post*, January 26, 2008, B06.
2. Andrew Rosenthal. "White House; Bush Says Raising Taxes Was Biggest Blunder of His Presidency." *New York Times*, March 4, 1992.
3. *Congressional Quarterly*, November 1990.
4. Congressional Budget Office, *Historical Budget Tables*.

5. Stephen Moore, "Why America Does Not Need New Taxes," *Heritage Foundation Backgrounder*, January 1989.
6. Stephen Moore, "Crime of the Century: The 1990 Budget Deal After Two Years," Cato Institute, *Policy Analysis no. 182*, October 12, 1992, http://www.cato.org/pub_display.php?pub_id=1042&full=1
7. Paul Craig Roberts, "Theoretical Foundations of Supply-Side Economics," in *Supply-Side Economics in the 1980s*, ed. Donald L Koch (Westport, CT: Quoram Books, 1982).
8. Howard Gleckman, "The Budget: Never Make a Tough Choice Today . . . ," *Business Week*, November 12, 1990.
9. Robert Barro, "How Tax Reform Drives Growth and Investment," *Business Week*, January 24, 2005.
10. Mathew Kibbe, "The Laffer Curve in Reverse," *Wall Street Journal*, July 22, 1991.
11. Paul Gigot, "Oops, Weren't We Going to Soak the Rich?" *Wall Street Journal*, July 9, 1993.
12. James Taylor, "Luxury Tax Sinks U.S. Boating Industry," *Wall Street Journal*, April 24, 1991.
13. Kim Strassel, "Reluctant Class Warriors," *Wall Street Journal*, August 3, 2007.
14. Joshua Cooper Ramo, "The Three Marketeers." *Time*, February 15, 1999, http://www.time.com/time/asia/asia/magazine/1999/990215/cover1.html
15. Jonathan Adler, "Clinton's Stealth BTU Tax," *Washington Times*, October 14, 1996.
16. Bob Woodward, *The Agenda: Inside the Clinton White House* (New York: Simon & Schuster, 1994).
17. Long-Term Budget Outlook, Congressional Budget Office, December 1995, http://www.cbo.gov/ftpdocs/69xx/doc6982/12-15-LongTermOutlook.pdf
18. Congressional Budget Office, Economic and Budget Outlook from April 1995.
19. Speech by President Clinton in NAFTA bill signing ceremony, December 8, 1993.
20. Rebecca Blank and Ron Haskins, *The New World of Welfare* (Brookings Institution Press, 2001).
21. Robert Rector and William F. Lauber, *America's Failed $5.4 Trillion War on Poverty* (Washington, DC: Heritage Foundation, 1995).
22. Michael Tanner, Stephen Moore, and David Hartman, "The Work vs. Welfare Trade-Off: An Analysis of the Total Level of Welfare Benefits by State," Cato Institute Policy analysis no. 240, September 19, 1995.
23. "Workers Must Earn 45k to Match Welfare," *New York Post*, August 2, 1994.
24. Authors' calculations based on Census Bureau income data.
25. Based on calculations from the NBER on months of peak to trough cycles.

Chapter 7. How George Bush Soaked the Rich

1. Interview with the authors, June 16, 2006.
2. Congressional Budget Office, *Historical Budget Tables*.
3. Art Laffer, "The Tax Threat to Prosperity," *Wall Street Journal*, January 25, 2008, http://online.wsj.com/article/SB120122126173315299.html?mod=opinion_main_commentaries
4. Calculations based on data from the Bureau of Labor Statistics.
5. Stephen Moore, *Bullish on Bush* (Baltimore, MD, Madison Books, 2004).
6. "Bill Clinton's AMT Bomb," *Wall Street Journal*, Review and Outlook, February 23, 2007.
7. "Dean Condemns Bush Administration Decision to Cut Soldiers' Pay," Howard Dean Press Release, August 14, 2003.
8. Stephen Moore, "The Laffer Curve Strikes Again," *The American Spectator*, Vol. 39, No. 7, September 2006.
9. American Shareholder's Association, "2003 Tax Cut Scorecard," Americans for Tax Reform.
10. Moore, *The American Spectator*, September 2006.
11. Bureau of Economic Analysis, *National Income Product Account Tables*.
12. Arthur P. Hall, Ph.D., and Gary Leff, Special Report No. 61A, Tax Foundation-Half Century of Small Business Federal Income Tax Rates and Collections. http://www.taxfoundation.org/news/show/728.html
13. Bureau of Labor Statistics, Employed Persons, available via www.bls.gov
14. Harold Meyerson, "Second Class Citizens," *Washington Post*, January 14, 2004.
15. American Shareholders Association based on Federal Reserve data.
16. U.S. Department of Treasury, "Topics Related to the President's Tax Relief." May 28, 2008.
17. "Their Fair Share." *Wall Street Journal*, Review and Outlook, July 21, 2008, A12.
18. U.S. Department of Labor, "America's Dynamic Workforce." 2006 and 2007. http://www.dol.gov/asp/media/reports/workforce2007/ADW2007_Full_Text.pdf.
19. Congressional Budget Office, *Historical Budget Tables*, 2008, http://www.cbo.gov/budget/historical.shtml
20. Ibid.
21. Edmund L. Andrews, "Surprising Jump in Tax Revenues Is Curbing Deficit," *New York Times*, July 9, 2006.
22. Congressional Budget Office, *Historical Budget Tables*.
23. Internal Revenue Service, *Statistics of Income*—same as earlier IRS data.
24. Stephen Moore and Phil Kerpen, "Show Me the Money! Dividend Payouts after the Bush Tax Cut," Cato Institute, Paper #88, October 11, 2004, http://www.cato.org/pubs/briefs/bp88.pdf

25. Robert A. Guth and Scott Thurm, "Microsoft to Dole Out Its Cash Hoard," *Wall Street Journal*, July 21, 2004, http://online.wsj.com/article/SB10903 5431245368850.html

26. Ibid.

27. Taub, Stephen Taub, "Dividends Are In Again," CFO.com. July 18, 2003, http://www.cfo.com/article.cfm/3009963?f=search

28. Stephen Slivenski, *Buck Wild: How Republicans Broke the Bank and Became the Party of Big Government*, Thomas Nelson, Nashville, TN. 2006.

29. Congressional Budget Office, *Historical Budget Tables*.

30. Stephen Moore and Phil Kerpen, "Who Lost the Budget Surplus?" *Human Events*, January 25, 2002.

31. Senator Tom Coburn's speech at CPAC, Washington, DC, February 7, 2008.

32. John Fund, "Den Young's Way," *Wall Street Journal*, February 7, 2006, http://www.opinionjournal.com/diary/?id=110007930

33. Mark Skousen, *The Making of Modern Economics*, M. E. Sharpe, 2001.

34. Internal Revenue Service, *Statistics of Income*.

Chapter 8. Bankruptcy 90210: As Goes California, So Goes the Nation

1. Census Bureau, 2008, *Statistical Abstract of the United States*.

2. Data from the National Association of State Budget Officers.

3. "CA median home price falls 32 percent," *Inman News*, May 27, 2008.

4. Arthur B. Laffer, "Proposition 13: The Tax Terminator. Revisiting the Great California Tax Revolt," Laffer Associates, June 27, 2003.

5. Ibid.

6. Ibid.

7. Arthur B. Laffer, "Revitalizing California's Economy, A Discussion of the Impact of Proposition 13," United Organization of Taxpayers, March 22, 1978.

8. See Note 4.

9. Jack Cashill, *What's the Matter with California?* Threshold Editions, 2007.

10. Data from the California Budget Project.

11. Kathleen Pender, "Google's April surprise for state," *San Francisco Chronicle*, May 9, 2006, http://www.sfgate.com/cgi-bin/article.cgi?file=/c/a/2006/05/09/MNGSVIO7NG1.DTL

12. Census Bureau, 2008, *Statistical Abstract of the United States*.

13. Cost is based on reservation date (1/12/08) and moving date (3/1/08). This quote is for use of a 26 truck. Data obtained using U-Haul online reservations, available at http://reservations.uhaul.com/ReservationsWeb/Default.aspx?sfc=main

14. Census Bureau, 2008, *Statistical Abstract of the United States*.

15. Felicity Barringer, "California, Taking Big Gamble, Tries to Curb Greenhouse Gases," *New York Times*, September 15, 2006.
16. Dr. Patrick Michaels, Press Release on Lieberman-Warner, The Cato Institute.
17. "The Red Ink State." *Wall Street Journal*, Review and Outlook, December 28, 2007, A-12.
18. Arnold Schwarzenegger, State of the State Address, January 2007, http://gov.ca.gov/speech/5143/
19. Tax Foundation, State Income Tax Rates, 2008 update.
20. "Meat Head Economics," *Wall Street Journal*, September 11, 2006.
21. Authors' calculations based on data from the California State Board of Equalization.
22. Rich Karlgaard, "Where to Get Rich," *Forbes*, October 6, 2003, http://www.forbes.com/forbes/2003/1006/039.html.
23. Zsolt Becsi. "Do State and Local Taxes Affect Relative State Growth?" Federal Reserve Bank of Atlanta, Economic Review, March/April 1996, 34.
24. United Van Lines migration studies, 2007, 2006, 2005.
25. John Tatom, "Are Higher Taxes Restricting Indiana's Growth?" Networks Financial Institute at Indiana State University, May 1 2007, http://mpra.ub.uni-muenchen.de/4307/1/MPRA -paper-4307.pdf.
26. Judy Lin, "Legislative analyst criticizes across-the-board reductions," *Sacramento Bee*, January 15, 2008, A3.
27. Stephen Moore, "The Unions Go to Town," *The Weekly Standard*, March 24, 2008, Volume 13, Issue 27.
28. Ibid.
29. Ibid.
30. Cashill, *What's the Matter with California?*

Chapter 9. Socialism, Non, the Laffer Curve, Oui: Supply-Side Economics Takes the World by Storm

1. Simon Kennedy, "Tax-Cut War Widens in Europe as U.K., France, Germany Jump In," *Bloomberg*, May 29, 2007. http://www.bloomberg.com/apps/news?pid=20601109&sid=aev_LMGsw3aw&refer=home
2. Interview with the authors, August 8, 2007.
3. Sean Dorgan, "How Ireland Became the Celtic Tiger," Heritage Foundation, June 23, 2006.
4. Scott A. Hodge, "U.S. States Lead the World in High Corporate Taxes," Fiscal Fact No. 119, March 18, 2008, http://www.taxfoundation.org/publications/show/22917.html
5. Interview with the authors, April 12, 2008.
6. Alvin Rabushka, "The Great Tax Cut of China," *Wall Street Journal*, August 7, 1997.

7. See Note 1.
8. Ibid.
9. John Thornhill, "Sarkozy vows to loosen the 35-hour work week," *Financial Times,* January 22, 2007, http://us.ft.com/ftgateway/superpage.ft?news_id=fto012220071328241641
10. Carl Schramm and Robert Litan, "Can Europe Compete?" *Commentary,* September 2007.
11. Jurgen Reinhoudt, "Achtung, Taxman." *The American,* December 13, 2007, http://www.american.com/archive/2007/december-12-07/achtung-taxman
12. Björn Borg, Come Home," *The Wall Street Journal,* April 11, 2007.
13. Interview with the authors, May 11, 2007.
14. Stephen Moore, "Reaganomics 2.0," *The Wall Street Journal,* August 31, 2007, A8.
15. Sean Dorgan, "How Ireland Became the Celtic Tiger," Heritage Foundation, June 23, 2006.
16. Carl Schramm and Robert E. Litan, "Can Europe Compete?" *Commentary Magazine,* September 2007.
17. Ibid.
18. See Note 15.
19. Aparna Mathur and Kevin A. Hassett, "Taxes and Wages," American Enterprise Institute, AEI Working Paper #128, June 2006.
20. Ibid.
21. Alan Reynolds, "A Depressing Situation," The Cato Institute, May 4, 2003.
22. Galbraith, *The Affluent Society.*
23. James Gwartney, "Economic Freedom of the World Report."
24. Adam Smith, *The Wealth of Nations.*
25. Stephen Moore and Julian Simon, "It's Getting Better All the Time," Cato Institute, 2001.
26. Julian Simon, "Communism-Capitalism-Economic Development: Implications for U.S. Economic Assistance," Heritage Foundation, December 8, 1989, http://www.heritage.org/Research/TradeandForeignAid/bg741.cfm
27. Stephen Moore, "Reaganomics 2.0," *Wall Street Journal,* August 31, 2007, A8.
28. Jerome C. Glenn and Theodore J. Gordon, 2007 State of the Future Report, United Nations, http://www.millennium-project.org/millennium/sof2007.html
29. "We're Number One, Alas": *Wall Street Journal,* Review and Outlook, July 13, 2007, A12.

Chapter 10. How to Create a Bull Market:
The Capital Gains Tax Validates the Laffer Curve

1. "A Capital Gains Primer," *Wall Street Journal,* October 17, 2007, A22, http://online.wsj.com/article/SB119240927948858793.html
2. Robert L. Bartley, "How Reaganomics made the world work," *National Review,* April 21, 1989.
3. Stephen Moore and Tyler Grimm, "The Bush Capital Gains Tax Cut after Four Years: More Growth, More Investment, More Revenues," National Center for Policy Analysis, NCPA Policy Report No. 307, January 2008, http://www.ncpa.org/pub/st/st307/st307.pdf
4. Stephen Moore and John Silvia, "The ABCS of the Capital Gains Tax," Policy Analysis no. 242, October 4, 1995, http://www.cato.org/pub_display.php?pub-id=1101
5. Dale W. Jorgenson and Kun-Young Yun, *Lifting the Burden: Tax Reform, the Cost of Capital, and U.S. Economic Growth* (Cambridge, MA: MIT Press, 2001).
6. Stephen Moore, "It's Getting Better All The Time," Cato Institute, 2001.
7. Paul Samuelson and William D. Nordhaus, *Economics* (New York: McGraw-Hill, 1985), 789.
8. John Goodman, Aldona Robbins, and Gary Robbins, "Elderly Taxpayers and the Capital Gains Tax Debate," National Center for Policy Analysis, 1990.
9. Ibid.
10. U.S. Civil Rights Commission.
11. Bureau of Economic Analysis and Bureau of Labor Statistics.
12. Stephen Moore and Tyler Grimm, "The Bush Capital Gains Tax Cut after Four Years: More Growth, More Investment, More Revenues," National Center for Policy Analysis, NCPA Policy Report No. 307, January 2008, http://www.ncpa.org/pub/st/st307/st307.pdf
13. Internal Revenue Service, *Statistics of Income,* Table 1.4, 2007.
14. Arthur P. Hall, "Issues in the Indexation of Capital Gains," Tax Foundation Special Report, April 1995.
15. Alan S. Blinder, "The Level and Distribution of Economic Well-Being," in *The American Economy in Transition,* ed. Martin Feldstein (Chicago: University of Chicago Press, 1980) 48.
16. Stephen Moore, "The Obama Bear Market," *Wall Street Journal,* Political Diary, July 14, 2008.

Chapter 11. Throw Momma from the Train:
The Unfair Estate Tax

1. William W. Beach, "The Death Tax Must Die," Heritage Foundation, March 1, 2001, http://www.heritage.org/Press/Commentary/ed030101b.cfm
2. "Death and Democrats," *The Wall Street Journal*, Review and Outlook, August 3, 2006, http://www.opinionjournal.com/editorial/feature.html?id=110008743
3. Stephen Moore, "Death by Taxes," *Wall Street Journal*, May 30, 2008, http://online.wsj.com/article/SB121212106984832153.html
4. Ibid.
5. Ibid.
6. American Family Business Institute, http://www.nodeathtax.org/STORIES/deathtaxtales.htm
7. Stephan Pollan and Mark Levine, *Die Broke: A Radical, Four-Part Financial Plan.* HarperCollins, 1997.
8. Richard Wagner, *Federal Transfer Taxation: A Study in Social Cost,* Center for the Study of Taxation, 1993.
9. "Arizona senator pursues fight against federal death tax," *Journal Record* (Oklahoma City), Mar 10, 1997.
10. Sergio Pareja, "Estate tax repeal under EGTRRA: A proposal for simplification," *Real Property, Probate and Trust Journal*, Spring 2003.
11. "Taxes Everlasting," *Wall Street Journal*, Review and Outlook, June 8, 2006, http://www.opinionjournal.com/editorial/feature.html?id=110008487
12. Internal Revenue Service, *Statistics of Income*. SOI Estate Tax Data Tables, Filing Years, http://www.irs.gov/taxstats/indtaxstats/article/0,,id=96442,00.html
13. American Family Business Institute, *Economic Reports*. http://www.nodeathtax.org/ECONOMICREPORTS/reports_index.htm

Chapter 12. Protectionism Then and Now:
The Smoot-Hawley Tariff Act of 1930

1. *USA Today*/Gallup Poll, March 2008.
2. Amity Shlaes, *The Forgotten Man: A New History of the Great Depression* (New York: HarperCollins, 2007).
3. Jude Wanniski, *The Way the World Works,* fourth edition. (Gateway, 1998).
4. Robert Shiller, *Irrational Exuberance* (Princeton, NJ: Princeton University Press, 2005).
5. See Note 3.
6. Census Bureau. *Historical Statistics of the United States,* millennial edition.

7. Consumer Electronics Association, Advertisement, *Politico*, January 16, 2008, 24.
8. Bill Clinton. "American University's Centennial Convocation." February 26, 1993. http://www.american.edu/media/speeches/1993centennial.htm
9. Stephen Moore, "It's Getting Better All the Time," Cato Institute, 2001.
10. Sang Foon Rhee, "Clinton steps up rhetoric against Obama," *Boston Globe*, February 18, 2008, http://www.boston.com/news/nation/articles/2008/02/15/clinton_steps_up_rhetoric_against_obama/
11. David Leohardt, "The Politics of Trade in Ohio," *New York Times*, February 27, 2008.
12. "Texas v. Ohio," *The Wall Street Journal*. Review and Outlook, March 3, 2008, http://online.wsj.com/article/SB120450306595906431.html?mod=opinion_main_review_and_outlooks
13. Ibid.
14. Ibid.
15. Holly Ramer, "Clinton Outlines Broad Economic Vision." *Washington Post*, May 29, 2007.
16. "Hillary, Obama told in S.C. to tone down," *Washington Times*, January 25, 2008, http://www.washingtontimes.com/news/2008/jan/25/hillary-obama-told-in-sc-to-tone-down
17. "BMW Announces Plant Expansion," BMW news release, March 10, 2008.
18. "MBUSI Builds Exceptional Automobiles in the US." *MBUSI Products*. Mercedes-Benz U.S. International, Inc., http://mbusi.com/pages/products_home.asp
19. Organization for International Investment. *Fact Sheet: Open Investment*, http://ofii.org/insourcing/Open%20Investment%20Fact%20Sheet.pdf
20. Department of Labor, Bureau of Labor Statistics http://data.bls.gov/PDQ/outside.jsp?survey=ce Series ID CES3000000001. AND "Total Nonfarm Employment—Seasonally Adjusted," http://data.bls.gov/cgi-bin/surveymost?bls Series ID CES 0000000001. AND "Employment Level—Nonagricultural, Private Industries Wage and Salary Workers," Series http://data.bls.gov/cgi-bin/srgate Series ID LNS12032189
21. Ibid.

Chapter 13. Many Happy Returns: The Flat Tax Solution

1. Tomoeh Murakami Tso, "Buffett Slams Tax System Disparities," *Washington Post*, June 27, 2007, D3.
2. Democratic primary debate, Los Angeles, CA, January 30, 2008.
3. "State Cigarette and Excise Tax Rates and Rankings," Campaign for Tobacco-Free Kids, http://www.tobaccofreekids.org/research/factsheets/pdf/0097.pdf

4. Thomas Kelly, Savers & Investors League, 1998, www.savers.org
5. DeWayne Wickham, "Do positions on evolution really matter in 2008 race?" *USA Today*, June 12, 2007, http://blogs.usatoday.com/oped/2007/06/do_positions_on.html
6. Internal Revenue Service, "About the IRS," www.IRS.gov
7. Tax Foundation, "Number of Words in Internal Revenue Code and Federal Tax Regulations, 1955–2005," http://www.taxfoundation.org/taxdata/show/1961.html
8. Arthur Laffer, *The Complete Flat Tax*, Arthur B. Laffer Associates, 1984.
9. Steve Forbes, *Flat Tax Revolution* (Washington, DC: Regnery, 2005).
10. See note 8.
11. Ibid.
12. Congressional Budget Office, *Historical Budget Tables*.
13. Daniel Mitchell, "Russia's Flat Tax Miracle," Heritage Foundation, March 24, 2003, http://www.heritage.org/press/commentary/ed032403.cfm
14. Neil Boortz and John Linder, *The Fair Tax Book*, William Morrow. 2005.

Chapter 14. The Death of Economic Sanity

1. Milton Friedman, "Supply-Side Policies: Where Do We Go from Here?" in *Supply-Side Economics in the 1980s* (Westport, CT: Quorum Books, 1982).
2. Stephen Moore and Tyler Grimm, "The Bush Capital Gains Tax Cut after Four Years: More Growth, More Investment, More Revenues," National Center for Policy Analysis, NCPA Policy Report No. 307, January 2008, http://www.ncpa.org/pub/st/st307/st307.pdf
3. David Leonhardt, "Closing Income Gap Tops Obama's Agenda for Economic Change," *New York Times*, February 2, 2008.
4. Ibid.
5. Stephen Moore and Tyler Grimm, "The Bush Capital Gains Tax Cut after Four Years: More Growth, More Investment, More Revenues," National Center for Policy Analysis, NCPA Policy Report No. 307, January 2008.
6. Michael Darda, "The Tax Time Bomb," MKM Partners, New York, NY, June 2008.
7. Congressional Budget Office, *Historical Budget Tables*.
8. "Bill Clinton's AMT Bomb," *Wall Street Journal*, Review and Outlook, February 23, 2007.
9. Patrick Fleenor and Andrew Chamberlain, "Backgrounder on the Individual Alternative Minimum Tax (AMT)," The Tax Foundation, *Fiscal Fact No. 26*, May 24, 2005, http://www.taxfoundation.org/publications/show/498.html
10. David Leonhardt, "For Clinton, Government as Economic Prod," *New York Times*, January 21, 2008.

11. Ibid.
12. Michael Bloomberg and Charles Schumer, *Sustaining New York's and the US' Global Financial Services Leadership*, http://www.nyc.gov/html/om/pdf/ny_report_final.pdf
13. Moisés Naím, "The Free Trade Paradox," *Foreign Policy*, September/October 2007.
14. Richard Vedder and Wendell Cox, *The Wal-Mart Revolution Print Mail: How Big-Box Stores Benefit Consumers, Workers, and the Economy* (AEI Press, 2007).
15. Authors' calculations based on gold price data from Global Insights.
16. "Oil and the Dollar," *Wall Street Journal*, Review and Outlook, January 4, 2008, http://online.wsj.com/article/SB119941453085566759.html
17. Ibid.
18. Congressional Budget Office, *Historical Tables*.
19. Citizens Against Government Waste, "Pig Book," 2007.
20. Interview with the *New York Times* editorial board.
21. Center for Disease Control, *Health, United States*, 2007, http://www.cdc.gov/nchs/hus.htm
22. Congressional Research Service, 1991.
23. "Another Ice Age?" *Time*, June 24, 1974, http://www.time.com/time/magazine/article/0,9171,944914,00.html
24. Arthur B. Laffer and Wayne Winegarden, "The Adverse Economic Impacts of Cap-and-Trade," Free Enterprise Education Institute, 2007.
25. American Council for Capital Formation. Analysis of the Warner-Lieberman bill, http://www.accf.org/pdf/NAM/ACCF-NAM-US.pdf
26. Patrick Michaels, "Cato Scholar Comments on Warner-Lieberman Climate Security Act," Cato Institute, http://www.cato.org/pressroom.php?display=ncomments&id=34
27. Tim Ball, "How the world was misled about global warming and now climate change," *Canada Free Press*, April 21, 2008.
28. Jason Riley, *Let Them In* (New York: Gotham, 2008).
29. Ibid.
30. Stephen Moore, "A Fiscal Portrait of the New Immigrants," National Immigration Forum, 1996.
31. Ibid.
32. Interview with the authors, January 28, 2008.

ACKNOWLEDGMENTS

No one will be surprised to hear that authors get a lot of help when writing a book, particularly one with as many moving parts and features as this one. That's the reason most books have an acknowledgments page, and this one is no exception. To begin, we want to acknowledge our spouses, who had to contend with the rigors of having a part-time author around the house. So our special thanks and gratitude to our best friends—our wives, Traci Laffer, Allison Moore, and Ann Tanous—whose support was invaluable.

This book never would have been completed without our expert research assistant Tyler Grimm.

Thanks to our colleagues, family, and friends who helped in many different ways, including Justin Laffer, Kenneth Petersen, Nancy Epling, Jeffrey Thomson, Mark Wise, Ford Scudder, Daniel Stephenson, Michael Kretschmer, Francesca Stabile, Patrick Manning, Hunter Armistead, Jim Witherspoon, Kim Strassel, Colin Levy, Jeffrey H. Marks, Deborah Pierdominici, and Matthew Gielfand. Thanks to our agents, Alexander Hoyt and Theron Raines, for their excellent work and counsel.

Special kudos to the hardest-working editor in the business, Pocket Books editorial director Maggie Crawford, who not only had to deal with a complex project but with three authors, to boot.

Acknowledgments

From all three of us, our deepest gratitude to all of our coworkers and colleagues at our respective "day jobs" who picked up the slack while we toiled away on this outside project. We are very grateful.

Arthur, Steve, and Peter

INDEX